STEPPING BACK

STEPPING BACK
Exploring South Island History

Mark Pickering

SHOAL BAY PRESS

DEDICATION

To those local heroes (and heroines) who badger councils, write letters to the editor and pester MPs to save our historical heritage.

First published in 1998 by
Shoal Bay Press Ltd
Box 17661, Christchurch 8

ISBN 0 908704 68 2

Printed by Rainbow Print Group, Christchurch

CONTENTS

ACKNOWLEDGMENTS

Although I have visited all of these walks personally, I have gathered specific historical information from a wide variety of sources, including standard reference works and the *Historic Places* magazine. I am grateful to the Historic Places Trust for allowing me to use the material in their magazine.

Books from which I have used extracts, and which I found to be most relevant, are listed at the end of each section. I am appreciative of the help of the staff of the Christchurch Public Library, in particular the New Zealand Room, for dealing with manifold enquiries.

I also want to acknowledge the help of pamphlets (many of which are now out of print), which established a good background for my own notes. To these mostly unnamed writers in the old Forest Service, Lands and Survey Department, and the newer Department of Conservation, I express my thanks. Any errors are of course mine.

Lastly, my thanks to my partner Rachel, who has supported and encouraged me throughout this project.

PHOTO CREDITS

Thanks to the following for permission to reproduce historical photographs: Nelson Provincial Museum for photographs on pages 18, 19, 28, 34 (Tyree Studio Collection) and 36 (G.C. Wood Collection); *Marlborough Express* for photograph of the *Edwin Fox* on page 37; Canterbury Museum for photographs on pages 41, 50, 73 (W.A. Taylor photo), 75 (Beken photo), 80 (Canterbury Pilgrims & Early Settlers Association Collection). 90 (W.A. Kennedy photo), 103 (*Canterbury Times* photo), 113 (Ring photo), 128 (Spencer Digby photo), 149, 174 (Thorpe Collection); Otago Museum for photographs on pages 133, 137 and 144. All other photographs were taken by the author.

INTRODUCTION

History is about how we got here, and why. Behind us, and getting larger every day, is a huge historical rubbish dump of our aspirations, follies and achievements. The amount of historical debris humans leave behind is remarkable, and alarming. People enthusiastic about history are rather like regular visitors to the recycling depot – they often come away with rather more than they took.

Stepping Back has been written to help people locate the gems of South Island history and fossick in our past without being overwhelmed by it. It's not about what's in museums but what's out there on the streets: the plethora of Maori, agricultural, military, gold and industrial ruins that were once crucial to the communities that brought them into being.

Admittedly New Zealand lacks romantically ruined castles and gorgeous palaces: the remnants of our history are often far more utilitarian – pa food pits, a whalers' blubber factory or a gold-diggers' water-race. The materials used were whatever was to hand: mud and tussock to make cob cottages in Canterbury, schist rock for the Chinese shelters of Otago, ponga fern trunks for the whatas on the West Coast.

Yet it is remarkable how many of these 'quick-fix' buildings have survived, and how out of improvisation and necessity certain vernacular styles of architecture developed and have endured more than a hundred years of use – the colonial 'lean-to' cottage for example, or the weather-beaten high-country hut.

Stepping Back has been written to encourage people to get out and have a look at their history. Walking about the landscapes where events took place gives you a much better understanding of our past. It's obvious why the French chose Akaroa, and why cattle were forced over the high, misty Paringa track. It's clear why Maori used the sea caves for shelter on the 'Wet' Coast, and chose a swamp for a home in Kaiapoi. And it does not take too much sweat on our part to look into a deep Otago gorge in midwinter and realise why gold-diggers from all nations drank hard, and dreamed about sweethearts they never had. It's just a step back to their world.

Not Just Buildings

This book attempts to represent a wide diversity of historic sites:

- Maori history, which includes pa sites and middens.
- European colonial buildings and gardens.
- Military sites from the two world wars.
- The goldmining era, including poppet heads, stamping batteries, packtracks and water-races.

- Agricultural history, including machinery, high-country huts, farm buildings.
- Coastal harbours and wharves.
- Historic icons, such as the Christchurch Cathedral and Dunedin railway station.
- Notable industrial and engineering sites, such as the concrete water tower by Addington Station in Christchurch and the railway tunnel at Kawatiri Junction.
- Unusual sites, such as Te Oru Mata cave by the Fox River and the memorial to McKenzie the sheep-stealer.
- Nostalgic places, such as Naseby in Otago, which have retained a timeless quality.

Sites were selected on the basis of having something to see, something to do and good public access. Most offer more than just 'look and click' history and encourage an active enjoyment of an area. There are usually walks, other areas to explore and often rather distractingly stunning scenery as well. Grandmas and grandkids alike should find something to interest them. A deliberate effort has be made to leave some aspects of each site undescribed, to allow for a sense of discovery.

Geographical Selection

Stepping Back tries to cover the South Island thoroughly, from Golden Bay down to Stewart Island, and to include the distinctive historic *imprimatur* of each province.

In many regions the wealth of historic sites has made the selection difficult, and many well-known sites have had to be omitted. Not every town's prize cob cottage will get a look in. Because of their significance to the community, churches have enjoyed a much higher survival rate than other historic sites, and most important churches have had to be excluded for lack of space.

Museums, monuments and memorials are generally are not included in this book, although where appropriate good local museums have rated a mention.

Public Access

These sites all have to have good public access, and for that reason several important places (in particular historic homesteads) are not included because they are still in private hands. Maraes are excluded because they also are not open to the casual visitor.

Some sites do make a small charge (such as the Fyffe Cottage in Kaikoura) but most of those mentioned in this book are free.

Walking

A good parka, food, thermos, map, camera and sturdy, comfortable shoes are good equipment to start with. Keep your plans modest if you are unfamiliar with the area (or the exercise). Take a note of the weather and tell someone where you are going. Walking times in

STEPPING LIGHTLY

Historic areas are both valuable and fragile and observing a few simple courtesies will help to preserve our history for future visitors.

Keep to the Tracks

Not only is this a good way to reduce unnecessary damage to a site, but it's a useful safety tip in mining areas, where old hidden shafts often lie uncovered.

No 'Souveniring'

Many sites in this book have all manner of 'junk' apparently lying about, some of it 'untidy', some of it 'dangerous'. Much of it would make a 'good souvenir'. However these remnants are important and integral to the site, so please leave them to tell their story.

Farm Courtesy

Leave farm gates as you find them, open or closed. If you have to cross fences, do so by the strainer post, and try not to disturb stock.

Dogs

Please ensure that dogs are kept under leash or voice control. Some walks forbid dogs, for instance national parks, and on others cattle and sheep are easily disturbed. Some dog owners treat the great outdoors as one huge dog toilet and dog fouling is a persistent problem on many walking tracks these days, making it unpleasant for other users. Most councils have bylaws that require that you clean up after your dog, so dog owners should carry a plastic bag to remove dog mess.

Vandalism and Graffiti

Because many of these walks are close to towns they periodically suffer from vandals wrecking signs, smashing glass, etc. If you see the aftermath of this behaviour please contact the controlling authority. If you actually see some of the vandalism, or some suspicious behaviour, take down the car's number plate.

Mountain Bikes

Mountain bikers should be aware of walkers. Slow down and give warning shouts. In fragile areas bikes can cause serious ruts to develop.

Closure of Walks

A number of these walks may be closed for certain times of the year. This is particularly true in rural areas during the lambing months of August to October. Other reasons for closure may be fire risk, or wildlife management. Please respect these restrictions.

this book mostly vary from 15 minutes to a half-day return walk, 4-5 hours. Some longer tramps are also included. It is notoriously difficult to be accurate about walking times but the times suggested here are designed for the slower, the less fit and family groups. Most averagely fit adults will reduce these times.

Some sites are in alpine regions, such as the Otago uplands, and the usual walking precautions should be taken.

Wheelchair and Disabled Access

Few of these walks are suitable for wheelchairs. However, many walks start in visually interesting landscapes, which are rewarding in their own right, so people with disabilities may not need to venture far to see spectacular places and interesting history.

Map Disclaimer

The maps printed with each walk are intended as a visual ready reference only and are not a substitute for a good topographical map. This is especially true for the more challenging mountain areas.

Information and Pamphlets

A good number of these walks have information boards on site. Quite a few had at one time or other pamphlets describing the walks in detail but many of these pamphlets are now unavailable.

Some pamphlets were produced by departments either now extinct, such as the New Zealand Forest Service, or that now have no official interest in the area, such as the Department of Survey and Land Information (DOSLI, formerly the Lands and Survey Department). But it is still worthwhile trying your local Department of Conservation office (DOC), which even if it has not reprinted or revised the original pamphlet, may well have inherited some of the old pamphlet stock.

Historic Places, the magazine of the Historic Places Trust, is highly recommended, with many in-depth articles on heritage areas. I found the *New Zealand Geographic* magazine invaluable, as was the *Mobil Travel Guide to the South Island* by Diana and Jeremy Pope.

Things Change

Every effort has been made to keep the information in this book up to date but nothing stays the same. Tracks get re-routed, ruins get damaged, and areas once open to public access get closed down. Anyone reading the text should make allowance for altered situations (and author fallibility).

If you do spot some real discrepancies please write to the publisher so every effort can be made to incorporate the changes in the next edition. No, you don't get your money back – enjoy the past!

GETTING RADICAL

One of the depressing aspects of historical places is the rate at which they disappear. Neglect on its own will not necessarily destroy a site, indeed perversely, many fine historic sites have been saved by a good dose of indifference and Kiwi 'dump it in the back paddock' habits. Usage often seems to be a key to survival, and perhaps this is why industrial sites are poor cousins to the colonial homestead. People can see the attractions of an elegant homestead, but a rendering-down plant?

However, most historic sites are knocked down quite casually, and legally, with little record, and little protest. Even when such protest does make the headlines it is usually too late, and if the building is damaged sufficiently, the developer can rely on that old standby that the site is now 'unsafe'.

The Historic Places Trust Act 1993 is an impressive 63-page document, yet it simply has not provided the protections that it supposedly promulgates. Being threatened with the act is a bit like being sucked to death by a toothless poodle: it takes too long.

The Historic Places Trust Act is also under the thumb of the Resource Management Act, which in itself has not proved particulary useful in preserving buildings and historic sites. Indeed, the assumption of the bill's famous 'level playing field' often disadvantages older sites, since concepts such as nostalgia, character and meaning are given less intrinsic weight than economic or commercial 'realities'.

The Resource Management Act is in practice entrenching a value system that is dollar-based. A 100-year-old structure that has seen seen generations of people working, living and loving within it becomes identified with those people, and in some sense belongs to them. Europeans have no trouble in assigning high value to their history, but New Zealanders are still coy about it. We don't want to block progress or look fuddy-duddy.

Even the Historic Places Trust must face some criticism. It is a taxpayer-funded body, undoubtedly well meaning but it moves at an archival rate. There is too much emphasis put into preserving individual buildings, and not enough into their context, or on precincts with a demonstrable character. Isn't there something ironic in the Wellington headquarters of the trust? It's a gingerbread palace surrounded by glass and concrete towers.

Of course we have to have new buildings, and new ideas, but we have over-loved the new to the point of promoting blandness and mediocrity. There are some glass towers that can count as elegant and witty, but there are many more that are merely vacuous.

But it's not just a case of saving old for old's sake; rather we should be saving quality, integrity and meaning. Some ugly historic sites mean a lot to their community, and some bare paddocks have an integrity because of what took place there. No doubt this may lead us to some odd situations, perhaps when people want to save a line of original parking meters, a shopping mall, or the first KFC outlet in New Zealand – but so be it.

It *is* hard to decide, but one thing is certain: if we are to save more of our heritage (and incidentally preserve the vividness and personality of our landscapes) then we are going to have to be more passionate, more bloody-minded, and a good deal less nice. The destruction of any important historic site is the theft of memories.

THE WALKS

ONEKAKA WHARF
WHARIWHARANGI BAY
PUPU HYDRO
EDWIN FOX
Nelson
SOUTH STREET
MAUNGATAPU TRACK
HOP KILN HIGHWAY
RUSH POOL ARGILLITE QUARRY
DENNISTOUN INCLINE
KAWATIRI JUNCTION
BIG RIVER
TE ORU MATA SEA CAVE
ACHERON ACCOMMODATION HOUSE
FYFFE HOUSE
Greymouth
CROESUS TRACK
KAIKOURA COAST ROAD
HOKITIKA PRECINCT
WAIKARI ROCK DRAWINGS
CHRISTCHURCH CITY
DEANS COTTAGE
BRIDLE PATH
GODLEY HEAD
INDUSTRIAL ADDINGTON
LYTTELTON PORT
ARTHUR'S PASS
KAIAPOI PA
DONOVAN'S STORE
Christchurch
BLACKBURN MINE
ORTON BRADLEY
OKAINS BAY
AKAROA
PARINGA CATTLE TRACK
TAUMUTU & KAITORETE SPIT
McKENZIE MONUMENT
BLUESTONE COUNTRY
Timaru
CASCADE HUT
WAITAKI DAM
HOMER TUNNEL
MT IDA WATER-RACE
Queenstown
TINKERS TOWN
WHITESTONE CITY
SAWPIT GULLY
SKIPPERS BRIDGE
MATANAKA FARM
THE DUNSTAN TRAIL
BANNOCKBURN SLUICINGS
Dunedin
DUNEDIN CITY
OTAGO PENINSULA
MAPOUTAHI PA
POURAKINO BUSH TRAMWAY
Invercargill
PORT CRAIG & WAITUTU VIADUCTS
QUEEN'S PARK
PORT WILLIAM

PUPU HYDRO WALK

FEATURES
Micro hydro-electric power station, viewing window into powerhouse, goldminers' water-race, native bush walking track and swimming hole.

HOW TO GET THERE
From Takaka drive 2km to the Pupu Springs turnoff, and follow the winding road 6km to the carpark at the end. Two small fords.

WALK DETAILS
Allow 3-4 hours return for the 8km walk. Because the narrow stopbank beside the water-race is also the walking track, small children should be kept in hand.

'A Little Gem'

Both elegant and ingenious, the Pupu power scheme has adapted an old gold-diggers' water-race which delivers crisp, crystal water to the top of a penstock, then plunges it down to the toy-like power station some 120 metres below.

The system works, and supplies electricity to the general grid, and has been doing so for over 50 years. The publicity pamphlet calls the hydro scheme a 'little gem'. It was developed in 1929 by the engineer H.R. Climie and, in fact it was almost too innovative, for in those days people were unsure what to use electricity for. The Golden Bay Electric Power Board had to start an advertising campaign to urge on people the benefits of this new source of energy. It was thought to be the smallest hydro scheme in the country.

It was closed in 1981 but the Pupu Hydro Society has since quite literally regenerated the power station to its present-day function.

From the carpark a short track leads around to the dinky power station, where a viewing window enables you to see the power turbines. From here a cable and trolley swing perilously up to the high terrace where the water-race starts. The track zig-zags up a steepish bush face to the top of the penstock

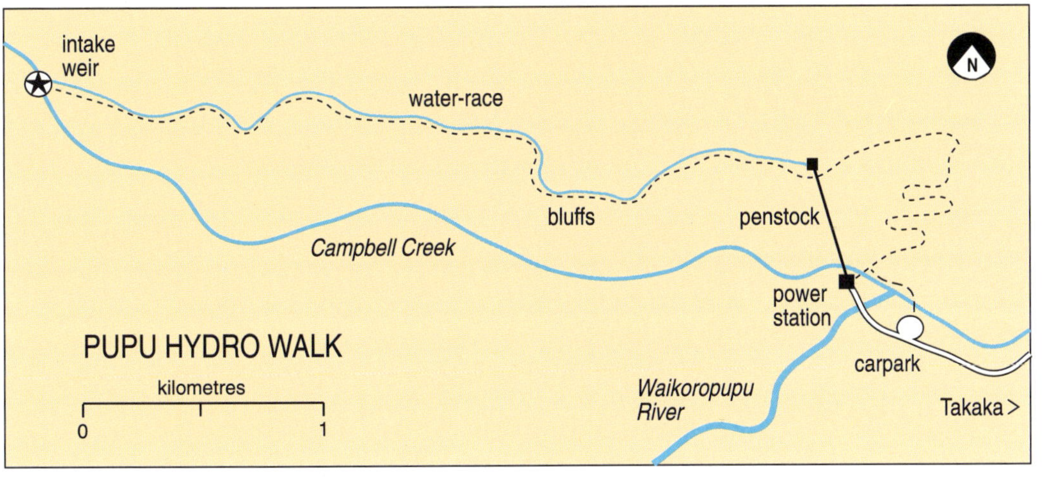

Cableway swinging up to the water-race

and the water-race which was built in 1901-02 to supply a head of pressure for goldminers in the valley. These gutsy men completed it in a remarkably short time of six months, chiselling it out of the rock bluffs and constructing wooden fluming across gullies. The water-race curves cunningly through bush and bluffs for some 3km before reaching the intake weir at Campbell Creek.

Some of the dry-walling built by the original goldminers still remains, and the society has built new stretches of concrete aqueducts.

Apparently the gold claim was one of the most successful in Golden Bay and only finally ceased operation in 1910, a long life for a gold company. The manager was Charles Campbell, and the creek was named after him.

There's a good swimming hole at the intake, and on a hot day it is a sanguine place for lunch. You can be sure the goldminers sat on the same rocks – and then turned them over to look for 'the colours'.

Further Reading

Pupu Walk (Department of Conservation pamphlet).

ONEKAKA WHARF

FEATURES
Derelict wharf, beach and estuary.

HOW TO GET THERE
Onekaka Wharf lies down Washbourn Road at Onekaka off State Highway 60, about 15km from Takaka. Parapara Inlet is another 3km further on from Onekaka down a 1km side-road.

WALK DETAILS
The Onekaka beach is wide and bright, and at low tide you can walk 3km along to Tukurua Point and Parapara.

The ironworks is currently on private land and very overgrown. A new hydro-electric proposal to utilise the existing company dam in the Onekaka Gorge may allow better access to this site in the future.

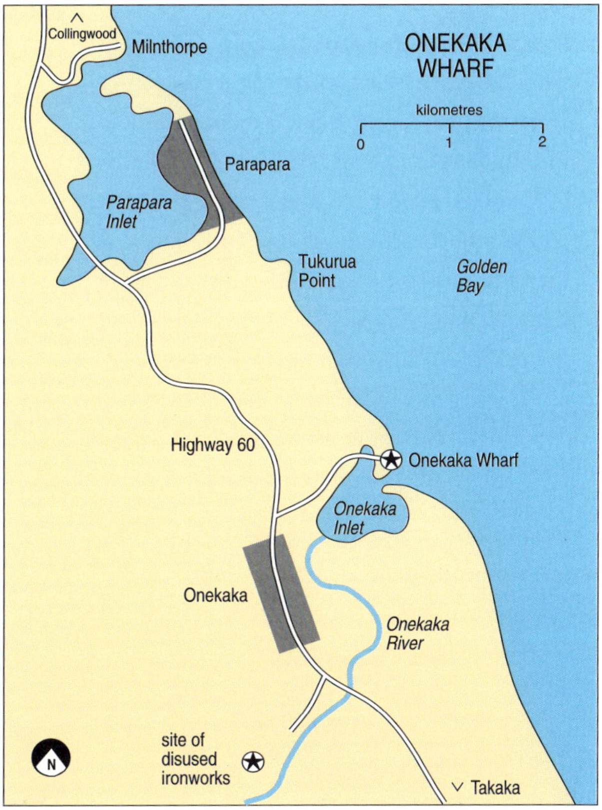

'A Brilliant Luminous Waterfall'

A shattered, spindly wharf lies on the Onekaka shoreline. Rust and tides have eaten the iron piles till they are mere wraiths of their former selves, adopting a sculptural pose for the few passers-by who visit. One of those was Canterbury artist Doris Lusk, who repeatedly painted the remaining piles, turning them into anorexic figurines delicately stepping out to sea.

In the hillside behind the beach there used to be the large Onekaka Iron & Steel Company works, with overhead cableways to bring out the rich iron ore. Pig iron bars were taken by rail wagon on a 2.4km tramway across the mudflats and onto the 370m-long wharf. Here the iron was loaded onto the ship, and West Coast coal taken off.

A trial run of pig iron was produced in 1922 and full production started in 1923, with 41,000 tons of iron exported before prices collapsed during the Depression and the works closed in 1935. The mining machinery was put 'in readiness' during World War II, but was never used and was sold and dismantled in 1946.

This dark, satanic and polluting industry was magic to a child, as local author Enga Washbourn recalls:

> Watching the furnace being 'tapped' at night was always a spectacular sight. Dazzling white-hot molten iron poured out of a hole into moulded pig beds. The tall black building became illuminated with orange-red light, which reflected on the damp shiny faces of the men as they worked in the heat. At more frequent intervals slag was drawn off and poured in a brilliant luminous waterfall over a cliff into a valley, turning into a hard glassy substance, reminding me always of the fairy story about the mountain of glass.[1]

People now come to Golden Bay for the peace and quiet, so it's hard to credit the industry that spawned on the back of an estimated 9 million ton lode of iron ore.

Kokowai

The soils at Onekaka and Parapara are rich in ochre deposits and the Maori were the first to exploit it, using the red iron ochre 'kokowai' extensively for decoration, drawing and face paint. At Parapara the Washbourn family ran the New Zealand Haematite Paint Company for 20 years, from the 1880s to 1906, producing high-quality paint pigment that ended up on many New Zealand railway wagons and goods sheds.

William Washbourn installed a battery of six heavy stampers and four berdans to process the ore, and a 30ft overshot waterwheel (which they built themselves) to drive all this

Onekaka ironworks quarry

machinery. A tramway was built to bring the ore to the crushing plant, and a water-race several miles long was dug to keep the waterwheel turning, generating 16 horsepower.

In the process of manufacture the iron ore was first calcined before going into a battery of six stampers, each weighing about 750 pounds. After being crushed, it flowed through berdans and then passed over nearly still water tanks in order to catch all the sediment. The paint was then dried in a kiln and afterwards pulverised through rollers and bagged ready for market.[2]

Onekaka ironworks wharf – then and now

It took about eight hours to dry a ton of paint. The Washbourns constantly experimented with different types of ironstone soils around Parapara to see what colours they could get. Mostly they produced red and yellows, but occasionally a good bright orange. They tried out the results on their own place. 'Our front door is very grand, with three colours on it ...'[3]

Now it's all gone. Much of New Zealand's industrial history has had a short life, and at Onekaka and Parapara there's precious little to show for 50 years of mineral exploitation and engineering achievement. The tramways have fallen down, the water-races have blocked up, the waterwheel rotted away. The ironworks could not compete with overseas imports, and neither in the end could the paint company. Useful machinery was removed, buildings pulled down, and gorse and manuka now cover the sites of the ironworks and paintworks.

The only reminder is the lean Onekaka Wharf, and soon even that will be recalled only in old black and white photographs, and the strong colour washes that Doris Lusk preferred – appropriately, she liked her reds.

Footnotes and Further Reading

1. *Courage and Camp Ovens*, Enga Washbourn, A.H. & A.W. Reed Ltd, 1970.
2. Ibid.
3. Ibid.

'Golden Bay Turns up Colourful Shades', Gerard Hindmarsh, *Christchurch Press*, 19 October 1996.

'Iron Fever Short-lived at Onekaka', Gerard Hindmarsh, *Christchurch Press*, 6 July 1993.

Landmarks: The Landscape Paintings of Doris Lusk, Lisa Beaven, Robert McDougall Art Gallery/Hazard Press, 1966.

WHARIWHARANGI BAY

FEATURES
Lonely bay and sandy beach, historic homestead and macrocarpa avenue, site of Abel Tasman's attempted landing in New Zealand, memorial to Abel Tasman in Ligar Bay.

HOW TO GET THERE
Access to Whariwharangi Bay is easiest from Takaka, following the coast some 15km past popular Pohara, Tarakohe and the Wainui Inlet. Then it is 3km down McShanes Road to the Whariwharangi carpark and information boards.

In Ligar Bay along the way there is a memorial to Abel Tasman and his crew, with the names of the murdered men. The memorial might be in the wrong place but there's a fine view over the bay.

The Totaranui road continues over a tortuous bush saddle and at Totaranui there is a small visitor centre and campground. There is a daily bus service to Totaranui in summer, which diverts up McShanes Road for Whariwharangi walkers.

WALK DETAILS
Allow 4 hours to walk from Wainui Inlet to the homestead and back. From Mutton Cove it's about 3 hours return and from Totaranui a full day return. It can get hot and dry in summer so take plenty of water.

The First Encounter

There's an old dusty road to Whariwharangi, zig-zagging up a dry hillside that must have broken the hearts of a few musterers. The saddle is hot and expansive. The last sheep would have got a good view as they came out this way, leaving the landscape to chance and chaffinches.

But hillsides once covered with gorse have replenished themselves, and the descent to the bay is through a moist forest of kanuka and native shrubs. The track brings you alongside the old homestead which DOC has renovated, retaining the original outline and keeping the dark wood interiors. The hut is two-storeyed and was built in 1897 by John Handcock, who lived here for 15 years.

A 1923 photograph shows the homestead with outbuildings and bare hillsides behind. It was last inhabited in 1926, then used well into the 1970s as a musterers' hut, but 'why worry' bay did not bring much farming success, and the hillsides became shaggy with gorse.

It's only 500 metres from the hut down to the long arc of the beach, a lonely bay of golden sand backed by a stand of melancholy macrocarpas. The wind seems to make them sigh. They provide shade, and space for contemplation of an event of singular importance to New Zealand.

Whariwharangi homestead, detail

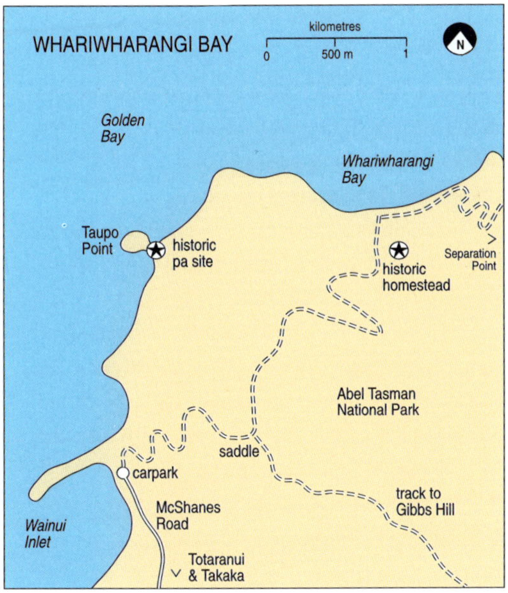

> On the 18 December in the morning having raised our anchor in calm weather; at noon estimated latitude 40 degrees 49 minutes, longitude 191 degrees 41 minutes course kept east South east and sailed 11 miles; in the morning before [we] had our anchor home, [we] have with the officers of the *Zeehaen* resolved that one Shall Try to get into this land, and Try to find convenient harbour ...[1]

The prosaic ship's log recorded the attempt of Abel Tasman's two ships to find a harbour in what they called 'Staten Landt', which only later became known as New Zealand. Australia was 'New Holland'.

Tasman had arrived on the West Coast near Cape Foulwind on 13 December 1642, and trailed along the 'low sandy Land' of Farewell Spit on the 17th. They had already seen smoke from fires, and this must have increased their curiousity to land. What happened next is well known. Maori canoes swarmed out to meet the *Heemskerck* and *Zeehaen*, caught a boat with seven Dutchmen in it rowing between the two vessels, and suddenly attacked.

> [They] struck the *Zeehaen*'s small boat with their stem on the Side, Dashed over that Same violently, whereupon the foremost in this canoe of rogues, pushed the quartermaster Cornelis Ioppen in the neck several times with a long blunt pike so fiercely, that he had to fall overboard, whereupon the rest of them set to with short thick pieces of wood (which we at first thought to be Heavy blunt parangs) and their paddles, overpowering the small boat, in which violence 3 of the *Zeehaen*'s people were killed, and the fourth through the heavy blows was mortally injured ...[2]

The crew of the two boats fired muskets and cannons and scared off the attackers, and amazingly the quartermaster swam to safety. Abel Tasman cursed 'this monstrous deed' and called the place 'Mordenaers Baij'. Such was the first meeting between European and Maori.

The precise location of this encounter has never been clearly pinpointed. The monument to Tasman overlooks Ligar Bay, but some people favour the area near Taupo Point, an important pa site between Wainui Bay and Whariwharangi Bay. Here a sandy isthmus connects a headland to the mainland, with a fresh stream nearby. Drawings by the surveyor John Barnicoat in 1844 show an occupied pallisaded village with canoes drawn up on the beach. The old pa on the peninsula was sacked by Te Rauparaha in 1828 and has remained unoccupied since.

A COMPANY MAN

There is something unconvincing about Abel Tasman the man. His explorations show little inclination to get to grips with the new lands he saw, and the ship's log notes are factual and spiritless – he was following instructions rather than taking the initiative.

In fairness, commercial preoccupations ruled the day for the Dutch East India Company, and Tasman did not have the luxury to explore with the freedom that Captain Cook enjoyed. The company's instructions were explicit and detailed, and any change of route had to be authorised by the whole command structure of the expedition.

Abel Tasman was through and through a company man, who started as a seaman and ended up as commodore of a small squadron. His whole career and life were spent in the company's service. Promotion was fast in the Dutch East Indies, as illness, disease and hardship took a rapid toll. Tasman was an excellent navigator, and loyal, not afraid to carry out the Company's dirty business, such as slave trading, and stealing gold from the Spanish.

But despite his innumerable voyages Tasman's career was uneven. He was criticised for a lack of thoroughness in examining new-found lands. He liked his drink, and was actually put on trial for attempting to hang a seaman while drunk. Despite his valuable qualities his promotion was baulked at a certain point; perhaps his humble background meant he never became truly part of the company culture. He died a relatively wealthy landowner in Batavia in 1659.

The Dutch in the Pacific

The history of discovery is an odd patriotic business, and each nationality claims for itself the prize of discovery, in ignorance or disdain of previous voyages – and whatever the local inhabitants think.

The Dutch were active in the South Pacific in the early 17th century. Schouten and Le Maire had pioneered the route round Cape Horn to Indonesia in 1616, and the Dutch had a large base in Batavia (Java). Like the Portuguese and Spanish they guarded their knowledge jealously and tried to keep secret any commercial information that might be useful to a rival. Consequently exploration of the South Pacific was in fits and starts, with bits of knowledge recorded, even mapped, then buried away in private archives or distorted in official journals.

By 1640 the Dutch had re-explored much of the northern coastline of Australia, right down to Perth. However, the Portuguese had pipped them almost a century earlier, down much of the same coastline. In their turn the Portuguese had gained tips from Timorese sailors (whom they frequently employed as crew). Then there was information from the Malay *beche-de-mer* voyagers, and hints of Arab and Chinese expeditions dating back even further.

The north coast of Australia was well known by Tasman's time, but what lay south? Mapmakers had persisted for years in placing a 'Great Southern Continent' in the Pacific to 'balance out' the northern land mass. Abel Tasman was issued clear instructions by the Dutch East India Company to look for this continent, to find gold and silver, and to prove a passage south. This latter he did; indeed to him belongs the dubious distinction of sailing around mainland Australia without ever seeing it.

He stayed in Tasmania for a few nights, but had a superstitious fear about what he thought to be giants, 'Very tall people' and 'people who must Be of unusual height'. After the Golden Bay fracas he sailed to the northern tip of New Zealand to the Three Kings Island, where he was again alarmed by men of 'tall stature', 'who made mighty large great steps'. He continued to Tonga and Fiji, then returned to Batavia, where his employers were unimpressed.[3]

There is skimpy evidence that the Dutch sent another expedition to Staten Landt in 1664, but there is no record of this voyage so for all intents and purposes Abel Tasman was the first and last 17th-century Dutch voyager to New Zealand. For almost a century his scanty outline of New Zealand appeared on European maps, whetting the appetite of explorers who thought at last this must be the Great Southern Continent. It took an altogether more brilliant navigator to lay the myth to rest.

Footnotes and Further Reading

1. *The Voyages of Abel Janszoon Tasman*, Andrew Sharp, Clarendon Press,1968.
2. Ibid.
3. Ibid.

Abel Tasman and The Discovery of New Zealand, B.J. Slot, Otto Cramwinckel, 1992.

SOUTH STREET WORKINGMEN'S COTTAGES

FEATURES
Restored working-class cottages both sides of a quiet cul-de-sac.

HOW TO GET THERE
Starting in Trafalgar Street in Nelson, walk to the cathedral end and turn right into and around Trafalgar Square to Nile Street West. South Street is signposted 30m down Nile Street West.

It takes only 10 minutes or so to sample South Street, a compact collection of old cottages in the heart of Nelson. Most of the cottages in South Street were built between 1863 and 1865, and many have only recently been saved from rack and ruin and restored to a glory that they probably never enjoyed in real life. Bright paintwork, flowerboxes, carefully detailed architraves and herb gardens have created a 19th-century precinct.

Many cottages received lean-tos and add-ons over their long lives, a typical response to growing families, and the modern restoration of the cottages has continued to adapt each house to modern needs. Rooms have been opened up and more sun let in.

Most of this work has been achieved at great cost and effort by a few dedicated people. In fact they have done their job almost too well, for there seems something rather toytown-like about the spruced-up street, despite the fact that the houses are lived in.

Jeanie White's two books on South Street show the diversity of original tenants and owners: there were tinsmiths, labourers, a priest, a baker, a storeman, a fisherman and probably a candlestick-maker. South Street was quite literally at the heart of Nelson life for many years.

Further Reading

Town Acre 456: Historic South Street 1851-1988, Jeanie White, 1998.

Window on the Past, Jeanie White and Phillip Edwards, South Street residents, 1995.

RUSH POOL QUARRY

FEATURES
Maori argillite quarry, flaking floor and argillite flakes, Rush Pool mountain tarn, views of Dun Mountain and Maungatapu Track, Maitai River picnic area.

HOW TO GET THERE
From Nelson city it is 10km up the signposted Maitai Valley to the Nelson waterworks reserve. The valley road is winding and delightful, with many rest areas beside the bush pools. There is a gate at the entrance to the waterworks which closes at set times, and there is a caretaker's house on the hill.

WALK DETAILS
For the return walk to the Rush Pool allow 4-5 hours, and carry water. An information board at the waterworks carpark shows the various tracks in the reserve, and this should be studied carefully. The signposting en route is sometimes not the best. The track to the Rush Pool follows a vehicle track up the south branch of the Maitai a short distance, then climbs up a pine forest spur to a saddle with excellent views of the Maitai reservoir.

Follow the vehicle track a bit further as it sidles around a hill to where a sign indicates the start of the Rush Pool track, which climbs steadily through an open rocky and scrub face to the beech forest. A short climb through the bush and you reach a flat point of the spur where the Rush Pool is tucked discreetly into a bushy dell. The argillite quarry is signposted a little way further, and the rock outcrops make a good lunch spot.

An Adze Industry

About 1000 years ago Polynesians arrived in New Zealand and gradually spread southwards. These early Maori had no metals so stone implements were crucial – for hunting, warfare and barter.

The discovery of argillite in the Nelson area inaugurated a period of 400-500 years of stone-age industry. Huge amounts of argillite were worked in the Nelson region, with big quarry fields on D'Urville Island, Croisilles Harbour and the Whangamoa River. So extensive were the workings in some places that the argillite flake deposits are almost a metre deep and vegetation is still unable to regenerate.

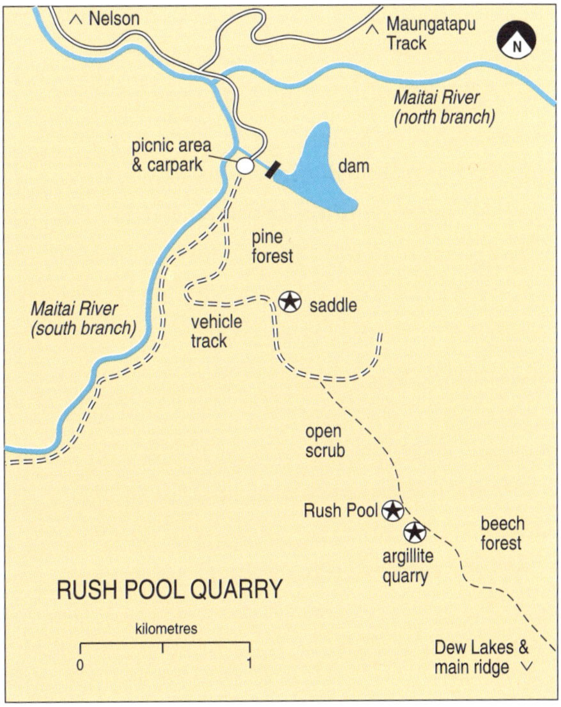

Argillite implements were traded throughout New Zealand, encouraging even more quarries in this labour-intensive, family-based industry. Then for some reason the argillite industry collapsed, around the turn of the 16th century, perhaps because of the discovery of the beautiful West Coast greenstone.

Aptly named Rush Pool

The process of making a stone adze has distinct stages. First the argillite rock has to be broken up and the blank formed, then the 'preform' is shaped from the blank, and finally the adze is given a cutting edge.

Argillite is an ideal stone for the manufacture of adzes because it can be flaked in a controlled manner in a much quicker process than the traditional grinding.

Hammerstones of a hard dense rock such as granodiorite were smashed onto the argillite and flakes of argillite were struck off as blanks. The hammerstones were often rounded boulders from the Boulder Bank at Nelson, some of them requiring two men to lift.

The next stage was to work the blanks into shaping the preform, using a smaller, harder hammerstone. This was skilled work and very few craftsmen would have had the skill to manufacture the long argillite adzes that have been found in some Maori burial sites. These would have been considered prestigious articles.

Shaping the preform usually took place near the quarry and the flaking floor of the Rush Pool is knee-deep in argillite flakes, a characteristic feature of all argillite workshops. As much as half the blank would be cut away.

The last stage was smoothing out irregularities and grinding the blade of the adze on a piece of sandstone. This work could be carried out more comfortably in the villages, and adzes were often bartered as preforms rather than as finished products.

The Rush Pool today is a romantic spot, and it is not hard to imagine a whole tribal family living and working on site. Yet back then it was a hard, unromantic life: the men smashing and shaping the rocks, the women gathering and cooking food, older children trying to mimic their parents, and the younger ones getting in everyone's way. Chips and flakes still litter the ground, and the mists roll eerily over the Maungatapu.

Further Reading

'Quarries and Mines in the Mineral Belt', Dan Witter, *Historic Places*, December 1991.

MAUNGATAPU TRACK

FEATURES
Original Maori trail, gold-diggers' packtrack, 'Murderers' Rock', Maitai Valley picnic areas, beech forest, Pelorus River.

HOW TO GET THERE
The Maungatapu 'Track' from Nelson to Pelorus Bridge is 40km long and crosses the Bryant Range. The middle section is a 12km-long 4WD road. Allow 1-2 hours to drive the Maungatapu in good conditions in a 4WD; fords can sometimes be a problem.

Ordinary cars can be taken 10km up from the Nelson side along the Maitai Valley to the forks by the Nelson waterworks. The Maitai Valley is an attractive drive with many picnic areas on the river flats. From here the Maungatapu Track becomes 4WD-only and climbs steeply through scrubland and pine plantations to the saddle.

Pelorus Bridge at the other end is a well-known beauty spot and it is easy driving for the10km alongside the river. The turnoff to the Maungatapu Track is well marked, but steepish at first, though in dry conditions a car can be taken from this end onto Murderers' Rock. The road winds up through beech forest to the saddle, and those not blessed with a 4WD will have to foot it.

'El Dorado'

The Maungatapu Track is several centuries old. The name is usually translated as 'sacred mountain', named not after the infamous events of 1866 but by a much earlier priest (tohunga) on a successful war party (taua), who erected a sacred place beside the track to recite his incantations. Early European explorers in the 1850s used the trail but it was really the discovery of gold at the Wakamarina in April 1864 that transformed the overgrown Maori route into the main highway between Nelson and this new goldfield.

Wakamarina was unfortunately in Marlborough province but Nelson was determined to have its share of the gold, and 'Sleepy Hollow' (as Nelson was dubbed) rapidly became sleepier as all casual labour headed off over the Maungatapu to the new city of Canvastown beside the Wakamarina River.

> We may safely assert that almost the whole male population of Nelson has been contemplating an exodus to the El Dorado with a view to actual operations or to inspect the

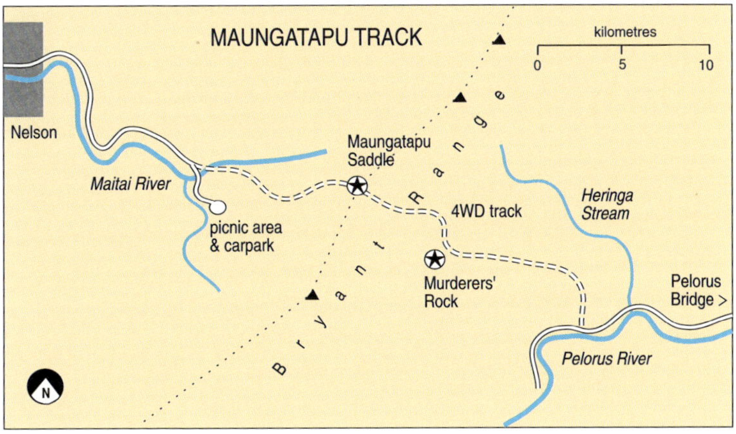

THE CONFESSION OF BURGESS

Richard Burgess

A great deal of mythology festers around sensational crimes and authors like to lay on the adjectives thickly. One book on the Maungatapu murders refers to the gang in the first three pages variously as 'lying Londoners', 'four thugs', 'work-dodgers', 'beasts of prey', 'four hoodlums', 'four desperados' and 'mentally awry'. Burgess is described as having 'the arrogant, determined look of the ruthless fighting Englishmen of the Norman-Gallic type, contrasted with the fair-haired, long-headed Anglo-Saxon strain'. He had a 'petulant mouth' and a 'scowling glitter in his hard eyes'.[3]

In fact Burgess was a rather ordinary-looking man who would pass as a prosperous publican, but this was the age of the phrenologist, where people thought that criminals had a certain head shape that revealed their criminal inclinations. Head and face casts were taken of all the three hanged murderers.

In fact Burgess (whose real name was Richard Hill) was mainly remarkable for his 50,000-word confession, written in a month before his trial. The most extraordinary criminal document in New Zealand's history, it is an explicit and detailed account of a life of crime. He wrote the confession to get back at Sullivan for turning Queen's evidence.

Burgess (Hill) was a professional pickpocket at 14 and was caught, flogged and sentenced at 16 to 15 years of transportation, the first 20 months in solitary confinement in a prison hulk. In Australia he became a bush-ranger, preying on gold-diggers, and admitted to killing at least two men – 'burking' in the criminal jargon of the days. He was caught again and there followed more flogging and a 10-year sentence, three of them to be spent in irons. The pattern continued remorselessly in New Zealand, described in a chapter Burgess called 'The Commencement of my Career in New Zealand'.

After more time in Dunedin Burgess and Kelly crossed Brownings Pass to the West Coast. They kept up the robberies despite the police keeping an eye on them, and killed George Dobson after mistaking him for the banker Fox. Burgess left a woman and his child on the West Coast and the gang shipped to Nelson, Sullivan noting that it would have been easy to rob the boat had there been any gold on board!

Burgess's confession is surprisingly well written and was probably dictated to Alfred Hibble, editor of the 'Nelson Colonist,' who visited Burgess frequently in prison. But Hibble's literary fluency does not disguise the extraordinarily brutal life Burgess led.

> scene of action and many hundreds have already taken flight. Clerks, mechanics, employees of every class and description have surrendered themselves willing slaves to the fascinating influence which operates so powerfully upon men's minds on such occasions.[1]

On one day in April 1864 137 people were recorded criss-crossing the Maitai River and stomping up the muddy trail. The corduroy on the track (thick poles laid side by side) made it difficult for the horses and was also disappearing into the mud. The roadmen had deserted for the goldfields, leaving the travellers to shift fallen trees themselves.

The track was entirely through thick beech forest, both romantic and threatening. Would-be miners often got lost or squatted out a wet night beside the track, complaining of deep mud and poor signposting.

> Wakamarina! My back is now breaking
> As I gaze up the steep Mokatap hill,
> 'Neath this heavy swag all my poor bones are aching,
> And yet, oh alas, I am clambering still.[2]

Accommodation houses sprang up alongside the track: Smith's, Dwyer's, Couper's and Lash's, the latter's chimney still a landmark. J.G. Lash was issued with a Publican's Bush Licence on 26 May 1864 but did not trade after 1866, such was the decline in custom. For the Wakamarina rush was a short-lived godsend and it is ironic that by June 1864 unemployed gold-diggers petitioned the Nelson provincial government to subsidise road work to the Maungatapu, where fewer gold-diggers now needed to go.

Murder on the Maungatapu

The Wakamarina goldfield attracted not only the hopeful and industrious but also four criminals whose murderous actions became the sensation of the colony.

Five gold-diggers – James Battle, Felix Mathieu (French), Jim Dudley, John Kempthorne and James de Pontius (American) – were killed by a gang of four men: Burgess, Sullivan, Kelly and Levy. The gang had already previously killed George Dobson on the West Coast and the gang's pledge to kill the men they robbed, to stop them alerting the police, led to the widely held suspicion that they had murdered many more men than they admitted to.

Three of the gang were hanged, while Sullivan was given life imprisonment as a 're-ward' for turning Queen's evidence against the others. His final fate is unknown.

This was *the* crime of the last century, but it has now mostly faded from public memory.

Footnotes and Further Reading

1. *Roads of Yesterday*, P.V. & N.L. Wastney, 1982.
2. Ibid.
3. *Murders on Maungatapu*, Frank Clune, Angus & Robertson, 1959.
4. *The Trial of the Maungatapu Murderers*, A.A. Grace, 1924.

Confessions of Richard Burgess, ed. David Burton, A.H. & A.W. Reed Ltd, 1983.

HOP KILN HIGHWAY

FEATURES
Hop kilns and old farm buildings, old railway line.

HOW TO GET THERE
Drive from Brightwater to Belgrove, about 18km one way, allowing 1-2 hours for driving and looking along the highway.

Most buildings can be seen easily from the road and since all of these structures are on private land you should seek permission if you want to inspect them at closer range. (See map on p. 33.)

A Visual Archaeology

Drive along State Highway 6 between Brightwater and Belgrove, following the sun-shrunk Wai-iti River, and you will find the whole history of the farming community strung out along the road – a sort of visual archaeology: derelict homesteads with weatherboards crusted with lichen, solitary huts in a swathe of untrodden grass, and Victorian farm machinery lost in the thistles.

Many New Zealand roads can boast rural relics but on this highway the ruins come thick and fast. Rust never sleeps, of course, but here it has been kind, mellowing the farmers' heritage with autumnal reds and yellows in a kind of curbside art.

Every now and then there is an odd-shaped building, cube-like and two-storeyed with vent hatches on top. These are hop kilns, a reminder of a once-thriving industry along this highway and throughout the Moutere and Motueka district.

Most of these hop kilns have now been turned into something else. A hole cut in the side makes a garage, a larger hole makes a barn or room for a tractor. A couple of windows and you have a garden shed; add a set of french doors and there's a summer cottage for you.

About 69 hop kilns still exist throughout the Nelson-Motueka region which, because of its warm, sunny climate and lack of wind, was (and is) ideal for growing hops. They were first grown here in 1842 and, despite the gloomy predictions, we have not seen the last

Hop kiln on Highway 7

> **'A SAWCY INTRUDER'**
>
> In the olden days hops were never used to make beer and the importation into 15th-century England of this new-fangled flavour was treated with great suspicion. Hops did the work of preserving the beer and flavouring it, reducing the dependence on spices and sugars. The result, of course, was a lighter beer. The English suspected adulteration of their heavy ales, or worse – a foreigners' plot: 'Hops, Reformation, Bays [baize] and Beer, Came into England in One Bad Year'. Hopped beer was called
>
> > ... a Dutch Boorish liquor, a thing not knowne in England, till of late dayes an Alien to our Nation, till such time as Hops and Heresies came amongst us, it is a sawcy intruder into this land ...[1]
>
> In time hops were added to ale and became much the same as beer, and by 1524 Flemish immigrants were growing hops in Kent. However, laws were passed in 1848 forbidding the use of hops in ale, and rules were established to distinguish the ale brewers from the nouveau beer brewers.

of the summer malts, for 830 tonnes of hops were grown in the Motueka district in 1996.

Most of the hop kilns are relatively new and made from concrete board, but some early hop kilns were made from cob, a combination of tussock, grasses and puddled clay. Only one of these still survives, but there are others made of brick, double brick and wood. About 20 kilns were built of concrete and the oldest, at Dovedale, had a shingle roof until it collapsed in a storm in 1989. It is now only a shell. Ewers kiln, built in 1900 in Upper Moutere, is the oldest complete concrete kiln still standing.

From Hops to Beer

The hop vine (*Humulus lupulus*) is a relative of cannabis. They are traditionally grown on poles and strings and, until recently, the hops were picked off by hand when the plant was mature and then dried in kilns.

> The drying part of the kiln was always square, its size varying with the quantity of hops grown on the property. On the ground floor was a brick furnace, standing a little over a metre high, fired by charcoal or coke and needing to be stoked every twenty minutes or so. About three metres above the furnace was the drying floor, made of scrim and horsehair. The harvested hops would be spread about two feet deep over the drying floor. After drying for about twelve hours, they were shovelled out using skuds (long handled wooden shovels) onto the cooling floor. When cooled, the hops would be swept down a shute into the press on the lower floor where they were compressed into bales.
>
> The drying process required sufficient draught to draw the heated air up through the hops, hence the tall ventilator cowlings on the tops of the kilns. The roofs of early kilns were steep and generally sheathed with totara shingles [tiles]. With the advent of electricity, automatic coal stokers could be installed, allowing twenty-four hour firing. Other growers opted for oil-firing and installed fans in the cowling to improve the draught. With these advances, the designs of

kilns began to change. New kilns had lower roofs made of corrugated iron.[2]

From the kilns the dried hops were delivered to the brewer. The medieval language of beer manufacture reflects the mystique of brewing.

Dry barley kernels are soaked and allowed to germinate, and this 'malt' is dried and kilned to reach the proper flavour and colour. The malt is 'mashed' in warm water, which results in a sweet brown liquid called 'wort'. Hops are thrown into the wort to provide bitterness and aroma. They are boiled with the wort and then fermented with yeast until the right balance of sugar and alcohol is reached. The liquid is clarified and sold as beer.

Not everyone regarded beer benevolently. One yarn is told of an early hop-grower named Benjamin Cropp in the Hoult Valley, Wai-iti, whose West Coast brother came to stay. When it came time for his brother to go home he spent the boat fare in the local pub. His family gave him more money and he did the same thing. His ever-loyal family tried a third time, with the same result.

Finally, in desperation, Benjamin took his brother onto the boat himself, and once he was on board paid the fare. Benjamin went home and pulled out all his hop vines, vowing he wanted no part of an industry that caused the ruination of people like his brother. His hop kiln is the only surviving cob kiln, built probably in 1890.

Footnotes and Further Reading

1. *On Food and Cooking: The Science and Lore of the Kitchen*, Harold McGee, Scribner, 1984.

2. 'Nelson's Unique Hop Kilns', *Historic Places*, December 1991.

Cast in Concrete, Geoffrey Thornton, A.H. & A.W. Reed Ltd, 1996.

KAWATIRI JUNCTION

FEATURES
Railway platform and tunnel, beech forest circuit walk, old stations at Wai-iti and Glenhope, windmill at Belgrove, Kohatu Hotel (the old Terminus Hotel).

HOW TO GET THERE
Kawatiri is 100km from Nelson and 35km from Murchison on State Highway 6. Rest area, picnic tables and toilets.

THINGS TO SEE
All along State Highway 6 from Nelson to Kawatiri you see hints of an old railway: cuttings, formed embankments, the last railway sign at Spring Grove. Wai-iti station still exists, between Wakefield and Foxhill (33km south of Nelson), and so do the Tui station yard and sheds, and the 1912 Glenhope station (93km south of Nelson). All are on private land but can be seen from the road.

The railway windmill at Belgrove was built in 1898 and is one of only two remaining in New Zealand. It stands 12 metres high, with a sail 4.8 metres in diameter, and once pumped water from a stream into a water vat for the Nelson railway. It was designed by George Troup, a well-known rail architect. Now restored, it stands on Department of Conservation land.

The Unfulfilled Promise

The curious platform at Kawatiri Junction seems at odds with the misty, bushed valley, and some visitors might think the station is perhaps an architectural joke. But nothing could be further from the truth: the Nelson railway was a passionately serious business.

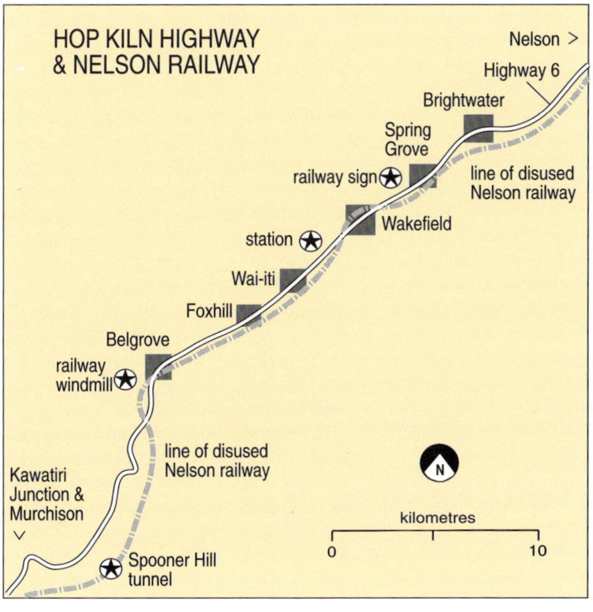

The history of New Zealand railways is one of unfulfilled promise. Nineteeth-century enthusiasts in New Zealand caught the tail-end of European railway fever and tried to reproduce its momentum here. The £10 million borrowed by Finance Minister Julius Vogel in 1870 helped, but a stubborn landscape and the depression of the late 19th century slowed progress.

With difficulty the main-trunk line snaked down the east coast of the South Island, but the numerous branch lines off to the side seldom made economic, geographic or social sense. Little River, Fairlie and Hawarden branch lines served the cause of Progress (with a capital P) but barely covered their running costs, and never their capital expenditure.

The Nelson branch railway was the most peculiar of all. There was no connection to the main-trunk railway at Picton, and no connection down the Buller River to the West Coast (Midland) line at Inangahua. It was built in limbo and remained in limbo, and therein lies a torrid tale.

'Toy Train'

Right from the beginning Nelson was obsessed with its isolation. Cut off by big mountains from the other provinces and perilously short of good, flat, arable farmland it had good reason to worry about losing people to more prosperous provinces. So Nelsonians wanted to make a stable communication link with the West Coast, which was in the 1860s part of the Nelson province. A railway was seen as a way to put Nelson on the map and the campaign began.

From the late 1850s to the 1870s Nelson newspapers hectored and badgered the administrators for action. The railway was always a hot issue in local government elections, and in 1872 a committee of influential local men was formed whose name summed up the preoccupation of the day: the Inland Communication Committee.

Midland railway works at Belgrove, c.1890

THE TUNNEL WALK

The 185m-long Kawatiri Tunnel was cut through granite in 1923, virtually the last great engineering effort of the railway. Lois Voller gives a good account in her book Rails to Nowhere:

> With hand-held drill and hammer, the tunnellers made holes for the plugs of dynamite. Later they loosened the rubble with picks and shoveled it onto the horse-drawn drays which removed it. The drilling of the holes by the hammer-and-tap method was by far the slowest part, yet they had to continue with it for 60 metres into the tunnel before a compressor was provided. This made the drilling speedier and two shifts could be worked each day. The second shift of men would do the firing at about 11 pm. Forty drill holes were charged with plugs of gelignite mounted on sticks, this being all that could be safely lit by hand before the first explosion.
>
> One night young Carl McDowell, the compressor operator, was recruited to light eight sticks and then hold the lantern while the rest were done. He found the experience nerve-wracking and was never persuaded to repeat it.[1]

These days the tunnel forms part of an attractive short walk that leaves the platform and goes through the tunnel and back over the top. Take a torch and read the above passage in the middle of the tunnel and you will come away with a good deal of respect for the tunnellers.

In 1873 the first official sod was duly turned, 3000 people turned up to watch, and the Railway Ball made a profit. It was a great event, but in 1876 when the Nelson-to-Wakefield branch railway finally opened there was only muted celebration. What had gone wrong?

Nelson felt it had been short-changed. Instead of a railway plunging down into the Buller Gorge and linking with the Midland line and thence to Christchurch (one in the eye for Picton), they had ended up with, as it was contemptuously called, a 'toy train'. The railway did not even go to the Nelson port, and the Nelson station had been built on the wrong side of the tracks.

John Rochfort's detailed survey of the proposed Buller line was disheartening: he estimated a cost of over £1 million. But despite these setbacks enthusiasm for the railway was maintained and by slow degrees the railway inched its way further south.

To Belgrove by 1881, Spooner Hill tunnel (1.4km long) in 1893, Kohatu (where the Terminus Hotel still stands, now named the Kohatu Hotel), Motupiko in 1899, Tapawera, Tadmor. Every foot of rail had to be teased out of a reluctant and poverty-stricken government. The Kawatiri tunnel was built in 1923 and the railway reached Kawatiri Junction by 1926. It was confidently expected that the line to Murchison would be completed by 1931, and embankments were taken as far as Gowanbridge in 1929 – but that was it.

The government decided the east coast railway was a priority, and the Depression and World War II left the Nelson railway languishing. Desperate appeals were made to 'fill the

Women stage a sit-in to protest against the closure of the Nelson railway in 1954. Veteran activist Sonja Davies sits on the rails at back, centre.

gap', but the last platform was at Kawatiri and the last train to it ran in 1954. The protests of a group of women against the closure of the Nelson railway made front-page news around the country, but to no avail. As far as Nelsonites were concerned, Progress had failed.

Footnotes and Further Reading

1. *Rails to Nowhere*, Lois Voller, Nikau Press,1991.

Guide to New Zealand Rail Heritage, John Garner, IPL Books, 1996.

Exploring New Zealand's Ghost Railways, David Leitch and Brian Scott, Grantham House, 1995.

THE EDWIN FOX

FEATURES

One of the oldest floating ships in the world and the only surviving immigrant ship to New Zealand, information centre and museum, Picton port and marina.

HOW TO GET THERE

The *Edwin Fox* is right by the Picton ferry terminal, with a museum and cooper's workshop. There is a charge for entering the *Edwin Fox*.

THINGS TO SEE

To explore the hulk and museum, allow about 2-3 hours. The museum is excellent – one of the best small museums in the country – with exhibits that are entertaining but not overwhelming.

Below is a proper cooper's shop, making barrels in the traditional manner (i.e. hoops of iron holding the staves together, with no glue or other fixing agent). The oak comes from old wine barrels and smells very evocative. Some of these barrels were bought for the replica of Captain Cook's ship *Endeavour*, which visited New Zealand in 1996.

A Roustabout Life

This massive and melancholy hulk is the oldest surviving large ship left in New Zealand: a gutted leviathan which, curiously, has not lost its dignity.

The outside is stained with colour – turquoise on the bow, warm reds and oranges on the streaked sides, dark heavy browns on the exposed teak timber – and the *Edwin Fox*'s history is equally colourful.

Born in India in 1853, she took tea to England, beer to India, soldiers to the Crimean War, convicts to Australia, and immigrants to New Zealand. She ran aground near Madras, and once got stuck on the Deal rocks in the English Channel.

The *Edwin Fox* made five immigrant passages to New Zealand, the first in 1873 – and what a voyage.

The *Edwin Fox* under full sail

THE IMMIGRANT VOYAGES

Numerous diaries have survived of early immigrant voyages, mainly kept by well-to-do passengers. Alfred Fell's diary records a voyage on the *Lord Auckland* in 1841 where there were 15 cabin passengers, 43 crew, and steerage of 60 married couples, 21 single men, 24 single women and 50 children. These numbers were fairly typical. Those who could afford cabins were expected to provide their own furniture, and were well advised to bring extra food as well. Ship's water was invariably bad so a forward-thinking Samuel Butler took along a charcoal filter.

Victorian ladies and gentlemen amused themselves with conversation, readings, debates, concerts and no doubt a little matchmaking on the side. In steerage things were a little less refined.

> A most amusing squabble took place below last night amongst the single women ... It seems they quarrelled amongst themselves, and about 12 o'clock it came to blows; then two or three of them went into hysterics, and a scene of confusion followed, I understand, rich in extreme.[1]

The goings on! Squabbles between passengers, drunken crew, riots in the steerage, wretched food: the complaints were endless. One captain was criticised for entertaining lady passengers in his cabin, and discharging a pistol when a passenger tried to remind him of his duty. He was arrested at Port Chalmers but fled on bail.

You could usually expect at least one decent storm, if not half a dozen, and the voyage would take anything from 90 to 140 days. Albatrosses, whales and icebergs would all be spotted, but rarely that most sought-after commodity – land.

This was the last fling of sail, before steamers finally took control of the trade. It was romantic and ghastly at the same time, and many immigrant ships were well past their best. Fares were rock bottom and profits were slim. Some ships had to stop off for repairs in South Africa or Australia; some ships never arrived at all.

The crew got drunk not long after leaving England, the ship sprang a leak during a storm and two people were drowned. Partially dismasted, she was rescued by an American steamer and towed to Brest. The crew received six months' hard labour for their sins and after six weeks of repairs the ship sailed again. This time scarlet fever broke out on board, killing four more people, and the *Edwin Fox* was forced to wait off Lyttelton heads for two weeks because of high seas. The voyage took 114 days all told: almost four months.

The ship had refrigeration equipment installed in 1885 at Dunedin and was used as a floating platform to freeze meat. Sheep were killed on shore, frozen on board the *Edwin Fox* and shifted onto vessels bound for England. She worked at this new and pungent endeavour at Lyttelton, Port Chalmers, Gisborne and Bluff, finally being towed to Picton in 1897.

Here she functioned as a stripped-down coal hulk, becoming increasingly dilapidated, until by the 1950s – although still floating –

she was practically derelict. She was towed and 'retired' at Shakespeare Bay in 1967.

By this time the *Edwin Fox* had been bought by the Edwin Fox Resoration Society for one shilling but it was to be 20 years before the society had gathered the resources necessary to move the ship on its last journey to its present berth in Picton. In 1986, after having nearly 400 tonnes of shingle ballast removed, the *Edwin Fox* was floated and manoeuvred around the point to Picton.

'Below the waterline'

The ship is much bigger than it looks from the carpark – registered at 836 tons with a length of 44 metres (144 feet). Most of the innards have been removed and the ship's back-bone of teak is revealed. Teak was the wood of choice for shipbuilders of the last century and the shipyards at Sulkeah in Bengal were some of the busiest in the world.

A discreet notice mentions that you are now 'below the waterline', which is a disconcerting thought. This ship is floating, alive still, and testament to a lively and lusty history.

Footnotes and Further Reading

1. *A Colonist's Voyage to New Zealand*, Alfred Fell, James Townsend, 1926.

The Story of the Edwin Fox, Edwin Fox Restoration Society, 1986.

A First Year in Canterbury Settlement, Samuel Butler, Blackwood and Janet Paul, 1964.

FYFFE WHALERS' COTTAGE

FEATURES
Original whalers' cottage, whale vertebrae piles, Maori pa sites, 1857 concrete retaining wall (earliest known use of concrete in New Zealand), magnificent views of the Kaikouras.

HOW TO GET THERE
From State Highway 1 turn off into Kaikoura and drive along the coast road some 3km to Fyffe House. A caretaker lives on site and guided tours take place at regular times during the summer season. Check at the Kaikoura Visitor Centre first. Nga Niho Pa site can be reached from State Highway 1, 1km along Scarborough Terrace.

WALK DETAILS
1 hour on guided tour around Fyffe House, 10 minutes for the Nga Niho Pa site.

'A Place Called Kia Kora'

Kaikoura waters run deep and these rich waters have produced rich pickings for human visitors: there is layer upon layer of human history on the Kaikoura Peninsula.

Fyffe House is built upon an ancient Maori site and remains a unique remnant of New Zealand whaling history. Whaling was one of the first industries of New Zealand, and one of the most cosmopolitan. A whaling contract was drawn up in 1843.

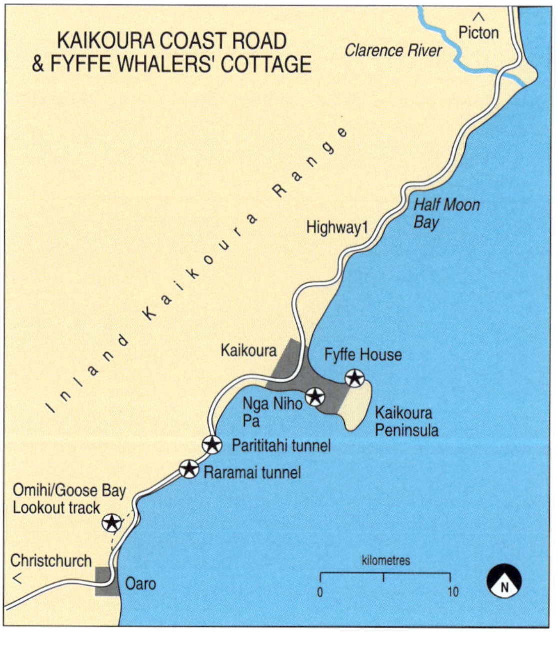

> Whereas the above named Robert Fyffe has agreed with Messrs Waitt and Tyser of Wellington, Merchants, to carry on a fishery for them at a place called Kia Kora in the Middle Island of New Zealand.[1]

The 29 men who signed up listed their place of birth as (variously): Ireland (2), America (1), 'British-America' (1), Saint Domingo (1), France (3), Scotland (1), Hawaii (2), Australia (5), England (10), India (2) and Germany (1). Their ages ranged from 18 to 50, with 10 men aged over 30. Most of them had already had many years' experience as sailors and whalers.

Shore whaling was dirty and dangerous. Once the lookout spotted a whale the longboats were launched, typically with a crew of six – four pulling oar, one boat steerer and one hand harpooner. As the whale began to tire from the loss of blood from the harpoon it was eventually killed with a lance, and the tail

Working the trypots

tendons of the whale were cut to prevent the huge fluke smashing the boat. The whale was towed ashore and cut up, the blubber melted in trypots and the oil skimmed off into barrels for export.

The first whaling season produced over 130 'tuns' of oil, worth at least £3000. They were killing hunchback and southern right whales (tohora), and other whalers moved into the area, attracted by Fyffe's success. But shore whaling was a quick-profit business – first in, first rich – and by 1847 the industry had virtually collapsed at Kaikoura, although whaling continued in a sporadic way until the 1920s.

The Fyffes of Fyffe House

Robert Fyffe was born in 1810 in Perthshire, Scotland, and he quite literally abandoned his dull life as an apprentice wheelwright and ran away to sea at th eage of 19. By 1836 he was working in Cloudy Bay as a whaler.

As the whales declined he expanded his sheep-farming activities, and by the time of his death from drowning in 1854 he had over 2000 head of stock, including goats. His personal estate was valued at £6000. His cousin George Fyffe continued to manage the station until 1866, and he also died by drowning in 1867.

NGA NIHO PA

Maori occupation of the Kaikoura coast goes back at least 1000 years. The full name of Kaikoura is Ka Ahi Kai Koura a Tama Ki Te Rangi: 'The fire on which Tama Ki Te Rangi cooked his crayfish'.

Food sources were plentiful – fish, crayfish, seals, penguins, shag and seagull eggs, and the occasional whale – and the Maori added to these resources by planting karaka groves up and down the coastline, some of which still survive. At Whalers Bay there is a cave that was occupied by Maori about 400 years ago.

As an important route between Marlborough and the Canterbury Plains the Kaikoura coast was at times hotly contested by Waitaha first, then Ngati Mamoe and Ngai Tahu. There were also incursions by Ngati Toa and Te Rauparaha in the early 19th century. The coastline favoured good defensive pa, with the sharp headlands providing lookout points and refuge. Takahanga and Nga Niho Pa on the Kaikoura Peninsula were both important.

This coastline saw many battles and subsequent cannibal feasts. One record states that the Maori name for Half Moon Bay was Umu Taoroa, 'the long cooking oven'. A record exists of a cannibal feast where 'the many dead were laid out in a circle, feet to the centre, and then cooked by the steam method'. The 'joints' were considered done when 'steam issued from uncovered mouths'.[2]

The Nga Niho Pa site has extensive earthworks, pits and terraces and is well worth a visit. The earthworks have been 'improved' at some stage, and the history of the pa is still obscure, but the site is a fine one.

Coopers or barrel-makers were crucial members of the whaling team: one, 24-year-old Thomas Howell from 'British-America' (Canada?), received £7 a month for his work and the oldest part of Fyffe House was probably built as a workplace for him. The shingles were hand-split totara and the piles were made from whales' vertebrae, still in place and still visible.

The house itself is built of pit-sawn timbers such as kahikatea, totara, rimu and matai, and the cavity of the timber frame was packed with a mix of earth and straw, which gave the house both insulation and fire protection.

It is believed that the two-storeyed addition to Fyffe House was built by George Fyffe in anticipation of his marriage to Catherine Douglas Fyfe, who was possibly a relation.

In August 1857 George Fyffe engaged two men to excavate for a store shed and they discovered the largest intact moa egg ever found in New Zealand. The humble concrete retaining wall built at this time is the earliest known use of concrete in New Zealand.

Joseph Goodall bought the house after George Fyffe's death and with his wife Margaret raised eight children. The house changed little, though a corrugated iron roof was added and wallpaper was used for the first time.

Like many other settlers, Goodall put his hand to anything that paid. He was first a policeman, then became clerk of the court and added the duties of customs officer and registrar to his functions. He later became wharf manager and in 1885 had the Pier Hotel built close to Fyffe House. This old hotel was cut up in 1909 and repositioned nearer the new wharf, where it still stands.

Fyffe House was sold in 1922 to James Johnston, who had previously operated the Clarence Bridge Accommodation House. His son was one of the new-generation whalers who used steam-powered launches and muzzle-loading harpoon guns. But they operated for only about five years, catching mostly humpbacks and the occasional sperm and southern right whale.

Fyffe House

The house was next occupied for almost 30 years by Joseph and Maud Low and their eight children. Maud 'Granny' Low was indomitable and after Joseph's death continued to make her own soap and tend her chickens and gardens. She still got her hot water from the coal range.

Maud died in 1951 and the house passed to her youngest child, George. George earned a reputation for oddness but at least he was not smitten by home improvement fever and when he, in turn, passed Fyffe House into the hands of the Historic Places Trust in the 1980s it was virtually intact – a unique whalers' cottage.

Footnotes and Further Reading

1. *Kaikoura: A History of the District*, J.M. Sherrard, Kaikoura County Council, 1966.

2. Ibid.

Tohora: The Story of Fyffe House, Jan Harris, New Zealand Historic Places Trust, 1994.

Kaikoura Coast: The History, Traditions and Maori Place Names of Kaikoura, W.J. Elvy, Hundalee Scenic Board, 1949.

The Past Today, Hundalee Scenic Board, Historic Places Trust, 1987.

Cast in Concrete, Geoffrey Thornton, A.H. & A.W. Reed Ltd, 1996.

KAIKOURA COAST ROAD

FEATURES
Almost 100km of spectacular coast and coastal highway, road tunnels, railway tunnels, seals and shags, bays and beachcombing.

HOW TO GET THERE
The scenic coastal highway runs from Oaro, 14km south of Kaikoura, all the way to north of Kekerengu, before the road turns inland to Ward. Drive time from Oaro to Kekerengu about 2 hours, with many rest areas, campgrounds and shanties selling 'cooked crays'.

WALK DETAILS
You could spend a few days exploring this coast, swimming, beachcombing, fishing and wildlife watching. There are several short walks, including the Kaikoura Peninsula walk and the Omihi/Goose Bay Lookout Walk.

The Omihi/Goose Bay Lookout walk is 20 minutes along a remnant of the original bridleway cut along the coast in the 1860s – the first European 'road' along this coast. At one time there was a deep pit on the spur, which was probably used as a lookout for the Maori sentinel who watched for enemies passing along the coast. The extinct laughing owl or whekau was often heard in this vicinity.

South of Omihi Stream is an old pa site, and Maori occupied this area for at least 1000 years. In the 1930s there were still traces of the maioro or defensive sea wall.

The Coastal Highway

We do take them for granted. They link our work with our home, our leisure with our duty, and have woven themselves into our lives so pervasively that we scarcely notice them – until we hit a pothole. Roads.

The Maori never had them; the early settlers craved them. Travellers in the 1850s navigated their way across the featureless Canterbury Plains with the aid of clumps of cabbage trees. Colonial newspapers were full of complaints about roads, the lack of them, the state of them, the cost of them. Nothing has changed.

Many modern highways still follow the approximate lines of old Maori routes. The European settlers first improvised bridle tracks along them, and after a fashion the 'road' was widened to accommodate bullocks and wagons, then improved further so that spring carts could tackle it. Bridges were slowly built and on many early topographical maps the status of the bridge was defined by the weight of traction engine it could safely bear. The early construction and upkeep of our highways took time and effort and roads still lie at the heart of a good deal of our economic and social history.

The Kaikoura coast between Oaro and Kekerengu is arguably New Zealand's finest piece of coastal highway: 100km of road as convoluted as the coast. Diving through tunnels, hugging bluffs, it twists and twines along the sea edge like a knotted piece of sailor's rope. The railway line has to share the same piece of turf as the road, shunted between an anxious sea and stark, rotten headlands.

Mountains rise severely some 2500m above the shore and seaweed slops to within inches of the road. Slug-like seals watch the cars

Double tunnel, Kaikoura coast road

pass, and cormorants congregate in committees on the rocks. If you are lucky, and look in the right place at the right time, you might see a plume of whale breath and the fluke of a tail.

This road now forms part of State Highway 1, the main drag between Christchurch and Picton, but for a long time it looked a most unlikely route for New Zealand's premier highway.

'Worn and Perforated Rocks'

> Our day's journey along the coast between Amuri [Haumuri bluff] and the Kaikoura peninsula was a rough one: we passed through two natural tunnels or caves in the headlands, one of which was about twenty yards long, and through which we had to crawl on hands and knees; the other, a noble archway crowned with bushes, would have furnished a good subject for the pencil: besides these underground ways we had also to climb over sundry creeks, and along the sides of curiously worn and perforated rocks.[1]

Frederick Weld struggled with the Kaikoura coast in 1851 and was pleased to catch a boat to bypass some of it.

As the small Kaikoura settlement developed early travellers were obliged to judge time and tides, and utilise the existing natural caves and tunnels.

> At the south end of Half Moon Bay horses – the bigger ones had to be unsaddled – scraped the roof as they were led through a natural cave beneath the bluff. At the middle they were liable to be terrified by the sudden appearance of light from the outlet ahead and would rear up, bash their heads against the rock, and half-stunned, would back out the way they had come notwithstanding beatings or blandishments.[2]

This cave still exists in part, half-filled with rubble and the sordid remains of teenage parties. You can crawl through it, just as Frederick Weld did. Parts of the roof look as if they might have been chipped away to raise the height of the cavern.

Bridle Paths and Dray Roads

By 1862 there was a bridle track between Blenheim and Kaikoura, and another one on to the Conway. But by 1869 the *Kaikoura*

OUT FOR A LARK

Arthur Lark did a spot of investigative journalism on the Kaikoura Public Works road gangs in November 1884. He volunteered for a spell of work to see whether the unemployed (there was a depression in progress) could be suitably occupied on roading gangs. It took him four days just to get to the works site, which was near the Mason River on today's inland Kaikoura road. Accommodation was a 12 x 10 tent, tools were in short supply, and so was food. It rained a lot.

> **On Monday morning Gang No. 22 duly commenced operations.**
>
> **About midday the gang's hands were very sore, seven blisters on each hand being about the average. We shifted about 18 cubic yards between us during this day; but the stuff was hard clay and part was rock, which took up a lot of time. All in bed at seven o'clock tonight – no euchre or singing. Up at 5.30 on Tuesday morning and started work a little before 8. We were very stiff and sore at first ...[3]**

Lark reckoned that it took a man 7-10 days to get up to any decent labouring speed and be able to handle the heavy work. He earned 4s 11d a day for his efforts at a time when food cost about 12 shillings a week; 'accommodation' was free of course. The 120 men were a real mix, ranging from

> **... the able-bodied West Coast digger, passing progressively through the strong able-bodied man who has done nothing but farm work, men who have done no work at all, worn-out old men of sixty years of age, mere boys, and, lowest of all in the grade, Salvation Army larrikins who made the night hideous with their horrid howlings.**

Herald was lamenting the fact that within the district there was 'scarcely a single mile of formed road which is passable for laden drays'.

The Provincial Council set aside land for accommodation houses along the coastal route at Kekerengu; the mouth of the Clarence River (1862); at the Hapuku River (1862-75); and at a bay then called the Boat Harbour (1865), which is present-day Claverley; and at the Conway River (1901). The houses were roughly a day's journey apart, which in the 1860s meant 15-25km.

With painstaking progress the roads were widened and were pushed along the coastline, and by the 1880s Kaikoura was connected to Blenheim by a reasonable dray road. Most headlands had been cut around but the Clarence River was a major obstacle.

The Clarence had a ferry over it in the 1860s. Passengers paid 2s 6d to be ferried across with their luggage; their horses swam. The first Clarence bridge was completed in 1887, at the same time as the inland road from Waiau was finally connected. Kaikoura had a party and erected a triumphal arch; at last Kaikoura was joined to the rest of the world – or so it seemed.

'Road Works'

In fact the inland route south, which is the current inland Kaikoura road, was unsatisfactory from the start. Snow made it impassable in winter and local runholders were not happy at being saddled with the cost of the road. Little maintenance was done. Ten years later a determined effort was made to cut a better road along the coast from Kaikoura to Oaro, and thence by the shorter Hundalees saddle.

Eventually two double tunnels, at Raramai and Parititahi, were blasted through (Raramai took seven months) and in 1901 the Hundalees route was established. But the vague road line up the Conway riverbed exasperated its users – 'as obvious as a politician's promise' – and this was not really sorted out until 1915. Bridges over the Waiau in 1911 and the Conway in 1915 at last gave a permanence to what has become State Highway 1.

Slips, slumps and washouts still damage the highway and as recently as 1992 the coastal route between Oaro and Kaikoura was closed for several days by a huge slip and people were forced over the tortuous inland route. New Zealand's roading system is fragile and still being worked on. There's always another discouraging sign ahead, reading 'Road Works' – when it clearly doesn't.

Footnotes and Further Reading

1. Frederick Weld, *Lyttelton Times,* 8 March 1851.
2. *Kaikoura: A History of the District,* J.M. Sherrard, Kaikoura County Council, 1966.
3. Arthur Lark, *Canterbury Times*, 15 November 1884.

Kaikoura Coast: The History, Traditions and Maori Place Names of Kaikoura, W.J. Elvy, Hundalee Scenic Board, 1949.

KAIAPOI PA

FEATURES
Stone monument, 15-minute walking circuit and lookout tower.

HOW TO GET THERE
From Christchurch drive north on State Highway 1 some 25km, to a side-road signposted to the pa. The pa site is 1km along this road.

WALK DETAILS
Today it is hard to imagine what the Kaiapoi Pa looked like in its heyday. Once waterways and swamplands stretched from the Waimakariri River right around through to Halswell and Ellesmere. But drainage and irrigation schemes in European times have made the original wetland pa site look little more than a paddock.

Apart from the huge and lonely Oamaru stone memorial, a lookout tower has been constructed with interpretation signs, and a short 15-minute circuit walk features signs that name the different parts of the pa.

Some efforts are now being made through native planting and the creation of lagoons to restore the pa to how it might have looked before it was sacked by Te Rauparaha in 1831.

Utu

Life in 18th-century Aotearoa before the coming of the European was no Arcadia. Maori were constantly engaged in inter-tribal warfare, and tribes based themselves in strong defensive positions in pas (or forts) to which they could retreat when threatened. Captain Cook was surprised to find on his return to Ship Cove in Queen Charlotte Sound (after three years' absence) that many of the original Maori he had met were gone.

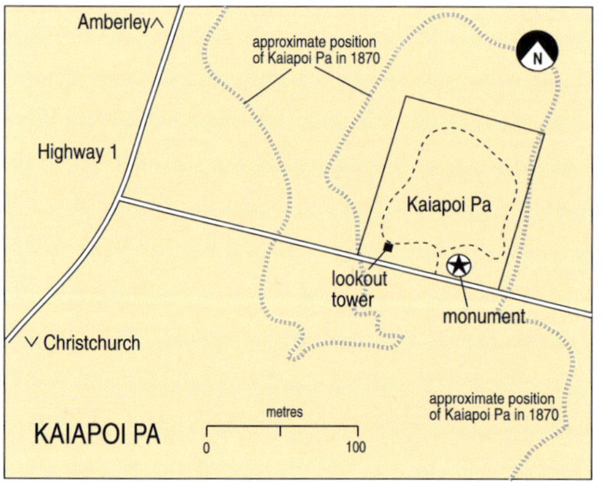

> From my observations, and from the information of Taweiharooa [sic] and others, it appears to me that the New Zealanders must live under perpetual apprehensions of being destroyed by each other; there being few of their tribes that have not, as they think, sustained wrongs from some other tribe, which they are continually upon the watch to revenge. And, perhaps, the desire of a good meal may be no little incitement. I am told that many years will sometimes elapse before a favourable opportunity happens, and that the son never loses sight of an injury that has been done to the father.[1]

Life was brutal and often short, utu (payback or revenge) was unforgiving and merciless, and the local Maori were surprised that Captain Cook did not seek to avenge the murder of a ship's crew some time before.

The avenging of one insult merely established another insult that had to be avenged in the future. Nothing was forgotten, and tribal alliances shifted as tribes repositioned themselves to gain an upper hand, or merely to survive. The victor expected to eat the vanquished, and women and children were enslaved or as quickly dispatched as the menfolk.

The introduction of guns only exacerbated the internecine warfare as tribes that managed to secure them hoped to avenge themselves before their enemies became armed. And no one seized more opportunities, was more ruthless, or more clever at securing European friendship than Te Rauparaha.

To some extent Te Rauparaha's fame rests on the fact that he had so many dealings with Europeans, who have recorded his activities. Te Rauparaha was clever and ingenious, as his subjection of many pas indicates, but he also had the devil's own luck, many times evading certain capture by his tribal enemies.

He was born in 1768 into the Ngati Toa tribe near Kawhia but the tribe was forced to migrate down the North Island, and eventually to Kapiti Island. At about the same time European sealers and whalers wanted to use 'Entry Island' as a base. Te Rauparaha was only to happy too oblige and a lively trade in flax and food for guns and gunpowder took place. As Te Rauparaha's tribal strength grew, so too did his ambition, and he sought to avenge insults that he had suffered from the South Island tribes.

The Prince of Pas

At the beginning of the 19th century Kaiapoi was the prince of pas in the South Island for the Ngai Tahu tribe. In a superb defensive position, it was bounded by waterways and swamps on three sides, with good food supplies close to hand, and well positioned along the main trading routes of the Maori. Ngai Tahu were able to take advantage of eels and flounder from Waihora (Lake Ellesmere), seals and whales from Kaikoura, and weka and kiore from the Canterbury foothills.

Ngai Tahu also crossed regularly to the West Coast and brought back the coveted greenstone. In a stone-age technology greenstone was the hardest substance available to the Maori, and the most prized. Only high chiefs would be expected to wield a greenstone mere or carry greenstone ornaments, and it was a mineral whose edge and lustre was quite literally worth dying for.

The fortifications at Kaiapoi were impressive, with high earthworks topped by pallisades, some of them six metres high. Totara posts held up the walls and on each were carved figures painted in ochre reds and with eyes of paua shell. In the front of the pa was

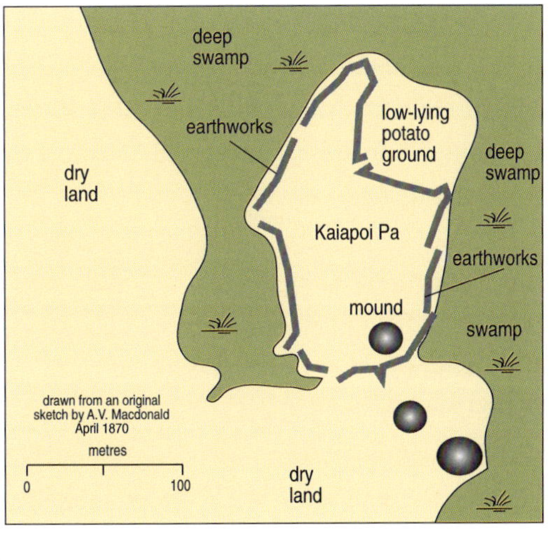

'Scene on the Horotueka of Cam/ Kaiapoi Pah/ Canterbury'. Watercolour by C. Haubroe.

a broad, deep ditch and there were earth mounds for observation points. The water supply was ample and the kumara gardens on the peninsula were easily accessible. Perhaps as many as 1000 men, women and children lived about the pa at the time of Te Rauparaha's first sally, in about 1828. It was a formidable fortress, considered by many to be impregnable.

The Sacking of Kaiapoi

Te Rauparaha had already attacked Omihi Pa in Kaikoura in 1828 and massacred most of its inhabitants. He arrived soon after at Kaiapoi with a hundred men professing friendship with Ngai Tahu, who were understandably doubtful of the honour. Te Rauparaha was too canny to enter the pa personally, but he happily sent in his high chiefs, unaware that some survivors from Omihi Pa had arrived and told Ngai Tahu what had happened there.

Ngai Tahu waited until eight of Te Rauparaha's chiefs were in the compound and then attacked and killed them. Te Rauparaha was stunned and could do little else but retreat to Kapiti, nursing grand schemes of vengeance. Two years passed before he returned and laid siege to the pa.

Te Rauparaha could see that the occupants were well equipped for a long battle and searched for some mechanism to overcome the pa's strong defences. He ordered his war-

KUMARA

The kumara fields of Kaiapoi Pa were integral to its strength and integrity. Frost is fatal to kumara, a tropical vegetable, and it says something for the skill and persistence of the Maori at Kaiapoi that so much was grown.

> **To regulate the temperature of the soil, and to secure perfect drainage, they covered the surface of the kumara plantations with fine gravel, to a depth of 6 inches [13cm], which was afterwards formed into mounds about 2 foot [26cm] in diameter, and arranged over the field with the precision of the squares on a chess board, and in these mounds the kumara tubers were planted. Breakwinds of manuka branches ... were erected every few yards apart, and in such a way as to secure the largest amount of sunshine and shelter to each plant.**
>
> **Both the planting and gathering of this crop were attended with peculiar religious rites, and only skilled persons were allowed to take part in a work, every detail of which was held sacred.**
>
> **The storing of the kumara had to be conducted with the utmost care, as the slightest bruise, or even abrasion of the skin, caused the immediate decay of the tuber.[2]**

riors to dig trenches with manuka and earth roofs that crept towards the pallisades and with this protection they began to stack manuka bundles against the pallisade walls. This was still a dangerous procedure because Ngai Tahu had firearms, and some 45 of Te Rauparaha's warriors were killed. But although Ngai Tahu constantly tried to clear the manuka bundles away at night, slowly the pile grew bigger until it became obvious that once lit, they would burn down the entire pallisade.

In desperation Ngai Tahu lit the manuka themselves in the hope that they could destroy it all, but a southerly sprang up and blew the flames against the pallisade. Many Ngai Tahu escaped before the northern warriors burst through the collapsed walls but even so there was a great slaughter. Twenty years later Europeans reported a great mass of bones on the site of the pa, and Charles Torlesse saw many skulls when he visited the site in 1849.

Footnotes and Further Reading

1. *Captain Cook in New Zealand*, ed. A.H. & A.W. Reed Ltd, 1951.
2. *Stirring Times of Te Rauparaha*. W.T.L. Travers, incorporating 'The Sacking of Kaiapohia' by Rev. J.W. Stack, Whitcombe & Tombs, 1906.

The Life and Times of Te Rauparaha, Tamihana Te Rauparaha, Alister Taylor, 1980.

Kaiapoi Pa (pamphlet), sometimes available from pa site.

CHRISTCHURCH: THE ENGLISH CITY

FEATURES
Provincial Government Buildings, cathedral, Arts Centre, Antigua Boatsheds, Shands Emporium, Hagley Park, Botanic Gardens, Peacock Fountain etc.

WALK DETAILS
Most of Christchurch's interesting buildings lie in a compact precinct from Cathedral Square down Worcester Street to the Botanical Gardens. Pedestrian malls, parks and boardwalks have made this area walker-friendly and there's no excuse to use a car. A 2-hour stroll would take in the Square and cathedral, the *Press* building, Provincial Government Buildings, Arts Centre, Canterbury Museum, the Peacock Fountain and the Botanic Gardens.

A longer 4-hour circuit could include the Spanish Mission facade of New Regent Street, Thomas Edmonds Band Rotunda and the Antigua Boatsheds. The tram circuit is an easy way to see most of the inner core, and they do an excellent historical commentary. Good historical pamphlets are available from the information centre, along with several books.

The Fondest Dream

Of all the cities in New Zealand, Christchurch is the most self-consciously English in design. A focal square with a cathedral dispatched four roads like earnest preachers to convert the Canterbury Plain into an English quilt. Smaller pretty squares and parks provide picturesque obstructions to the rigid order of roads, while a decorous river, nicely contained by banks of English willows and poplars, winds about a botanic garden.

Christchurch was established in 1851 by staunchly Anglican men, for whom the sentiments of William Blake's inspiring hymn 'Jerusalem' would have seemed quite appropriate. However it was not going to be an easy matter.

> Christchurch had been perhaps the [Canterbury] Association's fondest dream: a quiet university town of spires and quadrangles, lawns and trees. It was therefore a matter of some dismay to new arrivals who mounted the hill [in 1854] and saw the actuality spread out before them. For the town of some 600 inhabitants looked regrettably like a whistle-stop in the middle of the American prairie. It was exposed, it was utterly treeless, and it was dusty.[1]

Christchurch was built in a dry swamp, and the early settlers complained of getting lost in the flax and raupo (bullrush), but its prime asset was plenty of flat land, and a plentiful supply of good building stone in the Port Hills.

The discovery of the pastoral potential of the plains put Canterbury firmly on the map as *the* sheep province, and as the swamp was drained the city slowly grew. Gold fever helped things along in the 1860s, and the rural prosperity carried Christchurch through the depression of the 1880s and 90s. Many of the city's finest buildings went up in this period, which also saw many public and private

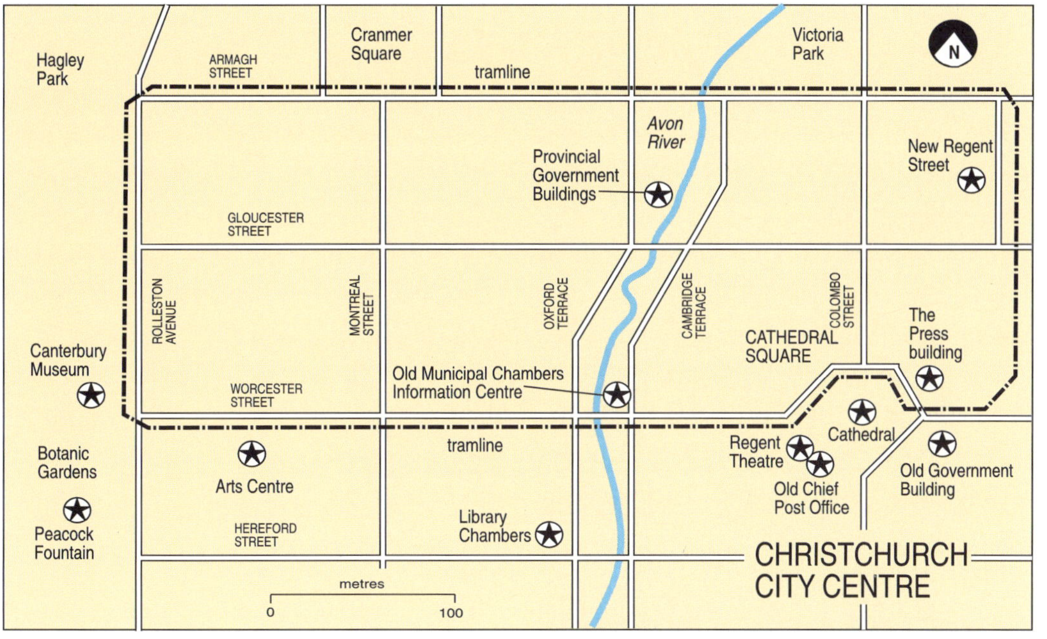

gardens established. Today the city core seems tidy, prosperous and erudite – exactly as the founders intended.

Their English vision is implanted in every street name: Worcester, Gloucester, Oxford, Manchester, Hereford. Many streets bear the names of the city's founding fathers: Bealey, Rolleston, Harper, FitzGerald.

The new immigrants also imported the then fashionable style of architecture dubbed 'imitation Gothic'. The icon of Christchurch, the cathedral, is a good example of this style, and despite being really only the size of a large church in England it is still the focal point of the city. It was started in the 1860s but not finally finished until 1904, with bits added as funding allowed and constantly slowed by prolonged and impassioned debate. The new visitor centre was added in 1996 (after another prolonged and impassioned debate), but

Christchurch Cathedral

there are still very good views to be had from the tower.

It is not an accident that the magnificent Catholic cathedral in Barbadoes Street lies just outside this Protestant core: these things mattered then.

Other imitation Gothic buildings to be found include the *Press* building, built in 1909 and still home to the city's daily newspaper, the Trinity Congregational Church (1874), the Library Chambers (1875-1923), and the Provincial Government Buildings (1859-1865), a fine assemblage of stone-flagged corridors and wooden-beamed ceilings in various styles.

Breakaways from the Gothic style are the former Chief Post Office in the Square, built in 1879 in the Italianate style to house all government offices, and the massive Renaissance palazzo Old Government Building (1911), across Worcester Street from the *Press*, now saved and converted into flats, offices and a restaurant. This was built to house the overflow of government offices from the Post Office building.

The original Municipal Chambers (1887) at the other end of Worcester Street is a rebel architecturally, built in Queen Anne fashion. This now houses the city's information centre.

The greatest conglomeration of stonework lies in the Art Centre (built 1877-1923), which originally housed Canterbury University College. The style is basically imitation English University, with cool stone colonades, pristine quadrangles and massive beamed interiors. You can visit Ernest Rutherford's den and historic classrooms. There is a guided tour every day which is well worth while.

Other interesting oddities to explore include New Regent Street, a pedestrian mall that boasts a Spanish Mission facade (1930s); Shands Emporium (1860) in Hereford Street, a simple, utilitarian survivor; and the Antigua Boatsheds (1882), with their cool-as-a- cucumber elegance beside the placid Avon River.

HAGLEY PARK

The city founders did not omit to provide space for a park and gardens, and Hagley Park is the green cravat on the sombre-suited Anglican dress. It boasts a nine-hole golf course, avenues of trees along the cycleways, duckponds, band rotundas, daffodil lawns and swathes of playing fields. The first race day was held at Hagley Park in 1851, and the first cricket match in 1852. The renovated cricket pavilion at North Hagley is 132 years old, built in 1864 and moved to the cricket oval in 1869.

The Botanic Gardens are 23 hectares tucked into Hagley Park inside a loop of the Avon, and are laid out in traditional English manner. There are lily ponds, a tea kiosk, a herb garden and herbaceous border, and many fine specimen trees date back to the 1860s.

An autumn's morning in Hagley Park is magical. The mist from the Avon half obscures the sweating cyclists on their way to work, and the lines of chestnuts and oaks are turning russet in a low illuminating sun. It is 'more English than England'; slightly improved, in fact, because here you are allowed to walk on the lawns.

Former Chief Post Office, the Square

What has saved most of these buildings is conversion. Almost all the stone buildings (except the *Press* building) have been altered from their original function. The fine Provincial Government Buildings are now the offices of architects and lawyers (and, appropriately, the local Historic Places Trust). The University College is now the Arts Centre: the old students' union a cafe and bar, the gymnasium a cinema, the normal school (1876) now a restaurant and flats.

The preservation of so many older buildings has made Christchurch an attractive and succinct tourist destination. However, the addition of a tram, a town crier, horse and carriage rides, a punting operation and a waterwheel have made some people worry that the city is becoming a 19th-century theme park. The founders would be delighted.

Footnotes and Further Reading

1. *A History of Canterbury,* 3 volumes, Whitcombe Tombs, 1957-1965.

The Arts Centre of Christchurch: Then and Now, Glyn Strange, Clerestory Press, 1994.

Canterbury Provincial Government Buildings, pamphlet, Christchurch City Council, 1996.

Christchurch Central City Walks (pamplets).

DEANS COTTAGE & MONA VALE

FEATURES
Two historic houses: Riccarton House with Deans Cottage and Riccarton Bush, and Mona Vale with fernery and bath-house.

HOW TO GET THERE
From Cathedral Square Riccarton House is about a 4km drive around Hagley Park and up Kilmarnock Street, or catch a bus to Riccarton. Mona Vale is on the way to Riccarton, via either Memorial Avenue or Kilmarnock Street, well signposted.

WALK DETAILS
To visit both houses allow 3-4 hours. They do Devonshire teas at Mona Vale, which cultivates an English sensibility. Riccarton Bush (or Putaringamotu) is a tiny 7-hectare fragment of the original forest of the Canterbury Plains. There are short walks among the kahikateas and wood pigeons, fantails and silvereyes are the popular and vocal native birds. There are lots of grassy areas for picnics and romping around in, and the Avon River completes a scene that is gently shielded from traffic noise by stands of fine old English trees.

'A Fine Grove of Trees'

The tiny Deans cottage was built in 1843 and is the oldest surviving building in Canterbury. The stately old Riccarton House next door has an original core dating back to 1856, and was gradually built in stages from then until 1900. The Deans family can fairly claim to be the European pioneers of pastoral Canterbury, the original squatters in fact. It's a remarkable story.

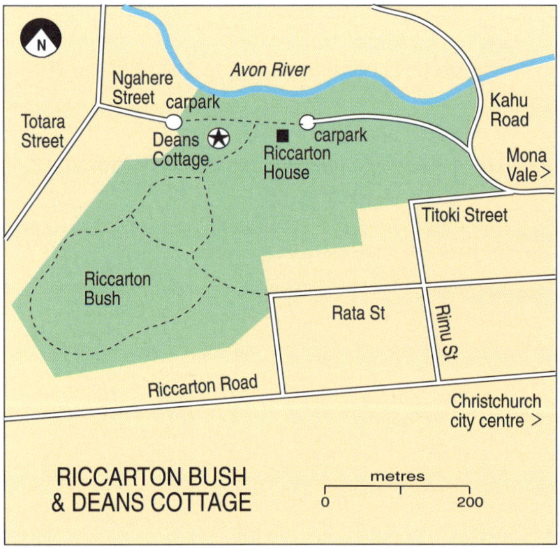

William Deans came out to New Zealand in 1840, and his brother John followed in 1842; they were aged 23 and 20. William arrived first in Port Nicholson (Wellington) and he quickly became dissatisfied with the land arrangements there.

Like many early colonists he showed great energy, and walked overland to Taranaki (in the company of the likes of Wakefield and Charles Heaphy). He later made a short trip into the Wairarapa ('would you believe it, no colonist but myself has been there').

John Deans had bought land in the Nelson settlement and thought he had been ripped off – 'the New Zealand Company have been guilty of the most notorious deception'.[1]

Meanwhile William had spent seven weeks on a cutter that serviced the whal-

Deans Cottage, 1843

Part of the display inside the cottage

ing stations, visiting Stewart Island and Akaroa. He liked the looks of the Port Cooper Plains (Canterbury) and the brothers shifted there in 1843.

Looking across the empty plains and wetlands on what is now Christchurch they saw only two isolated clumps of forest – at Papanui and Riccarton – and selected the latter, 'a fine grove of trees'. Riccarton Bush gave them shelter, firewood and timber for their first two houses, both built in 1843. The second house is now known as Deans Cottage.

The Pre-Adamites

The energetic Deans brothers quickly became the most prosperous of the 'Pre-Adamites', as the forerunners of the Canterbury Settlement were called, and the Deans farm became both a showplace and a haven for the few white people who visited them in the early years. At that time Akaroa was still the most substantial European settlement in Canterbury, so for many later colonists the Deans were shining examples, who had demonstrably proved that Canterbury was fertile and ripe for settlement.

William and John were careful to establish good relations with the local Maori, especially as the first group of Europeans to settle beside Riccarton Bush had left under a cloud. In 1840 a party of eight people grew wheat under contract for a season for Sydney millers, but the difficulties of access and the failure of the second crop after a plague of rats discouraged them and they left after a year.

The Deans entered a rental agreement with the local Maori tribe to pay £8 a year for a large grazing area – 'six miles in every direction' – including the present-day Hagley Park. But the legality of this tentative agreement was to cause considerable anxiety to the Deans brothers as the various land purchase agreements between the Maori and the Canterbury Association took effect. After some wrangling John Godley (who was land agent for the Canterbury Association) arranged a swap. The Deans could keep 400 acres freehold by Riccarton, but the grazing right was exchanged for 33,000 acres at Homebush, a run still in the Deans family.

William Deans drowned in 1851 and John Deans visited Scotland and returned with his wife Jane in 1853. Tragically John Deans died in 1854 (like William, aged only 34), and three of Jane's brothers came out and took over the running of the two farms.

The first part of Riccarton House was built in 1856 and was gradually extended as the clan grew. Jane Deans played a pivotal role in protecting Riccarton Bush and died at Riccarton in 1911, aged 87. She had been married only two years and had just one son, who had predeceased her in 1902. But John Deans II fathered 12 children, the foundation for a considerable Canterbury dynasty.

Both John and Jane Deans are buried in the Barbadoes Street cemetery.

Footnotes and Further Reading

1. *Riccarton Bush: Putaringamotu*, ed. Brian Molloy, Riccarton Bush Trust, 1995.

'Former Glory', Barbara Allison, *Historic Places*, March 1995.

Pioneers of the Plains: the Deans of Canterbury, Gordon Ogilvie, Shoal Bay Press, 1996.

MONA VALE FERNERY

The house at Mona Vale was designed by J.C. Maddison. It was a fine house with an expansive Edwardian garden and all the trimmings: a bath-house (now a conservatory), a lily pond, a brick archway folly, and wooden bridges over the Avon. Right at the back was the fernery. Threatened with demolition in 1988 it has now been completely restored, and new plantings are intended to revive its former glory.

The fernery was built for the International Exhibition at Hagley Park in 1906-07, and the then owner of Mona Vale, Annie Townsend, had it moved to her garden. Ferns in glass cases were popular in Victorian and Edwardian culture and larger indoor ferneries were *de rigeur* for those who could afford them.

Mona Vale's fernery is not fully enclosed and the roof allows filtered sunlight, mimicking a forest effect. A watercourse also trickles through the fernery and splashes over rocks. The circular brick wall is supported by concrete buttresses, and elegant cast-iron brackets support the rafters, their fretwork complementing the natural fern filigree. Part nature, part design: an entertainment.

INDUSTRIAL ADDINGTON

FEATURES
Concrete water tower, Wood Bros brick flourmill, St Mary's of the Virgin, workers' cottages.

HOW TO GET THERE
From Christchurch Addington is 2km from the Square. Either take the bus or drive down Lincoln Road.

WALK DETAILS
The water tower is beside the new Christchurch railway station, and the Wood Bros flourmill is on Wise Street. It's only a few minutes walk from the flourmill across Lincoln Road into the network of streets around Addington and to St Mary's church.

Addington cemetery is off Selwyn Street. Started in 1858, these days it shows the usual prevalence of vandalism and decay. There is one notably well-tended plot, and the camellia bushes provide a clue – it is that of Kate Sheppard, an early New Zealand feminist.

Industry is functional and disposable, a necessary architecture, and suffers quick renewal as society changes. Nowhere is this better illustrated than in Addington.

You can trace the changing face of Christchurch's industries by following the transport choices of the time. Woolston in the 1850s located itself conveniently beside the Heathcote River wharves, where coastal scows and barques provided the main transport in the early days of Christchurch settlement.

Addington grew up when the railway was king, from the 1870s through to the 1970s, but today's transport darlings are road and air, and modern industries position themselves near the airport, or close by the ring-roading system.

At the turn of the century the railway workshops employed over 500 men and women, and up to the 1970s the place was a buzz of industry. However, Addington's relationship with the railway was symbiotic, and once the railway declined the industrial suburb suffered. Now the largest railway workshops in New Zealand are an empty wasteland, and the only reminder is the starkly beautiful water tower, its unexpected isolation enhancing its lines.

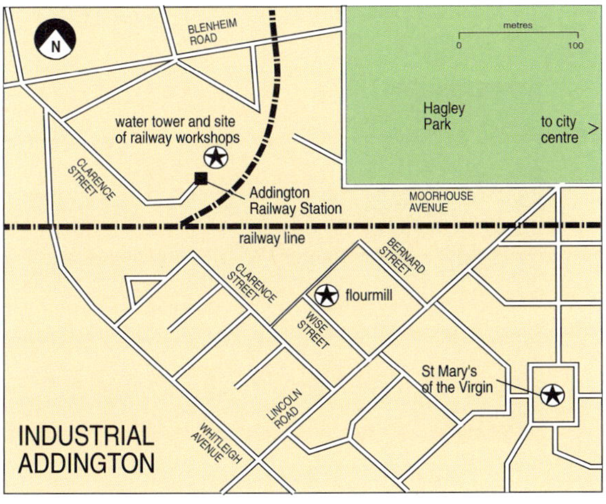

Railway Water Tower

The 18-metre tower was the first ferro-concrete (concrete reinforced with iron or steel) water tower in the world. It was built in 1882-83, utilising prison labour from nearby Addington Prison, and has a capacity of 114,000 litres. The tower was built on a layer of quicksand and settled (deliberately) some 230mm, but there is now a (less planned for) slight tilt.

The Addington water tower is notably ahead of its time. The metal was scrap steel, placed at 300mm intervals. It's claimed that this was the first 'real use' of reinforcing in New Zealand.

Industrial Addington lies in a tight-knot section of roads between Lincoln Road and the railway line. It still seems to be a male landscape, and the work ethic sprawls out on the street. Cars in half-finished paint jobs block the pavements, and spray painters and mechanics in blue overalls eat their sandwiches in the lunch break, having a smoke and a chat. Dogs sniff at interesting rubbish and the only greenery seems to be weeds.

There's not much left of Addington's historical warehouses and factories, with one notable exception – the Woods Bros flourmill.

You can hardly escape its presence: it dominates the area. It shows a typical industrial architecture, with the central building built in 1891 and flour stores and grain silos added on as needed. Extensions were made in 1896, 1913 and 1924, and probably other years in between.

For all this mish-mash of buildings, the central four-storey building has some splendid decorative trimmings, and its brick chimney is a beaut. The architect was J.C. Maddison, who specialised in industrial buildings. The brickwork glows a nut-red in the evening light.

The flourmill finally closed up shop in 1970, and now the Riccarton Players have occupied one corner of the building, while other parts are occupied by various small workshops and apartments.

Settlements for Hard Workers

Across Lincoln Road, residential Addington and Sydenham are still visually working-class suburbs, with quite a number of workers' cottages remaining, mostly grouped in twos and threes. Scott Street and Shelley Street in Sydenham, Poulson Street and Cotterill Street in Addington, and Rosewarne Street in Spreydon have quite a few samples.

Most of these cottages are tiny, with the characteristic 'lean-to' look of the rear roof. They managed to squeeze in two bedrooms, a kitchen and a drawing room or parlour area. Most would not have had bathrooms: the privy was at the back of the section. Many workers' cottages are now bastardised, sporting Decramastic tiles or new frontages, but every now and then you see one or two that have been brilliantly renovated. It's surprising what you can find exploring down these little side-streets.

Most of these cottages were built by devel-

Behind the Woods Bros Flourmill

CONCRETE

There's nothing new under the sun goes the cliché, and this seems particulary true for concrete. It was popularly believed that Romans invented concrete; certainly they made extensive use of 'pozzolanic cement' by 200BC, a mixture of volcanic sand found near the town of Puzzoli mixed with lime mortar. The fact that this new material set under water was an added boon, and it became the main structural building material of the Romans.

However, the Egyptians were making use of concrete at least as early as 1960 BC, as there is a mural at Thebes showing the various stages of concrete preparation. The Chinese were not so backward either: archaeologists have discovered a concrete floor in China dating back to about 3000 BC. It used similar ingredients to today's concrete: sand, stone, broken pottery (silica) and bones.

But the oldest known concrete has been found on the banks of the Danube in Yugoslavia: a floor of red lime, gravel and sand dating back to 5600 BC – that's neolithic times, 7600 years ago.

opers and private enterprise; the government arrived into housing relatively late. The first state housing in New Zealand was not promulgated by the mercurial John A. Lee in 1937, as often thought, but by the equally larger than life 'King Dick' Seddon in 1905.

Concern with overcrowding and unsanitary conditions led the government to establish 'Workers' Settlements' throughout New Zealand, and they ran a competition. 'Comfort', a house designed by Cecil Wood and Hurst Seager, won first place in the South Island section of the competition, and this 'free Tudor' two-storeyed house was set up as a workers' showpiece home at the International Exhibition in Christchurch in 1906. It seems far too elaborate for its intended tenants, but the idea was persisted with.

Flourmill brickwork

In Christchurch Workers' Settlements were established at Sydenham (Longfellow Street), St Albans (Chancellor Street), Linwood (Hulbert Street), and Riccarton (Mandeville Street). The latter was handily placed near the railway workshops at Addington, and six ferro-concrete houses were built with ornate verandahs to soften the exterior. Some of these houses still exist – numbers 21, 23 and 29, two of which have been turned into shop frontages.

By and large Seddon's scheme was a failure. A worker with a pay packet of £3 a week could not afford a 15-shilling rent, and the houses were rather 'grand' for the tenants. When the Mandeville Street houses were advertised only two of the applicants were railway workers – the rest had found cheaper accommodation.

'Comfort', the exhibition home, still survives, and was moved to Longfellow Street, to join a row of single-storey state housing. This settlement was called 'Camelot', a curious conceit.

Railway water tower

Addington does have a more successful connection with Richard Seddon, with a surprising oasis at its heart. St Mary's of the Virgin is the only parish church in Christchurch to be graced with its own square, enhanced by flowering kowhais.

The church was built in 1867, probably to a design by B.W. Mountfort. The separate bell tower is a memorial to Richard John Seddon, Prime Minister of New Zealand between 1893 and1906, and his son-in-law, Canon W.S. Bean, was vicar at St Mary's for 41 years.

Seddon popularised the expression 'God's own country' for this antipodean paradise, and he wouldn't have neglected to include industrial Addington on his political tours. Once there were a lot of votes here.

Further Reading

Cast in Concrete, Geoffrey Thornton, A.H. & A.W. Reed Ltd, 1996.

The Past Today, various authors, Historic Places Trust, 1987.

The Architectural Heritage of Christchurch, No. 9, Woods Mill, Christchurch City Council, 1996.

THE PATH OF PERSPIRATION

FEATURES
Historic (1850) track from Lyttelton to Heathcote, memorial to pioneering women, fine views of the Port Hills, Lyttelton and Christchurch.

HOW TO GET THERE
From Christchurch city it is about 7km to the Mt Cavendish gondola, and just beside it is the Bridle Path carpark. From Lyttelton the access is off Bridle Path Road, which is not as convenient for parking. Buses to Lyttelton and Heathcote will deliver you and bring you back.

WALK DETAILS
The Bridle Path is really a road: easy to walk up but steep. From the Heathcote end it takes 1 hour to walk to the pass on the Summit Road, and 2 hours for the crossing to Lyttelton. You can do a circuit walk by returning via Lyttelton back roads and up the Major Hornbrook Track to the top of the Mt Cavendish gondola.

For those whose uphill walking days are past, the gondola provides an easy way up the hill and you can walk back down the Bridle Path to the gondola carpark.

A pretty conical memorial shelter stands on the saddle for the 'Pioneer Women of Canterbury and their Families'.

Memorial to pioneer women and their families

'An Awful Pull'

In 1851 the Bridle Path was an object of fear, scorn and loathing. After five months at sea the pioneer European settlers were itching to get onto the promised land, but the Port Hills seemed of Himalayan proportions.

Their luggage was piling up on the Lyttelton foreshore and there was not even a horse and cart to get it to Christchurch. The prospect of hauling their baggage over the hill was dismaying, and to the frustrated settlers Lyttelton seemed a prison.

The Bridle Path is a steep track, constructed in a hurry over the Christmas period of 1850-51, and finished in the second week of January 1851. Every early account of the Bridle Path makes it sound like an endurance test of a settler's soul.

> After dinner I and another commenced the ascent of the hill between port and Christ Church. We had not gone far before we put our knapsacks on the back of the pack-horse that goes over the hill every day (poor pack-horse!). It is indeed an awful pull up that hill; yet we were so anxious to see what was on the other side of it that we scarcely noticed the fatigue ... So we continued to climb, panting and broiling in the afternoon sun, and much admiring the lovely view beneath. At last we near the top ... I must confess that the view, though undoubtedly fine, rather disappointed me. [1]

How had the Canterbury settlement, so well planned, so thoroughly organised, ended up with a dog of a track instead of the promised highway to the plains?

A 'Road' to the Plains

Captain Joseph Thomas was the principal surveyor and overseer of works for the Canterbury Association, and was given the job of preparing the settlement for the new immigrants. This meant surveying the towns of Lyttelton and Christchurch, building storehouses and temporary accommodation blocks for the settlers and cutting a dray road through to the plains from the port.

For the road he had logically chosen the line of Evans Pass, a low pass of only 600 feet (193 metres), but the roadworking in 1849 proved hard and frustratingly slow. It was not an easy construction job, and the road had to be cut out of volcanic rock walls and edged around steep bluffs.

After a year Thomas had spent most of the association's money and the 'Sumner Road' was still uncompleted. With the settlers due to arrive in December there was a panic on for some sort of pathway, and a fund of £2200 was put towards the 'bridle-road', which would be made passable for horses at least.

It was a tight finish. Charles Torlesse only started to survey the road on 3 November 1850 and the *Charlotte Jane*, the first of the immigrant ships, arrived on 16 December.

'Only Pedestrians'

Six months on board ship hardly prepared a person for a strenuous life in the colonies. It is true that some people walked around the ship for exercise from time to time, but that

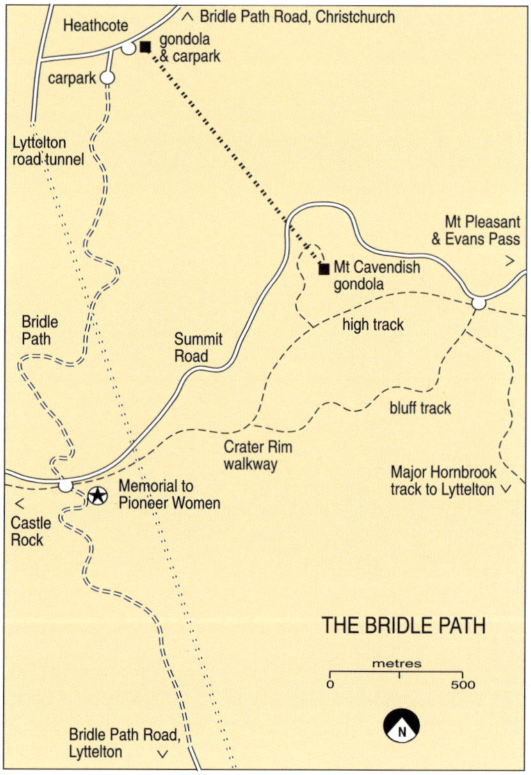

Bridle Path in sunshine, gondola on skyline

was not encouraged and probably thought rather odd. Among middle-class Victorian women there was a culture of delicateness and frailty, a sensibility exacerbated by tight corsets and broad crinolines.

Now they faced a narrow and twisting path climbing up some 1000 feet (300 metres) from the Lyttelton quayside, and then a steep descent on the other side. From the start the name was optimistic, as most settlers quickly realised.

> ... the bridle-path will eventually take the western side of the spur, winding round the steep crags and basaltic dykes, up to the lowest point of the ridge which encircles Erskine Bay. Just now, however, some of these stubborn dykes, although attacked, have not yet been fully pierced by the blasting powder; so that only pedestrians can follow the road along its whole distance.[2]
>
> Once over the pass the settlers had to follow the margins of the swampy Heathcote estuary to the ferry (Ferrymead) where 'the traveller finds a cluster of newly erected temporary huts, and a ferry-boat kept by Mr Hughes, who will put him across the river for 6d'.[3]

The road from Ferrymead to Christchurch was only properly begun in February 1851, with a road gang of 'sixty Englishmen and forty Maories'. It was mostly toetoe, thick grass and cabbage trees leading to the bare site of Christchurch where you pitched your tent.

No Place for a Piano

The Bridle Path was unsatisfactory from the beginning and any modern walker can see why. It is just too steep. In November 1856 the *Lyttelton Times* asked for suggestions to solve the vexed 'roading problem', and the letters to the editor column ran hot:

> 'I thought one Bridle Path was a bug bear, why then make two? And waste money in raising Evans Pass to such unenviable notoriety ...'
>
> '... construct a tramway on the face of the hill...'
>
> '... widen the Bridle Path to 8 or 10 ft and make it passable for light carriage...'
>
> '... should prefer a hole, but would like to get over the difficulty anyhow...'
>
> '... my opinion on the easiest mode of transit from the port to the plains? Try *early rising* ...'[4]

REFRESHMENTS

Henry Williams having commenced a stall for the sale of Ginger Beer and other Refreshments AT THE TOP OF THE BRIDLE PATH, begs to solicit the patronage of the public of Lyttelton and Christchurch, and to assure them that he will endeavour to keep on hand the best articles, and with the greatest possible variety.

Advert *Lyttelton Times*, 8 November 1851[5]

THE LIGHT AT THE END OF THE TUNNEL

The Lyttelton Rail Tunnel was the grandest and most expensive work of the young colony, and it was no toy. Canterbury Superintendent Sefton Moorhouse was an enthusiastic protagonist for the scheme, and although there is a statue of him in Hagley Park, it is the tunnel that is his memorial.

Lyttelton was an excellent port, sheltered and with deep water, but it was imprisoned by the volcanic crater rim. Although Evans Pass was finished by 1857 it was an awkward road and not suitable for shifting big loads. Moorhouse had been to England and no doubt caught some of the railway fever that was sweeping that rapidly industrialising country. The railway became not just an economic necessity if Lyttelton was to survive as a port, but a statement of the prosperity of the colony.

The tunnel was started on 17 July 1861 and broke through on 29 May 1867. The first passenger train went through on 9 December 1867. Quite oddly, in the process of digging the workmen discovered a freshwater spring that ran at a temperature of 70 degrees Fahrenheit (21 degrees Celsius). The tunnel cost about £300,000.

Although by January 1851 there was a daily packhorse over the Bridle Path, most people shifted their heavier luggage by boat over the estuary bar and up the Shakespeare (Avon) or Heathcote rivers. There's no evidence that any settler was game enough to take a piano over the Bridle Path.

The path was gradually improved and turned laboriously into a 'road', and the first spring-cart loaded with luggage was drawn over it by bullocks on 17 March 1857. An entrepreneur set up a refreshment stall selling ginger beer on the pass in November 1851.

Evans Pass was not finally pushed through until 1857, and although the main horse and cart traffic went that way, people still regularly used the Bridle Path as the quickest way to the plains. The Provincial Council spent £5400 on the Bridle Path between 1853 and 1864.

In 1867 the 'hole' of Lyttelton Tunnel was finally cut through and the path that cost so much sweat to the pioneer settlers was finally relegated to the past. History could mop its brow.

Footnotes and Further Reading

1. *A Year in Canterbury Settlement*, Samuel Butler, Blackwood and Janet Paul, 1964.
2. *Lyttelton Times*, January-February 1851.
3. Ibid.
4. Ibid.
5. Ibid.

Place Names of Banks Peninsula, J.C. Andersen, Govt. Printer, 1927.

GODLEY HEAD MILITARY INSTALLATIONS

FEATURES
World War II coastal defence batteries, 110-metre tunnel and searchlight emplacements, former cave dwellings, ingenious seaside baches, views of Lyttelton Harbour and Banks Peninsula, Scarborough Head sea-cliffs.

HOW TO GET THERE
From Christchurch drive through Sumner to Taylor's Mistake beach, about 14km, or else drive up through the back of Sumner to Evans Pass and turn left along the Summit Road to the top carpark. Picnic area and toilets at Taylor's Mistake.

WALK DETAILS
This is a justly popular and substantial walkway that has plenty of good views and some curious facets of military history. The area is one of the driest parts of Canterbury, with annual rainfall as low as 350mm.

The walkway can be completed in a circular track, or you can shorten the distance by driving along the Summit Road to the carpark and choosing smaller sections of the track. Allow 4-5 hours for the full walk from Taylor's Mistake to the tunnel and back.

'Ungodley Head'

Scattered around the New Zealand coastline are the remains of military emplacements built hastily during both world wars as a defence against the Germans and Japanese. These works were costly and ineffective: it is doubtful whether a single coastal gun battery fired against an enemy anywhere around the New Zealand coast.

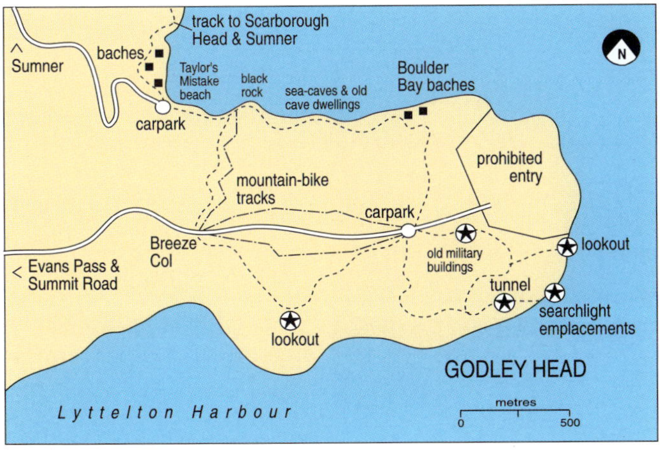

From the famous disappearing guns at Taiaroa Head (Dunedin) and Ripapa Island in Lyttelton Harbour, from North Shore in Auckland to Makara near Wellington, groups of military personnel drilled, trained, marched and watched and waited ... and nothing happened. 'Pill-boxes' watched fruitlessly, barracks beat with endless drill, searchlights probed an empty sky. A lookout's job from Godley Head must have been dead boring.

Only research done after World War II revealed that in June 1941 a German minelayer, *Adjutant*, laid a pattern of 10 mines at the harbour entrance, though no one saw the ship or the mines.

There are fine views on both sides of the Godley peninsula but after five years of cold sea-mist rain and lashings of southerlies these must have worn a bit thin at the sentry outposts at 'Ungodley Head'.

The Maori knew Godley Head as Otokitoki, which has been translated as 'the place of axes', but the Europeans named it after John Robert Godley, co-founder of the Canterbury Association and undisputed leader of the Canterbury Settlement. An early name was Cachalot Point, perhaps named after a French whaling ship when the French corvette *Heroine* visited Port Cooper (Lyttelton) in 1838. *Cachalot* is French for sperm whale.

The Cave-dwellers

The track starts at the far east end of Taylor's Mistake beach, wriggles past some precarious baches and follows a cliff coastline eaten out into bays and caves. In the late 19th century, long before the Resource Management Act forbade this sort of romantic activity, various caves were adapted into weekend baches, and in some cases permanent dwellings.

The three Kennedy brothers, well-known mountaineers, are thought to have been the first to camp in caves here, and by the 1890s Thomas Archbold had made one into a comfortable house, complete with rainwater-supply and fireplace. Next door in 1903 came Alfred Osborne, known as 'The Pilgrim', who had a telephone line to his neighbour held by insulators made from lemonade bottles ...

Probably the most impressive was one called the Hermitage, whose main cave was 60ft by 25ft and 14ft high. It was fitted out by two men, Cameron and Cropp, with material salvaged from the 1906 Exhibition, and was later bought by a city dentist, Jesse Worgan, who furnished it with a piano, brought around from Sumner by rowing-boat.[1]

Nesting sites for spotted shags and the white-flippered little blue penguin are found along this coast. The track cuts cleanly around the headlands to a few more baches at Boulder Bay, then climbs onto the top of the peninsula and crosses the Summit Road to the carpark and toilets.

Walking track and caves

There are several track choices here. The tunnel track descends past the remains of old military buildings (also a short circuit side-track to a coastal lookout), then zig-zags sharply down to the 110m tunnel, which can be walked through to the two searchlight 'pill-boxes'. There are splendid headland views and on a fine day this is a great place for fishing.

Searchlight 'pill-box'

In 1939 two 6-inch gun batteries were built on the headland, and a third in 1942 at the height of the Japanese scare. The first two had overhead concrete covers but the third was open, with a 360-degree firing arc. The lighthouse was shifted to clear the field of fire, and the battery had radar able to scan halfway to Wellington.

SEASIDE BACHES

The word bach is a contraction of bachelor, the original idea being that a single bloke can bolt away to a little hermit hut by the seaside for somewhere to swim, fish and drink beer with his mates. Baches have been described as 'architecture with jandals on', both indigenous and ingenious, and on the west side of Taylor's Mistake are some gems of kiwiana. Baches are clumped under the cliffs, hanging as perilously as shags' nests.

They're built on the Queen's Chain of course, and probably break most health and building regulations, but for all that they're cute and colourful. There has been a long-running controversy over a plan to demolish them but bach-owners are rather like the limpets on the rocks – difficult to shift and scarcely worth the effort.

Searchlight emplacements were built at sea level to shine across the harbour entrance and the tunnel dug to give foot access to them. Also built were concrete magazines, barracks, messes and a kitchen for the 11th Coast Regiment.

A different trail can be taken from the tunnel on the return to the carpark and old military cookhouse site.

The main ridge track back to Taylor's Mistake rambles along the crest of the tussock peninsula, past a lookout, and down to Breeze Col. It then descends dramatically to the bay. Several mountain-bike trails have been constructed on the peninsula and these can be utilised by alert walkers.

Footnotes and Further Reading

1. *Sumner to Ferrymead,* Walter de Thier, Pegasus Press, 1976.

A History of Port Lyttelton, W.H. Scotter, Lyttelton Harbour Board, 1968.

LYTTELTON PORT

FEATURES
Port town and historic walk, Pilgrim's Rock plaque, old police station, steam tug *Lyttelton*, Timeball Station, Lyttelton Gaol site, graving dock, steep scenic settlement with many old cottages and buildings.

HOW TO GET THERE
From Christchurch it is a 10km drive to Lyttelton, or take the number 28 bus. Ripapa Island can only be reached by tourist launch, but Quail Island can be reached via the Diamond Harbour ferry.

WALK DETAILS
The information centre has a pamphlet entitled *Lyttelton Historic Walk* which describes a 2-hour self-guiding walk giving a first-class historical introduction to the port town of Lyttelton.

The walk starts at the signal box and includes the Pilgrim's Rock plaque, which commemorates the first landings of European settlers in 1849, the site of Canterbury's first printing press (1851), the Lyttelton police station (1880), the Lyttelton Gaol site with the two remaining cells and the head warder's house, Dr Draper's house (1852), the Anglican church (1860) and many other historic buildings and sites.

Down at the port side there is the steam tug *Lyttelton* (1907), and the graving dock or dry dock (1883), which was used to repair Captain Scott's two Antarctica ships, *Discovery* and *Terra Nova*. Up on the hill is the distinctive castle-like Timeball Station (1876), one of only five in the world still working, and managed by the Historic Places Trust. See the information office for access details to these sites.

Tang & Texture

Port towns are located somewhere between the solitariness of the sea and the sinfulness of shore. For centuries sailors have been returning after long voyages charged up with a surplus of hormones and thirst, and it is the port towns that take the brunt. Lyttelton is typical, and still has more pubs per head of population than the rest of Canterbury. 'Grease shops', 'ship girls', 'coastal hostesses' and hotels provide entertainment until all too soon the ships, like the sailors, unload one cargo, gorge themselves on another, and slip away.

There's always something happening. Cranes sway heavily in the stiff nor'easters and water slops anxiously against the jetty piles. The gulls peck away at scraps from the rust-camouflaged fishing trawlers, and from the container wharf come the loud bangs, thumps and whinings of machinery.

Lyttelton has a dramatic site between the harbour and the steep volcanic cliffs of the crater rim. There's precious little flat land, and everything and everyone is jammed up against each other. While the port has had to continually re-invent itself to stay profitable, the township has lagged well behind. A type of domestic architecture called 'anything goes' mingles with sleepy collections of old cottages and shops with battered Victorian facades, all densely packed in the natural ampitheatre.

Polite sailors with ill-fitting clothes and incomprehensible accents peer through shop windows during the day; the new cafes lure a smarter crowd in the evenings. The hotels

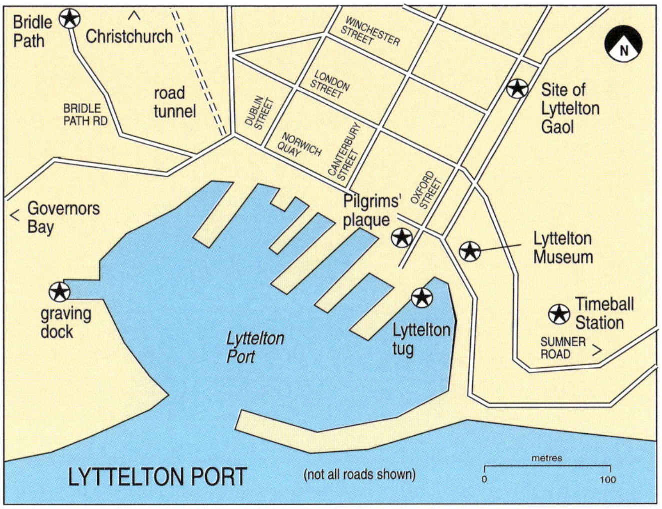

TWO HISTORIC ISLANDS

Ripapa Island has seen a lot of warlike activity. It was a Maori pa site, involved in a bloody battle as a result of the kai huanga feud, and in the 1890s became a European fortification, with two 8-inch guns and two 6-inch guns on 'disappearing' carriages.

Fort Jervois was built to scare off the Russians, but they didn't come and it is now an historic site, having done stints as a quarantine station, a prison (Maori prisoners from wars of the 1850s to the 1880s, and Count Felix von Luckner in World War I), a sea-cadet training area and a shipping company store. There are now tourist trips organised from Lyttelton to view the tunnels and the disappearing guns, which were never fired in anger.

Quail Island is an enjoyable coastal walk that can be reached by the Diamond Harbour ferry. Arriving by boat is a novelty and establishes an unhurried frame of mind well suited to the lazy solitude of the island.

It was precisely this solitude that has caused most of Quail Island's interesting history. A leper colony was housed here (the cemetery can still be seen), and so were Scott's dogs and ponies in transit to Antarctica in 1910. (Neither dogs, ponies nor Scott came back.) And there is dumping on a grand scale in the ships' 'graveyard' on the western side of the island.

Ships' graveyard, Quail Island

The information centre on the island is a surprise. From the outside it's a plain house, but inside the walls are covered with dramatic paintings of the island's natural and human history. There are also 'hands-on' exhibits.

For the smaller (and bigger) kids there are two excellent and safe beaches.

Allow 2 hours for walking around Quail Island, but you can easily use up a whole day.

offer a defiantly 1950s style of booze barn while up the hillside sit the immaculately restored villas with dormer windows and ornamented verandahs.

The history, seediness and charm of Lyttelton are still tangible. Different parts of it are working-class or yuppie, beautiful or bedraggled, according to how much view and sun they get. Some see Lyttelton as a town with a personality; others see it as a sunless hole. One of the great pleasures of Lyttelton is that these contrasts can be enjoyed easily on foot.

The First Four Ships

Lyttelton began life abruptly in the winter of 1849 as the town was prepared to take an influx of the first 'pilgrims' of the Canterbury Settlement. Streets were laid out, a jetty and barracks for the immigrants were built, and by late 1850 25 houses or more were dotted on the bare hillsides overlooking the town.

A good deal of the European mythology of Canterbury was generated because the first four immigrant ships arrived within close proximity of each other. The *Charlotte Jane* arrived at 10am on 16 December 1850 and the *Randolph* at 5.30pm the same day. On the 17th the *Sir George Seymour* arrived at noon, and the *Cressy* was a tardy 11 days later on 28 December. Some 700 people had arrived within a fortnight and Lyttelton bustled with Christmas expectation and apprehension.

A closer acquaintance of Lyttelton revealed certain drawbacks for the immigrant, among them a lack of sun in winter, a shortage of water, a lack of space to develop, and a steep hill to climb to escape the port and reach the Canterbury Plains. In fact the future of the port remained in doubt until the railway tunnel was built in 1867. The tunnel made Lyttelton viable, but also took away some of its independence.

Further Reading

A History of Port Lyttelton, W.H. Scotter, Lyttelton Harbour Board, 1968.

Lyttelton Historic Walk (pamphlet).

SIGN OF THE PACKHORSE

FEATURES
Original stone rest house (Packhorse Hut), 1848 shepherds' hut, waterwheel, agricultural machinery, information centre and extensive picnic areas, views of Mt Herbert and Mt Bradley.

HOW TO GET THERE
Drive from Christchurch via Gebbies Pass or Dyers Pass to Charteris Bay, about 30km.

WALK DETAILS
Orton Bradley Park is a charming out-of-town destination for families, would-be strollers and sun-bathers. It's a 653-hectare working farm-park and provides a valuable public space on this part of the peninsula. There is an information centre, historical machinery, and large tree-lined grassy areas for the kids to go berserk in. A small entry charge may be made in summer.

There are short walks to features of interest, such as the Big Rock, the rhododendron walk and mill race, a waterwheel, millpond and a small 20m waterfall fed by a natural spring. There are wheelchair toilets and picnic tables. For a longer walk you can climb up to Mt Herbert peak and back (a full day), or do the Tableland Circuit (2-3 hours).

To reach the Packhorse Hut a poled side-track (off the Tableland Track) sidles under Mt Bradley and slowly climbs to the saddle (a day return). The views from the hut are excellent. It has bunks, a fireplace (no wood, of course), a rain-water tank and toilet. The water tank is unreliable so it's probably better to take your own supplies.

The Packhorse sits in the centre of a web of tracks. For the fitter, a poled track leads behind Mt Bradley and connects with the Mt Herbert Walkway and the Orton Bradley tracks. A full circuit would take a day, 6-7 hours. You could also walk over Mt Bradley itself.

Only 10 minutes from the Packhorse Hut are the Remarkable Dykes, a great slash of volcanic rock like sharks' fins. This poled route continues down to Gebbies Pass, 2-3 hours one way. Another well-marked track leads down to the Kaituna Valley carpark, 2 hours one way.

Out on a Limb

The Sign of the Packhorse Hut is perched in a sort of limbo on a blustery saddle that looks from Lyttelton to Kaitorete Spit. In a style that could be called volcanic vernacular, the Packhorse looks more like a rock outcrop than a hut, sitting alone on the tussock pass.

No real roads lead here – only paper roads scratched on an old map – yet solitude suits the Packhorse and lends it some gravity. Any visitor is bound to ask why is it here? Who built it? For what purpose?

The original idea was for a series of hostelries punctuating the continuous sentence

Sign of the Packhouse (date unknown)

of the Summit Road, from Christchurch to Akaroa. Several were built, including the baronial Sign of the Takahe (now a restaurant),

THE WATER TECHNOLOGY OF ORTON BRADLEY PARK

Orton Bradley Park has many notable historic features. Included among them are an original stone shepherd's hut (1848), believed to be the oldest stone hut in Canterbury, the Charteris Bay School (1878), a flax mill (1870-90s), a quarry (1938-85), a replica of the original homestead, groves of exotic trees with 159 different species and, most important, the ruins of a complex water technology established by Orton Bradley.

Stables and stone hut

The water was used both for three-tier irrigation of his extensive tree plantings and to drive the waterwheel, built at the turn of the century and still in full working condition. It powered a smithy, saw, lathe, drill press, oat-crusher and a generator for electric lighting.

Reverend Bradley bought the property in 1858 for £1000 and was succeeded by his son Orton in 1892, who lived there for 50 years. Orton was either a romantic or a visionary. Steam-power systems were perfectly adequate to power his mechanical devices, but he chose water power. He was a keen horticulturalist, also a bit of a technology freak, fascinated by mechanical devices, and a passionate metal-worker. These interests melded to produce an ingenious system of water supply.

Water from a millpond was let down a 'leat' (an open watercourse), over an aquaduct over the river to a lower pond, where part of the water was taken off for irrigation and the remainder to the waterwheel. It is a 3.3-metre overshot waterwheel, with 32 one-metre-wide buckets each holding 53 litres (12 gallons). About 9-11 horsepower connected to a power chain drove the various implements. It has been estimated that the saw could only run for 50 minutes in the summer before the millpond was too low, while in the higher rainfall of winter it could run for seven hours.

So involved was Orton Bradley in his project that when he died in 1943, leaving the estate to 'the people of New Zealand', the farm was badly run down. However, restoration work is beginning to revitalise the farm and the historic ruins. The water is trickling again.

the Sign of the Kiwi (opened in 1917 and recently returned to its old function as a tearooms), the Sign of the Packhorse and the Sign of the Bellbird. The latter is just a shelter now, rebuilt from the ruins of the original 1913-15 caretaker's cottage and tearooms.

It required a vivid imagination to conceive the plan, and Harry Gordon Ell was the man for the job: a feisty, infuriating man who probably made an enemy for every friend. He was a Member of Parliament and a genius, someone remarked, as long as you did not have to work with him.

He was constantly in debt, constantly fighting for his beloved road, and constantly battling bureaucracy. He and his wife lived at the Sign of the Kiwi and the Sign of the Takahe at various times. Ell was seldom hobbled by either detail or inertia, and Gordon Ogilvie's book on the Port Hills has a marvellous chapter on the man, who was not one of life's quitters. Tracks on the Port Hills are named after Harry Ell and his wife Ada.

Later on, Banks Peninsula was the unlikely cradle of youth hostelling in New Zealand. The energetic Cora Wilding returned from a trip to Europe fired up by the concept of hostelling, and founded the Youth Hostel Association in Christchurch. Walking holidays were popular in the 1920s and 1930s and by 1932 there were 11 hostels on the peninsula, with a well-established walking circuit between them.

The Sign of the Packhorse came to be utilised in the hostel system and early photos show a homely place, with curtains by the windows and flowers on the table. At the hostels it cost a shilling for a bed, a shilling for dinner, and lunch (thick bread and butter with cheese) was sixpence.

Further Reading

The Port Hills of Christchurch, Gordon Ogilvie, A.H. & A.W. Reed Ltd, 1978.

Orton Bradley Park (pamphlet).

The Water Technology Orton Bradley Park, Neil Challenger, Dept. of Lands & Survey, 1985.

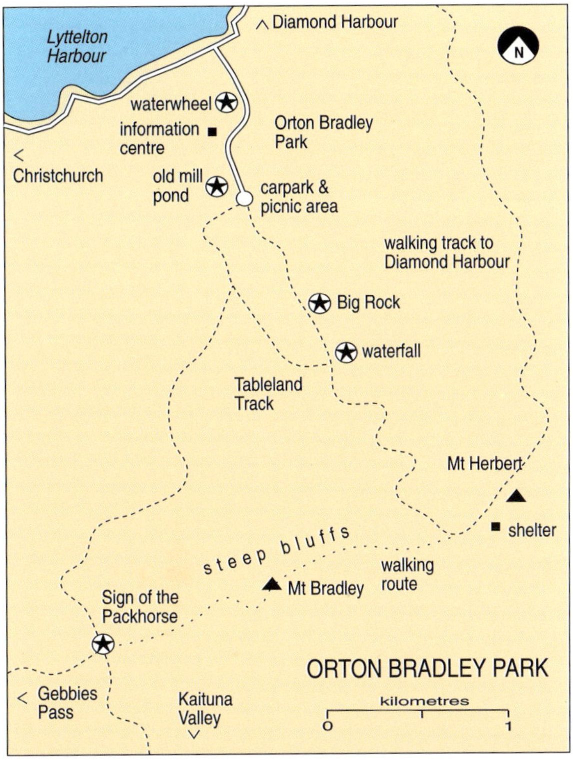

Interior of Sign of the Packhorse, c.1910

OKAINS BAY

FEATURES
Many colonial-style buildings, St John's Anglican church (1863), original store (1878), beautiful beach and bay.

HOW TO GET THERE
From State Highway 75 just past Duvauchelles (6km short of Akaroa) turn off up the Okains Bay Road, 4km to the hill saddle, then 6km down into the long valley to the Okains Bay settlement.

THINGS TO SEE
To look around some of the buildings, the Okains Bay museum and have a dip in the sea, allow yourself 2-3 hours. The museum has a 19th-century precinct of old buildings, plus Maori artefacts, farm implements and a cornucopia of other exhibits.

There is a large picnic and rest area in the dunes and pine trees at the end of the road, a mere stroll away from the wide, estuarine beach.

When Europeans arrived to settle Banks Peninsula forest covered most of the land, right down to the waterline. Maori settlements were sprinkled along the coast but the population had been debilitated by internal feuding, European diseases and Te Rauparaha's raids. But although each bay was isolated, and the European pioneers had to fend for themselves, the pattern of development was strikingly similar from bay to bay. Okains Bay was typical.

First there was shore whaling, and some shipbuilding or repair work. The first farmers hacked out homesteads from the bush but used inshore boats to communicate with other bays and the wider world. Okains Bay had some of the finest totara on the peninsula and gradually this timber was extracted, exported or burnt off, and early bridle tracks cut through to the other bays.

The area of farmed land slowly crept up to the skyline and by the turn of the century cocksfoot grass seed and dairying had provided prosperity. Every valley on the peninsula had at least one cheese factory. Nowadays most bays are dominated by sheep farming, with a sprinkling of tourism enterprises and quite a number of newer retirement and lifestyle settlements.

But for some reason Okains Bay has escaped these later modernisations and has

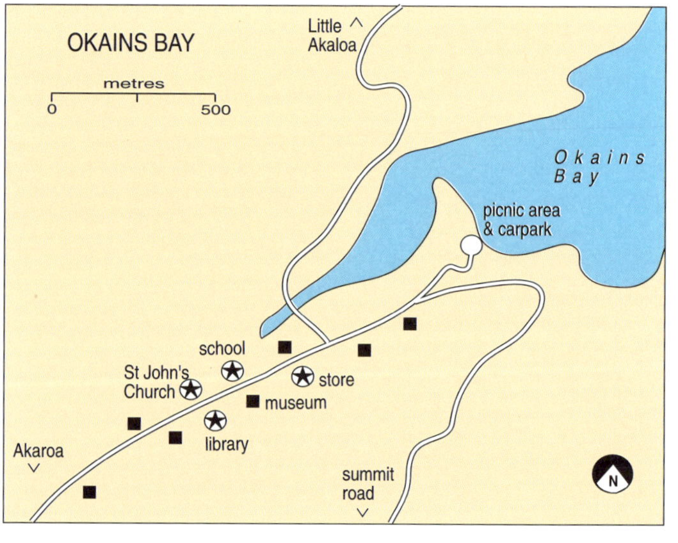

remained quietly itself. It is rather rumpled and down-at-heel, with an assemblage of buildings that date back to another century – a vale of history.

A typical peninsula road

Original homes with steep colonial-type roofs lurk among the trees and could do with a lick of paint, yet look better without it. Care-worn pioneer cottages with their characteristic lean-to additions and old sheds and steadings make a brief appearance through the shrubbery. There is a remarkable absence of modern or new building.

St John's Anglican church was built in 1863 for £554 by Edward Morey, a stonemason. He had already built Lyttelton's Holy Trinity Anglican church, which was the first stone church in Canterbury. The stone was brought to Okains Bay from the creek and local quarry and wood from valley timber mills. The bricks were locally made and the white stone came from Quail Island, the slate and stained glass from England.

The Okains Bay Circulating Library was established in 1860, the first public library on the peninsula, and the building opened in 1865 where it still stands, opposite the church. The school, built in 1872, is now a car-repair shop. The store was built in 1878 and still lies at the heart of the community.

In those days each bay had to look after itself: school, shop, post office, library, church, smithy, jetty, pub. Okains is perhaps the last bay on the peninsula to still retain a sense of that Victorian (and Kiwi) self-sufficiency.

Okains Bay Circulating Library

Further Reading

Banks Peninsula: Cradle of Canterbury, Gordon Ogilvie, GP Books, 1990.

FRENCH AKAROA

FEATURES

Original French settlement, cottage gardens, one of the two oldest houses in Canterbury, historic lighthouse, museum, compact attractive town, beaches and fishing wharfs.

HOW TO GET THERE

Akaroa is 82km from Christchurch on State Highway 75, an interesting road that on the way climbs over the Hilltop saddle with spectacular views of Akaroa Harbour.

HISTORIC PLACES AND WALKS

There are a number of interesting short historic and recreational walks around Akaroa, and many of them join together. This backyard network of tracks is an excellent way to explore the views and unexpected corners of the town.

On the main street (Rue Lavaud) is the 1863 Criterion Hotel (now a store-cum-dairy) and the 1878 courthouse. The Langlois Eteveneaux House was partly pre-fabricated in France in the 1840s and built between 1840 and 1845, rivalling Deans Cottage as the oldest house in Canterbury. The rooms have been laid out in the furnishings and style typical of the period. The adjoining museum (open daily) has many displays on Akaroa's history.

The old French cemetery (1842) is signposted up a short steep hill, and walks from here connect up with Rue Balguerie and Settlers Hill Road.

The former Akaroa Heads Lighthouse (1880) is well worth the entrance fee as the original mechanism of the lighthouse is intact. Across the road you can wander into the Akaroa Cemetery, which in turn connects up with the confusing network of tracks in the Garden of Tane.

The Britomart Memorial is not particularly memorable but it has a good outlook over the harbour and makes a very passable picnic site. The inscription says it all:

> Here on 11 August 1840 Captain Owen Stanley HMS *Britomart* raised the Union Jack to demonstrate British Sovereignty to the people of Banks Peninsula and to the French corvette *L'Aube* which arrived on 17 August.

Perhaps the most distinctive buildings are the small cottages, quite a number built 1850-80, and now faithfully restored. Smartly painted, they look bright-eyed and fresh and their fragrant gardens soften the salt air.

A Sense of Place

Akaroa is an historic place for three peoples – Maori, French and English – who met, mingled and interbred here in unusual, stressful and sometimes ironic circumstances.

By 1840 the Maori population around Paka Ariki (Akaroa Harbour) had all but disappeared. Bitter local feuds, European diseases introduced by the whalers and Te Rauparaha's murderous visits in 1829 and 1831 had left a poor and debilitated population.

The original purchase of Banks Peninsula by French whaler Jean Langlois in 1838 for 1000 francs was of doubtful legality and the Akaroa Maori refused to recognise it when the colonists duly arrived, sponsored by the Nanto-Bordelaise Company. So they had to re-buy the land they squatted on. The intention had been to found a French colony in the South Island to rival the English machinations up north, but by the time the French settlers arrived in August 1840 the British had got wind of the plan and sent down the frigate *Britomart* to erect a flag and fire a cannon to announce to a surprised local population that Akaroa was theirs.

The French were stranded, and in the end dismissed by their own government: on the wrong side of the world and totally committed, they decided to make the best of a bad job. Despite everything the British and French maintained good relations (an irony in itself) and the oddness of the colony's position was glossed over as the two sets of settlers got on with the business of survival.

Putting Down Roots

The Nanto-Bordelaise Company was not well equipped and the French settlers found themselves among an unhappy Maori population and a scurrilous bunch of whalers, convicts and deserters who had gravitated to this idyllic corner. In 1839 there were 30 French whalers and 13 American in the peninsula's waters, using Akaroa Harbour for repairs and re-stocking. However distasteful some of their occupants, these ships provided a useful source of income for the vegetable growers and farmers of the struggling community.

The French settlers were not the first European farmers at Akaroa. James Robinson Clough had lived with his Maori wife for two years in the harbour, and in 1839 the barque *Eleanor* had deposited cattle owned by W.B. Rhodes, stockman Thomas Creed and overseer William Green and his wife and child. It was the first cattle station in the South Island, pipping Johnny Jones in Otago by a few months. William Green much preferred

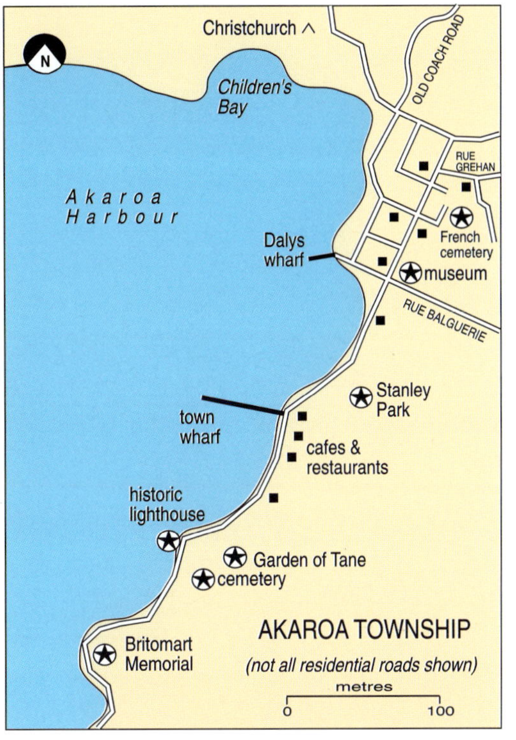

other activities, and the absence of a hotel in the new colony was soon corrected.

> ... he used to purchase any grog he could from the whaling vessels that visited the port, and, as there was no hotel, it was a standing joke with the colonists to say that they were going to have a glass of milk at Mr Green's ... William Green ... left his employment and established the first legitimate hotel on the harbour – without doubt an occupation more congenial than looking after cattle, and one for which his talents were singularly well adapted.[1]

No doubt the French settlers also appreciated the facility as they toiled to bring the land under control. By 1842 it was reported that they had all been offered a belated free

Akaroa c.1896

passage home but 'they refused to a man – the fact is they never were so prosperous thoughout their lives as now'.[2] A bakery, a coffee shop, a smithy, William Green's Victoria Inn and a few weatherboard houses had all emerged by 1842, and by slow degrees Akaroa grew. By 1846 Akaroa wheat was being processed through an Akaroa flourmill.

But the arrival of the first English immigrants to the Canterbury colony in late 1850 pointed to an obvious fact. Although most early settlers thought Akaroa a far more pleasant spot than bleak, windswept Christchurch, nevertheless the opportunities of the generous plains inevitably led to Akaroa's commercial decline. But ultimately this has meant Akaroa has remained a charming and prosperous backwater which has retained the wooden cottages and overflowing gardens of another century. The French have been absorbed, but their presence lingers.

The final irony is that people have lately 'rediscovered' Akaroa as a pleasant place to visit and retire to and the town has become something of a tourist trap. This has brought back European refinement to a sleepy Kiwi town, and along the waterfront are a line of outdoor cafes selling fine dining with frothy cappucinos and croissants, a French touch that would have delighted the early settlers.

Footnotes and Further Reading

1. *George Rhodes of The Levels,* A. E. Woodhouse, Whitcombe and Tombs, 1937.
2. Ibid.

Banks Peninsula: Cradle of Canterbury, Gordon Ogilvie, GP Books, 1990.

TAUMUTU

FEATURES

Taumutu church and pa site, Te Waihora (Lake Ellesmere), Kaitorete Spit and beach, Timber Yard Point picnic area, boat ramp.

HOW TO GET THERE

From Christchurch travel some 40km to Leeston, and turn off to Taumutu another 12km. Timber Yard Point is signposted 8km before Taumutu and has picnic areas, toilets and boat-ramp facilities.

WALK DETAILS

At Fisherman's Point there are a few private dwellings and baches beside the lagoon but the best access to Kaitorete Spit is down the side-road past the church. A makeshift footbridge crosses a side-stream and you can walk out onto the bleak beach landscape and along to the lake entrance, which is usually gravelled up. Among the shingle banks is a very old-style horse-drawn wagon, still in good condition.

On the Spit

At Taumutu there is a small, lonely church, the only coloured spot on the open beach plain. On one side the waves from the Pacific graunch against the gravelled shore, while behind lies the huge shallow waterway of Te Waihora. Between them is Kaitorete Spit, a lonely and seemingly lifeless peninsula where the wind sounds like a hymn and clouds shape a restless Sistine Chapel.

The Hone Wetere (John Wesley) church, was built in 1885 on the site of Te Taumutu or Te Pa o te Ika Mutu pa. Its original shingled roof has been replaced with corrugated iron and the small belfry removed. Battered macrocarpas shelter the small graveyard.

Taumutu is one of Ngai Tahu's important pa sites, both past and present, and the harshness of the present site should not blind the visitor to its geographic advantages. The pa was positioned for food and access.

Te Waihora (Lake Ellesmere) was regarded as the richest food basket in the South Island, with tuna (eel), patiki (flounder), awa (mullet), inanga and uaua (whitebait), koura (freshwater crayfish) and many wetland birds.

Besides food there were plentiful supplies of raupo and harakeke (flax) from the lake shore, and pingao for weaving from the spit. A special black mud, paruparu, was used to dye fibres.

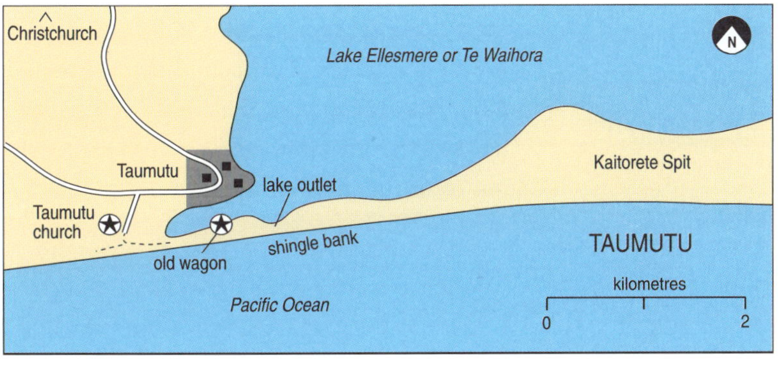

Taumutu had good access north to Banks Peninsula and the pa sites at Poranui and Kaiapoi, and south to

Eels drying

The original pa has been eroded into the sea but some earthworks remain. Originally the lake would have been two metres higher and the pa sat on a tongue of dry land surrounded by swamp – a good defensive position. It straffled Maori trading routes and was well able to sustain its mana and trade in greenstone with plentiful food. But all this changed with the arrival of the European.

The inter-tribal feud of kai huanga, Te Rauparaha's attack in 1831 and European diseases had drastically reduced the Ngai Tahu population in Canterbury. Europeans settled at Fisherman's Point at Taumutu to exploit the riches of the lake and at one time upwards of 250 people lived there. A flourishing commercial fishery was established, with little control or management, and by the turn of the century the lake was quickly becoming fished out – but there was worse to come.

Te Maru (Timaru). We have a description of Taumutu by George Rhodes in 1852, who was droving 28 head of cattle from Banks Peninsula to The Levels Station at Timaru:

> Travelling by way of Aorere our course lay around the shore of Lake Ellesmere to the Taumutu Maori Pa, near the lake outlet. It was at this pa that some of us had our first experience of the Maori. We found a number of natives sitting round a fire on the beach, and on the fire was a large iron pot in which ducks were stewing, the birds having feathers and all on. The head of the family dug a long pointed stick into a duck and thus took it out of the pot. Having pulled the duck apart, he handed a portion to each member of the family, and he continued the operation till all present were served. The wing feathers of the ducks were used in place of spoons to convey the soup to the mouth. The Maoris placed at our disposal a newly-erected whare, and as it rained heavily the following day we remained there a second night.[1]

Opening the Lake

European farmers wanted more land and a regime was established whereby Lake Ellesmere was permanently and perpetually lowered. The first European opening was in about the 1860s, and the Maori complained in 1865 that this took no account of the fishing or of the land purchases:

> Friend Mr FitzGerald. Here is one word to you about our land about Waihora; you yourself have seen that sheet of water which lies

behind the mountains of Port Cooper [Christchurch]; the Maoris catch eels there, and now we wish to sell that land (?water), because during the time that the lake was full of water, Mr. Kemp and Mr. Mantell laid down their money (in payment for the surrounding land); therefore they thought it not necessary to make any further payment for that land, and now the water is being let off by the Pakehas, that is to say by the Government, so as that land may be made a sheep station by the Europeans, and now there is very little (or no) water, it has to be left for two or three years before there is sufficient water to overflow so as to enable us to catch eels; but no, it is being drained off by the Government so as to be a source of emolument for them.[2]

Bulldozers opening Lake Forsyth

These days the lake is lowered by bulldozers to prevent flooding of surrounding land. They work slowly backwards and forwards over several days, leaving a small dam of gravel to hold back the lake waters as they dig a dry channel to the sea. At some stage the gravel holding dam is pushed down and the lake waters do the rest, scouring a deep exit channel. It might take a week or two for the lake to lower sufficiently that the lake water can no longer push back the tides, and a southerly will heap gravel and block the entrance again.

The lake's lowering has remained a running sore, affecting the vitality of the lake, its fishery potential and the mana of Taumutu Maori. Recently the bed of the lake has been returned to Ngai Tahu but there seems to be no solution to the issue of lowering the lake. If the lake were returned to its natural level it would lap at the portals of Lincoln University.

Footnotes and Further Reading

1. *George Rhodes of The Levels,* A.E. Woodhouse, Whitcombe & Tombs, 1937.
2. *A Compendium of Official Documents Relative to Native Affairs in the South Island,* Alexander Mackay, Government Print, 1873.

'The Food Basket of Rakaikautu: Taumutu', *The Past Today,* Historic Places Trust, 1987.

ACHERON ACCOMMODATION HOUSE

FEATURES
Historic cob-constructed accommodation house, high-country landscape and Clarence River. Hanmer Springs spa town.

HOW TO GET THERE
From Hanmer Springs go over Jacks Pass 8km (Jollies Pass is a four-wheel-drive route only) and turn right at the Clarence River junction. It's another 15km to the locked gate and the accommodation house just over the bridge.

THINGS TO DO
It's about 40 minutes' drive one way from Hanmer Springs to the old Acheron Accommodation House, with several picnic places and rest areas beside the upper Clarence River. Hanmer Springs itself has an information centre and a host of short walks – and of course the hot pools.

The Acheron Accommodation House was a 19th-century high-country hotel, crude by any standards, though few modern hotels could boast such a view. Scenic photographs evoke a spacious, almost sensuous land but conceal the fact that the high country is as tough and leathery as a musterer's old boot.

In the 1850s and 60s taking sheep from Nelson to Canterbury meant going through Molesworth country and few musterers viewed the prospect with any pleasure. The journey was as dull as a Sunday sermon and the land as painfully empty. The tussocklands were brittle and dry in summer, with temperatures soaring into the high 30s, while winter brought deep snows and clumps of ice drifting down the half-frozen Acheron River. There was little shelter for man or beast.

The first sheep, a mob of 1800, were taken from Nelson to Canterbury by the inland route in March 1852 by Edward Lee and Edward Jollie. By 1856 the Nelson Provincial Council had admitted a responsibility to 'set aside resting places for the

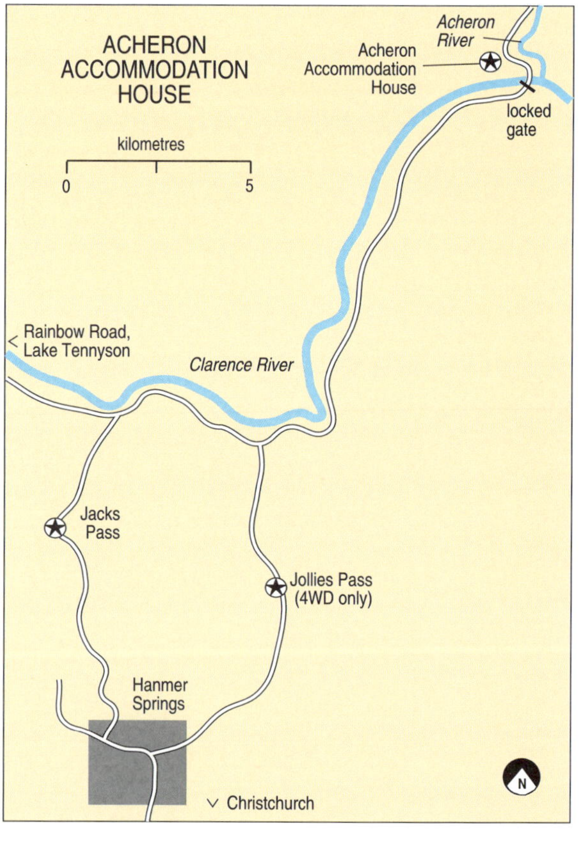

Acheron Accommodation House

accommodation of travellers and stock' and to relieve farmers whose hospitality was strained by too many weary travellers.

In 1862 funds were ear-marked for a 'House of Accommodation, Acheron Valley' and in 1864 a 2500-acre (1000-hectare) reserve was set aside. The first licence was taken up by Thomas Carter, who held the neighbouring Acheron and Clarence runs.

By 1865 seven such houses existed between the Hurunui River and Tophouse, near St Arnaud. From Tophouse the route went up the Wairau River to the Tarndale Accommodation House, and then over Alma Pass down the Yarra River to the Acheron. Then it was over Jollies Pass to an accommodation house at the foot of the pass, near present-day Hanmer Springs, and on to the Hurunui Hotel (1869). Three of these accommodation houses still stand.

'Beds 1 Shilling Each'

The accommodation house at the junction of the Clarence and Acheron rivers was built entirely of local materials. Wood was out of the question of course, and stone was too slow. The answer was cob, a slurry of tussock and mud, stomped down and dried in the ample supply of hot nor' west winds. It is a low, snug building, roofed with undressed mountain beech and tied with flax, and thatched with snowgrass tussock. Eleven small rooms were laid out in the plan supplied by the Nelson council, with bunks made of birch (beech) poles and manuka, and three rooms had fireplaces.

In order to encourage people to take up the licences of the accommodation houses the council offered special deals that exempted proprietors from a normal publican's fee, but they were still particular about the standard. For example, Thomas Dickenson of the Hapuku hostelry on the Kaikoura coast in the 1860s had to supply for travellers:

> ... one good sitting room with boarded floor, proper table and chairs, fire and lights; two bedrooms with boarded floor, each bedroom to contain at least three boarded bedsteads furnished with clean bed blankets and sheets and all proper and usual chamber accommodation; that all travellers be supplied with meals of tea or coffee and meat, also butter or cheese and bread; and all other usual appliances, at 1/6 each meal, beds 1s each; stable to be provided, convenient to the house, containing two stalls of sufficient size, with proper manger, rack and fastenings; good hay to be provided at 2s for every 14 lb, corn ditto at 6d per quart, standard weight

Hurunui Hotel

and measure, the above charges for ready money only ...[1]

Accommodation houses were supposedly strictly regulated: hours from 6am to 10pm on working days, 1pm to 7pm on Sundays, Christmas Day and Good Friday. Saturday was deemed a working day then of course. However, as one 1863 licensee bitterly commented, it was often not a profitable occupation:

Of the number of travellers passing to and from Otago, Canterbury and Nelson, nine-tenths not only cannot pay for what they eat at the house, but have to be assisted in the way of stores to carry them on the road, the stronger parties *demanding* and the weaker ones begging the same.[2]

The Acheron Accommodation House provided hospitality throughout the late 19th century and then became an outstation for the St Helens run. The house was abandoned in 1950 but restored as a shell in the 1980s, a reminder of civilisation in the wilderness.

Footnotes and Further Reading

1. *Kaikoura: A History of the District*, J.M. Sherrard, Kaikoura County Council, 1966.
2. Ibid.

Historic Buildings of New Zealand: South Island, Historic Places Trust, 1983.

WAIKARI ROCK DRAWINGS

FEATURES
Maori rock drawings, limestone overhangs, rural scenery and historic railway.

HOW TO GET THERE
From Christchurch turn off to Waipara at the State Highway 2 junction, then drive through Weka Pass to Waikari township – about 70km in total.

WALK DETAILS
This short (2-3-hours) return walk starts from Waikari township (just up from the Yorkshire Teapot). Initially it follows the old railway line before turning sharply uphill and climbing beside the fenceline to where it dips into a limestone valley, part of the Timpendean farm, which is private property. A sign turns you right after a few minutes to the obvious rock overhang and the striking display of Maori rock drawings – perhaps the best surviving in Canterbury, if not New Zealand.

Some of the drawings have been touched up by house paint and however objectionable this may be from an archaeological point of view, it does help to sort out for the layman the confusing array of shapes, figures and drawings. The drawings are believed to be around 600 years old. The walkway is closed during the lambing season.

On dozens of limestone overhangs throughout the South Island are the fading inscriptions of another race. Weathering, cattle rubbing and vandalism are diminishing the impact of these drawings, many of which have become as unfathomable as the reasons for their creation.

What were the drawings? Doodles? Religious icons? A guide for hunters? Marking of property or territory rights? An early system of writing or memory aid? Art? The comic strips of their time? All have been suggested. We cannot even assess the skill of the drawers: they could be the work of children or of high chiefs. How would people 1000 years on interpret our graffiti?

Evidence suggests that at the time of the drawings the area around Waikari was

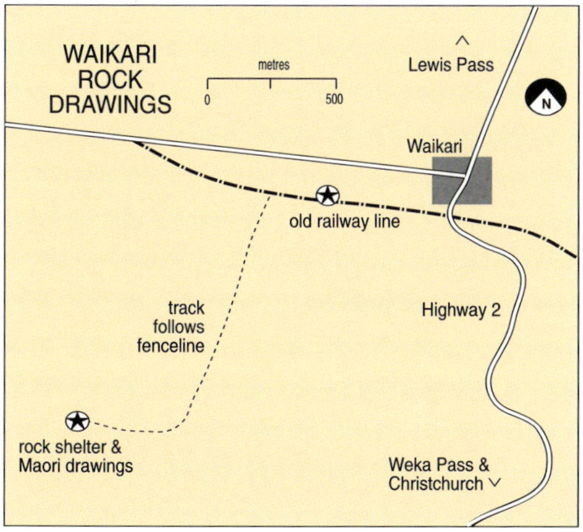

MAORI RECIPE FOR PAINT

First burn branches of monoao tree.
Collect the resulting soot off a tipaki [flax mat] placed to collect it and scrape it into an ipu [carved wooden basin].
Meanwhile collect gum from tarata tree and rautawhiri berries.
Grind berries and hang it in whitau [flax bag] over fire so juice drips out into the basin.
Add oil of weka and mix to right consistency. Not too thick nor too thin.
This will produce an ink that will stand forever.[1]

Rock drawings at Waikari

forested and Maori used the limestone shelter as a temporary camp. Birds such as kaka, weka and quail and the Maori rat (kiore) were hunted, and flaked stone tools, bones and shells have been found in the cave floor.

Limestone was obviously the rock of choice for the rock painter. It is light coloured and smooth and has many convenient overhangs and caves. The drawings were made mostly using charcoal and red ochre (kokowai), a haematite not readily available in Canterbury, though there are good supplies in Golden Bay. Red had important symbolic significance to the Maori, for painting faces and carvings, and also to colour the bones of the exhumed or mummified dead.

Some drawings clearly resemble human stick figures, fish or dogs, but many are too sketchy to identify at all, or possibly represent abstractions or ideas. Clearly rock art was practised after the arrival of Europeans as some sites show horses and sailing ships. One significant omission is the stencilled hand. Handprints have been found in practically every assemblage of rock art, from Australia to France, but not in New Zealand.

Footnotes and Further Reading

1. *Maori Rock Art*, Paul Thompson, GP Books, 1989.

Weka Pass Walkway and Historic Reserve (DOC pamphlet).

ARTHUR'S PASS RAILWAY VILLAGE

FEATURES

Short historic walk (featuring tunnellers' cottages, railway turntable and Otira Tunnel), original single men's dining hall, Punchbowl Falls, mountain scenery.

HOW TO GET THERE

Arthur's Pass is a 158km drive from Christchurch on State Highway 73. Facilities at Arthur's Pass include an excellent Department of Conservation visitor centre and museum, three cafes, public shelter and toilets, and several walking tracks.

Alternatively (and appropriately), you could catch the Tranzalpine Express to the pass, spend 3-4 hours looking around and catch the train on its return to Christchurch from Greymouth later the same day.

WALK DETAILS

A walk around the short historic circuit takes about 30 minutes but if you include a visit to Punchbowl Falls and a look at the DOC museum you could soak up 2-3 hours without any problem. If you are going on any of the harder walks around the village you'll need boots and should notify DOC via the Intentions Book in the visitor centre lobby.

There is a DOC pamphlet to guide you around the historic circuit, and there are picture plaques at appropriate points. Quite a few of the tunnellers' cottages are at the top end of the village (near the Chalet Restaurant) and can be seen on either side of the main road, with various idiosyncratic add-ons and lean-tos.

The original core of the large Outdoor Education Centre building was the single men's dining hall for the railway workers. It was enlarged by adding in part of the Otira schoolhouse and opened as a guesthouse in 1923. Oscar Coberger's shop was built in 1926. The old-style turntable behind the public shelter was big enough to carry the Kb steam locomotives and two men can easily swing the well-balanced loco around. From the stopbank here you get a good view of the Otira Tunnel.

A Hard Road

On a grey nor'wester day Arthur's Pass can be cheerless. Thick rain funnels into the confined valley and semolina clouds occasionally lift to reveal shiny rock faces and tops flecked with new snow. It is a dark, deep valley whose rivers start to roar as they flood. Many a passing driver sees Arthur's Pass as a quick coffee-and-bun stop, but when it fines up Arthur's Pass shows a wild and romantic face. It is a place steeped in history and overshadowed by undaunted mountains.

Because of the discovery of gold on the West Coast, or West Canterbury as it was known then, there was an intense need to establish some sort of track over the Southern Alps. But the prospects for building a road were discouraging.

Harper Pass was known about but was too indirect. Browning Pass was too alpine, Whitcombe Pass just too hard. Samuel Butler had spotted a likely-looking pass up a side branch of the Waimakariri as early as 1860 – one sometimes used by the Maori as a greenstone route. The first Europeans through it were the Dobson brothers, Arthur and George, in 1864; they found it hard going in the gorge on the other side.

Arthur's Pass 1914

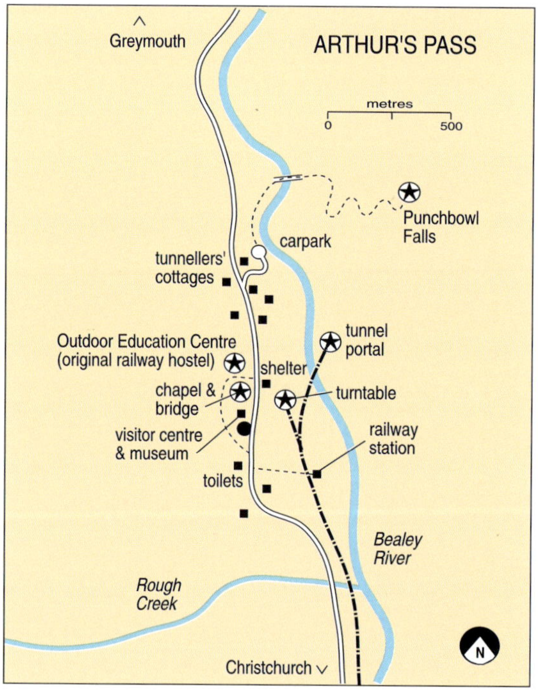

The ultimate decision ironically rested with their father, Edward Dobson, the Chief Engineer of the province, who took the advice of his sons that 'Arthur's Pass' was the best of a bad lot. A bridle track was cut through in the vicious winter of 1865, over the pass and down the Otira Gorge. Parts of today's highway still follow the same line and indeed do not seem much improved.

Gradually the road was widened to accommodate horse-drawn coaches, but the descent was harrowing and clearly a longer-term solution was needed. A railway to the West Coast was an attractive option. Harper's Pass was surveyed again as a possible rail route, but for sheer di-

Turntable and train

rectness Arthur's Pass was the logical choice.

By the turn of the century the railway line was creeping towards Arthur's Pass from both sides, though the railhead from Christchuch did not reach the village until 1915. The Otira Tunnel had been started in 1908 and it was to take 15 years to complete. The first coast-to-coast train made the journey at last in 1923.

Arthur's Pass has remained a railway village with all the accoutrements: sidings, signal lights, turntable, old rail coaches and a railway shed that has been ingeniously turned into a squash court. It is still a town of baches and beech trees, and seems to be in its own little warp of history. There has been little development because it is inside a national park, and the only modernish building is the ugly 1966 railway station, built after the original station burnt down.

Summer and winter the coal trains trundle through, probably keeping the line profitable. Despite the altitude heat can buckle the lines in summer, and winter snowfall gives the landscape intensity and grace, softening everything except the two parallel lines of steel.

OTIRA TUNNEL

The Otira Tunnel is 8.5km long with a gradient of 1 in 33, which means that for every 33 horizontal metres the line goes down 1 metre vertically. There's a total fall of 278 metres. Although the two ends of the tunnel were actually joined in 1918, with an alignment accurate to within 3cm, World War I labour shortages and harsh weather delayed the opening for five years. It was the longest tunnel in the British Empire when it was opened and the seventh-longest in the world.

Steam trains were only replaced by diesels on the Midland line in the late 1960s and special steam excursions often make the journey from Christchurch to Arthur's Pass. Of course steam trains were not allowed through the tunnel then, as now, and electric trains were used to haul the steam locomotives through the tunnel.

Tunneller's cottage turned into a ski bach

Further Reading

Arthur's Pass Village Historic Walk (Department of Conservation pamphlet).

BLACKBURN MINE

FEATURES
Coalmine and worked faces, jig line and ruined wagons, Quarry Cottage, lime kilns, tussock landscapes and views, beech forest, river walks.

HOW TO GET THERE
Mt Somers township is 100km from Christchurch: the best access is State Highway 1 south to Rakaia, then turn onto Thompson's Track. From the Mt Somers township take the Ashburton Gorge Road (to Erewhon) and after about 10km turn off down a signposted gravel road 3.5km to the Coalminers' Flat picnic area. This is a large, grassy and sheltered picnic area and campsite, with information boards and toilets. Wasps can be a nuisance in late summer.

WALK DETAILS
From Coalminers' Flat follow the Black Beech Walk for 10 minutes through black and silver beech, which wanders beside Woolshed Creek then picks up the old tramway road to the foot of the jig railway incline. The Miners' Track zig-zags up the jig incline for 20 minutes to the Blackburn Mine.

There's a different return track called the Sidewinder Track, which drops steeply back through old beech forest to the creek again. For the entire circuit allow 4-5 hours walking time. If you plan to stop off at the Whitestone quarry cottage and the lime kilns (signposted from the Ashburton Gorge Road) then you can easily fritter away a whole day.

In the high country above the Blackburn Mine the wind scythes the tussock and churns up duststorms on the shallow shingle beds. About 10 kilometres away is the 3000m Mt Arrowsmith massif, a glittering prize for early mountaineers, and beyond that lie the distant headwaters of the Rangitata River, the mythical land of Erewhon made famous by Samuel Butler.

But it was not for romantic reasons that the coalminers came up here. Glancing away from the shimmering Southern Alps, just five minutes below the ridge, is the bare, bleached plateau of the Blackburn Mine. Gritty banks of coal still sour the soil with dark colours, and tortured pieces of metal have lain on the same spot for nearly 50 years. The only thing uglier than a working coalmine is a derelict one.

Coal was discovered in the Mt Somers area as early as 1856 and by 1864 the first coalfield was opened in Woolshed Creek.

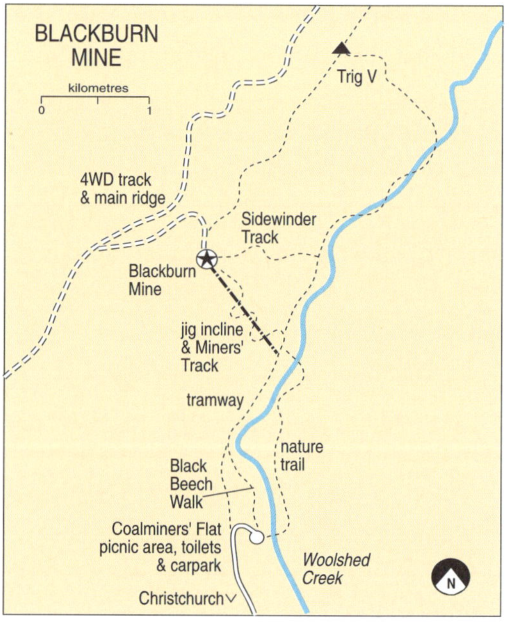

QUARRY COTTAGE

This old limestone cottage was built in 1909 and is in good condition. The first limestone was worked in 1865, and the quarry nearby from 1872 to 1925. Inside the cottage are some practical objects nailed to the walls, and intriguing information panels. Outside there are great blocks of old and fresh stone from the nearby quarry along with a detonator drum, an explosives bunker and the foundations of an outside bread oven.

Mrs Iris Rose lived in another stone hut close by in the harsh Depression years of 1933-36 and recalled:

> My basin was used for washing hands, dishes, clothes, bathing the baby, watering the garden, catching leaks in the roof, collecting rain for battery water and even 'other things' during the coldest of winter nights.[1]

Eventually a tramway went from this mine all the way to Mt Somers village, where it joined the newly completed main-trunk railway line in 1887. The tramway up Woolshed Creek itself was built in 1908 but the McClimonts Mine was closed in 1915.

The Blackburn Mine started life in 1928, the jig line being hacked out by pick and

Detonator lock-up

shovel. Its steepest incline was 1-in-2.5. Full four-tonne hoppers of coal would plummet down from the mine and, by means of a self-acting ropeway, pull up the empty hoppers. Invariably a few hoppers ran off the rails and one such mangled hopper lies at the foot of this incline.

A reconstructed mine entrance has been built, where you can learn about 'Gutsers' and 'Banjos', and marvel at the sheer hard slog of the miners during the Depression years, 760 metres above sea level.

The coal was low-quality lignite and burned poorly, and the mine became uneconomic in the Depression and closed down. However, it was later worked again in fits and starts until about 1954, when several underground fires finally closed the mine. Apparently it still smokes from time to time and a whiff of sulphur taints the otherwise pristine mountain air.

Footnotes and Further Reading

1. Interpretation panel at cottage.

Mt Somers Resource Study, Department of Lands and Survey, 1985.

BLUESTONE COUNTRY

FEATURES

Bluestone bridges, rural downlands and road zig-zags, St David's Church (Cave), St Mark's Church (Otipua).

HOW TO GET THERE

A road map and a tendency to wander are useful accessories. From Timaru drive south out of town and turn into Beaconsfield Road (just across the Saltwater Creek bridge). This road leads you to Otipua, but it is well worth detouring into Pudjeck or Wards Road. From Otipua you can follow Beaconsfield Flat Road and then continue on past a bluestone farmhouse on Cliffs Road up the Briggs Zig Zag. This in turn leads past Whalebones Corner toward the Taiko Zig Zag, etc.

DRIVING TIME

It's about an 80-100km round trip from Timaru, so allow about 2-3 hours' driving, as well as some looking-about time.

Kent with Cabbage Trees

If you drive south of Timaru and turn inland at, say, Beaconsfield Road you gradually enter a landscape of downlands, with a criss-cross network of lanes, stone bridges over sluggish streams, copses of trees and occasional stone churches with square Norman towers – a thoroughly English-looking landscape. And this of course was not an accident.

When strangers arrive in a new land they bring a whole paraphernalia of their plants, animals, customs and aspirations. Often the easiest way to cope with the strangeness is at first to ignore it, and then to try to replace it with your own institutions.

New settlers often yearn for a visual sense of belonging. It would be surprising if the Maori had not tried to plant coconut palms on the North Island coastline, and the English became equally earnest about the recreation of their 'home'. In a pocket of country between Timaru, Cave and Claremont they almost pulled it off.

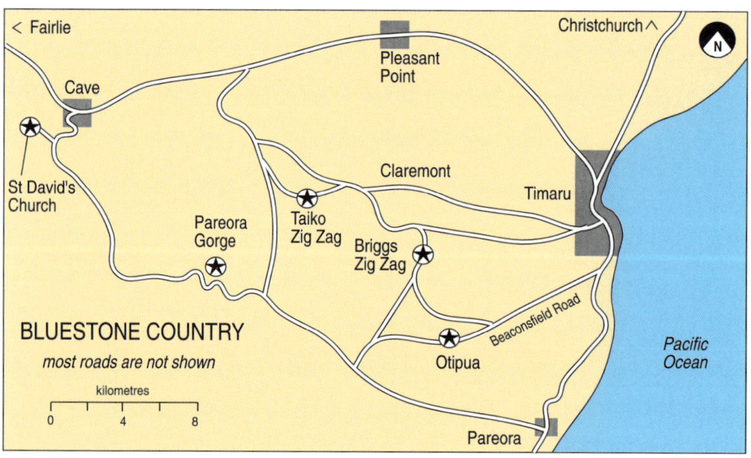

These soft fertile hills encourage small farms and the numerous rural service roads that are forced into occasional zany zig-zags bring to mind 'the rolling English drunkard [who] made the rolling English road' of G.K. Chesterton's patriotic

ST DAVID'S PIONEER MEMORIAL CHURCH

St David's is a simple, powerful church. From a distance it looks like pure England with its stone walls, square Norman tower, steep slate roof and deep windows, yet its inspiration is pioneer New Zealand. It was built in memory of Andrew and Catherine Burnett, who took up the Mt Cook Station in 1856, and their efforts are ingrained in the very structure of the church.

The pulpit is constructed from hearthstones from their first hut at Mt Cook Station, the font has a hub of the Burnetts' bullock dray, and in the stone porch is an inscribed greywacke slab that was used by Andrew Burnett as an impromptu table for his mustering camp in the Jollie Gorge. The exterior is sternly grey, the interior light and inspirational – a husband-and-wife landscape.

The church is unfashionably patriotic ('It is noteworthy that all the men engaged in the building of this church were British born') and you can feel their resourcefulness, energy and sweat. The pews are hand-adzed, the boulder-stone walls arduously knapped, the totara top of the pulpit is burnished a deep nut-brown red.

The church was built in 1930 and construction conceived and overseen by Andrew and Catherine's son, Thomas Burnett. It won an architectual award in 1934 and the sheer rawness and ebullience of the materials have not dated the design a bit.

Undoubtedly the best first view of St David's is from Cave itself as you climb a narrow lane up to a war memorial and look down on a little piece of England.

poem. Unlike much of rural New Zealand these downlands are a well-planted landscape, with lines of silver birch, oaks and Lombardy poplars. Only the cabbage trees give the game away.

Many stone bridges and culverts have been built out of the local volcanic bluestone, a hard, stable and attractive rock. The bridges date from 1865 through to the 1880s. Cement was used for the foundations only, then a frame was constructed and the bluestone blocks were angle-shaped and locked together with a crucial keystone, using some lime mortar. Recent renovations showed that the mortar has often leached out.

There are two splendid churches, St Mark's at Otipua and St David's at Cave. Both are superbly set, slightly on the side of a hill, and both retain superfluous fortress-like crenellations, an effect emphasised by the uncompromising stone walls. Yet the smallness of the churches makes them almost toy-like.

In spring the deception is complete. Mists clog the valleys, lambs bounce among clusters of daffodils and the squat stone church tower peeps out above the birch trees and settles and soothes the landscape as in Gray's *Elegy*:

'Rural scene, a rural scene,
sweet especial rural scene'

The curfew tolls the knell of parting day,
The lowing herd winds slowly o'er the lea.
The ploughman slowly plods his weary way,
And leaves the world to darkness, and to me.

Further Reading

Articles on South Canterbury stone arch bridges and St David's Church, Cave, *Historic Places*, May 1994.

THE McKENZIE MYTH

FEATURES
Mackenzie Pass, McKenzie Monument, Taiko Flat, Dog Kennel Corner plaque, Church of the Good Shepherd (1935), statue of the sheepdog.

HOW TO GET THERE
From State Highway 8 at Burke Pass township turn into Rollesby Valley and drive 10km to Mackenzie Pass Road, then continue 5km on to the pass. Another 2km on is the McKenzie Monument and the road can be followed 20km back to Dog Kennel Corner on State Highway 8.

The Church of the Good Shepherd and sheep-dog statue are on the lakefront at Tekapo town. Taiko Flat can be reached via Sutherlands Road, turning off 8km north of Pleasant Point. Such are the complexity of roads here that a good road map is useful.

DRIVING TIME
Allow 2–3 hours for a circuit drive taking in Taiko Flat, Mackenzie Pass, Dog Kennel Corner and the church and statue at Tekapo.

The Myth and the Man

On the brink of the Mackenzie Country is a peculiar memorial to a man who accidentally lent his name (albeit misspelt) to this region. The monument is three-sided and written in three languages: English, Maori and Gaelic.

> In this spot James Mackenzie the freebooter was captured by John Sidebottom and the Maoris Taiko and 'Seventeen' and escaped from them the same night 4th March 1855.

The monument was placed there in 1917 by T.D. Burnett and sits below what is now known as Mackenzie Pass, a lonely, wind-eaten spot, with stalking pylons shepherding the electricity lines from the Mackenzie on to the coastal cities. No one remembers Sidebottom or the two Maori, but everyone knows the story of James McKenzie.

The story goes that he was a Highland sheep-stealer who spoke only Gaelic, discovered Mackenzie Pass and rustled sheep between South Canterbury and Otago. He was finally caught near Mackenzie Pass in 1855 stealing 1000 sheep. His demon dog was said to be capable of rounding up sheep unaided and there is a memorial statue to the dog at Tekapo beside the church. A nasty judge ordered the dog hanged. McKenzie escaped from Lyttelton Gaol numerous times and was eventually pardoned, on the condition that he never darken the shores of New Zealand again.

These are the bare bones of the McKenzie myth, yet many of these facts are unreliable; many palpably untrue.

First, it seems his Christian name might not have been James. Herries Beattie in his account *Mackenzie of the Mackenzie Country* found that people mentioned John far more

---

Note: The spelling of James McKenzie's name is the subject of much dispute but O.A. Gillespie in *South Canterbury: A Record of Settlement* (Caxton, 1971) states that the man signed his name McKenzie.

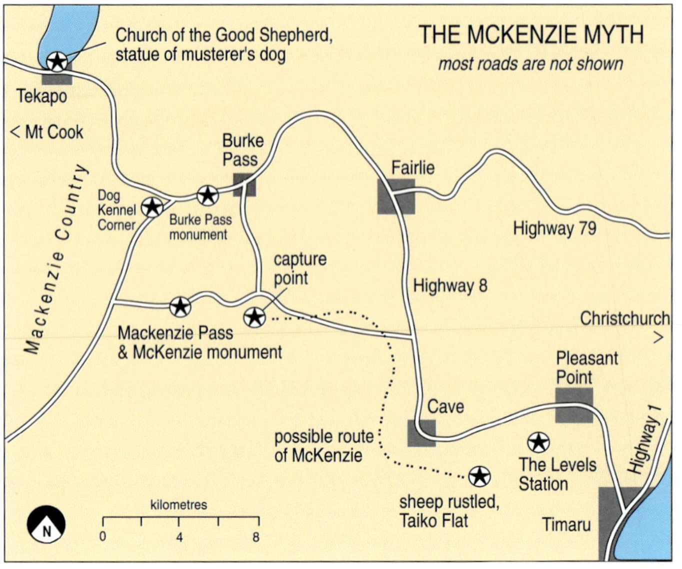

agree that McKenzie was 'a splendid man with sheep'. A first-hand description described him as a 'tall, raw-boned Highlander', and the police reward notice noted: 'height, 5 feet 11 inches; hair, light; eyes, small and grey; nose, large and aquiline; face, long and thin; body, spare and muscular'. An athlete's build in fact, and quite an impressive figure.[2]

often than James, although James was listed on the petition for a pardon. And his surname might not have been McKenzie.

The Lyttelton Police Lock-Up Register-cum-Correspondence Record Book noted at the time of McKenzie's arrest:

> *Date*, 15.3.55; *time of admission*, 10pm; *charge*, sheep stealing; *by whom charged*, Sergeant Seager; *property found on prisoner*, £21.11s. & knife; *decision*, committed for trial, sentenced to five years hard labour April 17th, 1855; *name of prisoner*, John Douglass *alias* James Mackenzie.[1]

McKenzie did speak Gaelic, but whether he was solely Gaelic-speaking is open to doubt. Some said his English was minimal; others that it was excellent.

It is true that McKenzie was a Highlander, and it is believed that he emigrated to Australia about 1845 and came to New Zealand as a shepherd around 1851. Several accounts

Don't Fence Me In

It is important to realise that at this stage of the colony's development the Canterbury Plains were covered with sheep stations but there were no fences. You can imagine the difficulties this posed, and the ease with which sheep could stray, or be stolen.

In March 1855 the Rhodes partnership at The Levels Station near Timaru found that 1000 ewes had been spirited away and their overseer, John Sidebottom, accompanied by two Maori trackers, caught McKenzie 'red-handed' with the sheep near the pass.

McKenzie never denied he was droving the sheep but he claimed he had been hired to do so by someone called 'Mossman' who had told him the job was legitimate and paid him £20. But 'Mossman' fled, leaving McKenzie to carry the can.

James McNeish has pointed out in his book that in Highland slang a 'moss-man' was a sheep-stealer, 'one who dwells on the peatmoss and stocks up by raiding'.[3] Sidebottom had noticed that there were the tracks of at least two men with the sheep, possibly three.

Was Mossman a real person? Did McKenzie have accomplices? The Rhodes brothers thought so, and indeed you would have to be very clever (or very foolish) to try to rustle 1000 sheep over 50km of rough country singlehanded. McKenzie was taken to Christchurch and arrested.

At the trial little account was taken of the possibility that McKenzie had been hoodwinked by any Mossman and he was convicted of 'Mute of Malice' for refusing to speak in English, which several witnesses said he could do. He was sentenced to five years' hard labour and incarcerated in Lyttelton Gaol.

Enter a saviour. Henry Tancred was the sheriff at the time of McKenzie's imprisonment and took pity on him. Tancred drafted a petition that eventually secured McKenzie's pardon, arguing that because McKenzie could understand English imperfectly the trial was hardly fair. 'I conceive that the ends of justice require that the matter ought to be further investigated.' Since the Governor was coming to Lyttelton it was thought McKenzie 'was a most proper object for His Excellency's Clemency on the occasion of His visit to the Gaol'.[4]

The pardon came promptly and may have been influenced by McKenzie's three widely publicised escapes from Lyttelton Gaol, and his growing reputation as a folk hero who had been done an injustice.

THE DOG

The famous Tekapo dog statue has nothing to do with McKenzie but is a tribute to all high-country mustering dogs. There is also a rather forlorn plaque at the aptly named Dog Kennel Corner that reads: 'In early times before these roads were fenced, a boundary dog was kennelled here to hold back station sheep.'

And what became of McKenzie's famous dog? William Ayson, who knew McKenzie, remarked tersely: 'A great deal has been said about his dog, but I think a lot about it was invented after it was dead, as I never saw anything wonderful about the dog he had.'[7]

James McNeish pointed out that there was a well-known Highland story of a canny sheepdog called Yarrow that could round up sheep unaided, needing only a few whispered instructions from its master. This may well be the basis of the supposed supernatural abilities of McKenzie's dog.

The dog in fact was not hanged and it seems likely that she ended up on The Levels as George Rhodes's pet, renamed Friday.

McKenzie was pardoned on 11 January 1856 but, contrary to popular belief, it was not conditional on his leaving New Zealand. There is some eye-witness evidence that he returned briefly in 1857-58.

Creating a Hero

The Rhodes brothers posted a reward notice in March 1855, at the time of McKenzie's trial.

> **£250 Reward**
>
> Whereas a person of the name of James Mackenzie and others, did on or about the 1st of March, steal and drive away about 1000 sheep from the Timaru station, and as there is reason to believe that the same men have, on previous occasions, stolen both Sheep and Cattle, and driven them away, the owners are of the opinion that there is a regular organised gang of thieves and receivers either in this or the Otago province.
>
> The above mentioned reward of £250 will be paid to any person or persons who shall give such information as will lead to the conviction of all the parties concerned, and the recovery of the whole of the stock.[5]

Clearly the Rhodes brothers had lost sheep before: in fact some 500 sheep had disappeared three years before the McKenzie episode. A further reward notice was posted by the Rhodes brothers in June 1856, after McKenzie's trial and pardon, offering a reward of £100 and 750 sheep for the return of the original 500 sheep. The stolen sheep were said to 'have since been traced over the north branch of the Waitaki River (between which river and the Bluff, in the Otago district, they are now supposed to be)'.[6]

A good deal of the McKenzie legend grew from these reward notices. They publicly supposed that the sheep were in Otago and that the notorious freebooter McKenzie had spirited them away. The public's imagination did the rest, filling in the details of how McKenzie got the sheep there – through the romantic and largely unknown Snowy Mountains.

Herries Beattie fueled the legend by supposing that McKenzie took these 500 sheep across the Mackenzie Country via Omarama, Alexandra and beyond Gore to present-day Edendale – some 300 kilometres at least. Not a bad effort for one man and a dog.

There is not the slightest evidence of this cross-country rustling, although early settlers do recall that McKenzie was at Edendale, in Southland, in late 1853. He built a slab hut, planted potatoes and made an application for land in April 1854.

Did McKenzie even discover Mackenzie Pass? On Charles Torlesse's map of 1849 the pass is clearly shown as Manahouna, and it was said this gap could be clearly seen by vessels approaching Timaru Harbour. Maori had used the Mackenzie plains for centuries and, according to Torlesse, they claimed that stock could be driven over the pass.

Sheep and cattle were the business of Canterbury in the 1850s, and it was almost exclusively a grazing culture, literally at the ends of the earth. Perhaps this 'empty land' needed heroes to fill it, but why McKenzie?

Perhaps the shepherds on their lonely beats needed someone to glamorise their lonely

Church of the Good Shepherd, Tekapo

harsh life and poorly paid skills. Perhaps the graziers needed an explanation for their sheep losses and poor management. Perhaps the early settlers needed a lovable rogue to give their end-of-the-earth settlement a personality.

There is always a need for heroes and the supply is always short, so perhaps we create from unpromising material what cannot be supplied from the natural course of history. The legend of McKenzie continues to bloom and it is curious that although the purpose of the lonely monument was not to commemorate McKenzie, that is in fact exactly what it does. And by the way, the monument is in the wrong place. Practically everyone agrees that McKenzie was arrested on the east side of the pass, near Lockharts Stream.

Footnotes and Further Reading

1. *The Mackenzie Affair,* James McNeish, Hodder & Stoughton, 1972.
2. Ibid.
3. Ibid.
4. Ibid.
5. *Lyttelton Times*, March 1855.
6. Ibid.
7. *Mackenzie of the Mackenzie Country* (Cadsonbury Publishers, 1994) and *Mackenzie the Sheep Stealer* (*Otago Times and Witness,* 1959) Herries Beattie.

George Rhodes of The Levels, A.E. Woodhouse, Whitcombe and Tombs, 1937.

DENNISTOUN INCLINE

FEATURES

Gravity-powered incline, poppet head and machinery, packtrack to Conns Creek, mountain plateau, Coalbrookdale Mine Walk.

HOW TO GET THERE

From Westport it is 14km north to Waimangaroa. Conns Creek, the base of the incline, is 5km up the creekside, but to get to the top follow the signposted Dennistoun road as it winds remorselessly up onto the 2000ft (700m) plateau.

The township of Dennistoun is a patchy collection of old coalminers' houses, sheds and rusting machinery. Down the side-road is the carpark and lookout over the top of the incline.

WALK DETAILS

You can spend quite a bit of time just inspecting the poppet head tower and machinery remains at the top of the incline. A well-signposted walking track zig-zags down in thick bush, and a side-trail goes to Middle Brake, where you can get an idea of the steepness of the incline. An old viaduct is below Middle Brake but it is unsafe; indeed the incline itself is generally too steep and insecure to walk on.

The main packtrack continues down to touch the plateau road at One Mile Log, then continues down to Conns Creek. Obviously if you can arrange to be dropped off at the top of the incline and picked up at Conns Creek this makes for an excellent down-trip: about 2-3 hours one way downhill.

Another productive mine, Coalbrookdale, was linked with the Dennistoun Incline by a rope-hauled railway and aerial cableway. There are plenty of remains, including the fan house, wagons, tramway tunnel and bridges, and more pieces of rusted wire than you would believe. It is easy on a misty day to imagine the wagons clanking and groaning along the track, and hear the bellicose shouts of the miners, helmeted like warriors.

Allow 1 hour for the return walk around the mine site.

Somewhere on this bleak and grimly beautiful plateau there might be a plaque that says 'profit comes first'.

Once Dennistoun kept 250 miners and their families up on this mountain land, sweating, singing, laughing and crying. In 1895 Dennistoun was New Zealand's most productive coalfield and ultimately 12.6 million tons of coal were carted by the full wagons as they tipped over the edge of the incline and trundled down to sea level, pulling up the empties as they did so. But in 1967, after 87 years of operation, the mine closed and the plateau became lost to mist and memories.

There is still one private coalmine up here, taking only a pittance of 'black gold' compared with the mighty Dennistoun Incline which, when it was built in 1878-79, was proudly considered New Zealand's biggest and best engineering project. Water-operated brakes slowed the coal-laden wagons in a de-

Dennistoun miners' houses 1912

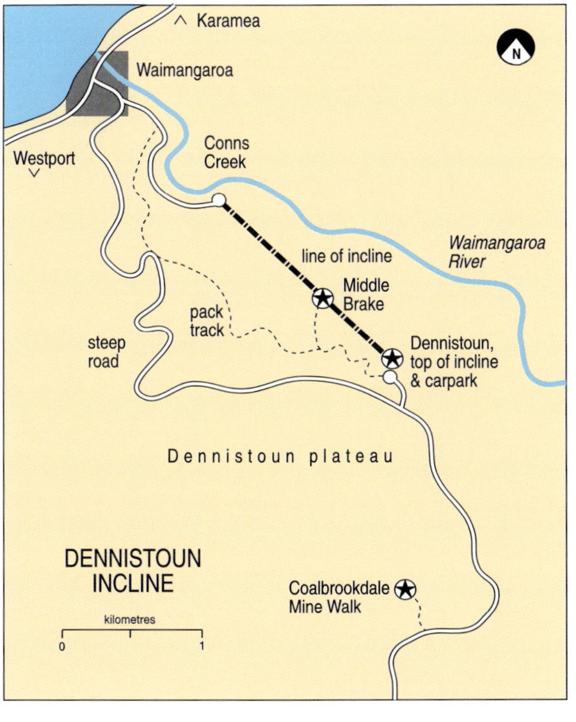

scent that was as steep as 1 in 1.69. The 548-metre drop took place over two stages: from Upper Brake down the No 1 incline to Middle Brake, and then down the No 2 incline to the railhead at Conns Creek.

Dennistoun existed for the work, not the views. The climate was wretched. Pea-soup cloud hung about the township for weeks at a time, and steady drizzle kept the washing wet and the machinery runny with rust. In 1887 there were three hotels, four general stores, three butchers, three bakers, one post office and a school for a resident population of 500. Few trees, fences or gardens embellished the rows of corrugated-iron houses.

Dennistoun drive tower, top of the incline

The community of miners and their families bred a hard, isolated and proud spirit on 'The Hill'. There is a kind of primal working-class romance in coal: the sweat, the camaraderie born of shared danger, the wresting of fire from geological bowels. But men wore out quickly on coalfields, tired from overwork or coughing their lungs out from emphysema. Communities shared a lot – then dissolved when the profits ran out.

Damn Dennistoun
Damn the track
Damn the way both there and back
Damn the wind and damn the weather
God damn Dennistoun altogether.[1]

Footnotes and Further Reading

1. 'Dennistoun pulls back the faithful', David Gee, *Christchurch Press*, 13 February 1996.

TE ORU MATA SEA CAVE

FEATURES
Huge natural sea cave, Fox River and estuary mouth, historic road bridge and road cave, natural arch.

HOW TO GET THERE
From the Paparoa National Park visitor centre at Punakaiki drive 10km north to the Fox River bridge. There is a good carpark and picnic area on the north side of the bridge. The Fox River is 46km south of Westport; 54km north of Greymouth.

WALK DETAILS
Allow 1-2 hours to explore around the Fox River and Te Oru Mata sea cave. The cavern is 'inside' the prominent headland on the south side of the Fox River. There's a good carpark on the north side of the river. From there you can walk across the historic Fox bridge and down a track that dives under the highway and goes past some baches to the cave entrance.

The cave is best visited at a low tide, for then you can wander around the headland past sea-stacks and smaller archways onto the beach south of the Fox River. Beside the Fox bridge there is also an old road cave to explore, and a fine natural arch opposite the baches.

'A Remarkable Cavern ...'

This is a punishing shoreline. Westerly waves beat against iron headlands; the forest is drenched with sea-sweat. Pebbles growl at every wave surge, while underwater coal seams are torn open and pieces of sea-coal thrown up, smooth and polished like obsidian.

The coast from Westport to Greymouth was difficult for any early traveller to negotiate. The Maori took an inland route through the pakihi country at Charleston, and then came down to the coast at White Horse Creek. There was an easy beach to the Fox River and Te Oru Mata sea cave was a natural stopping place – plenty of kai. There were eels from the river, shellfish off the rocks, and fresh fish quite literally thrown up on the beaches sometimes. Even a seal or two, or little blue penguins in the coastal scrub.

Maori used the cave for food and shelter for centuries. 'Oru' means deep hole or cave, and 'mata' headland. The constant roar of the sea from inside the cave must have been disconcerting, sounding as it does like an animal scrabbling at the entrance.

The spectacular T-shaped cavern at the Fox River was visited by Charles Heaphy and Thomas Brunner in May 1846:

> Crossed the Potikohua stream [Fox River], a mountain torrent, running strongly, and immediately entered a remarkable cavern, teonumatu. A large mass of conglomerate rock, about 150 feet square and 80 feet high, stands out at the edge of the beach, and through its base this cave has been hollowed, apparently by the action of the adjacent stream, at some remote period ere the coast line has been elevated by volcanic agency, the signs of which are in many places apparent.

The vault is in the form of a cross, and penetrates the rock at right angles from its four sides, the eastern entrance, however, being blocked up. It is about 30 feet high, 150 feet long, from north to south, and about 50 crosswise. In it the natives have erected bed places, and stages for the purpose of drying dog-fish, which in the summer time the people from Araura catch on an adjacent isolated reef.[1]

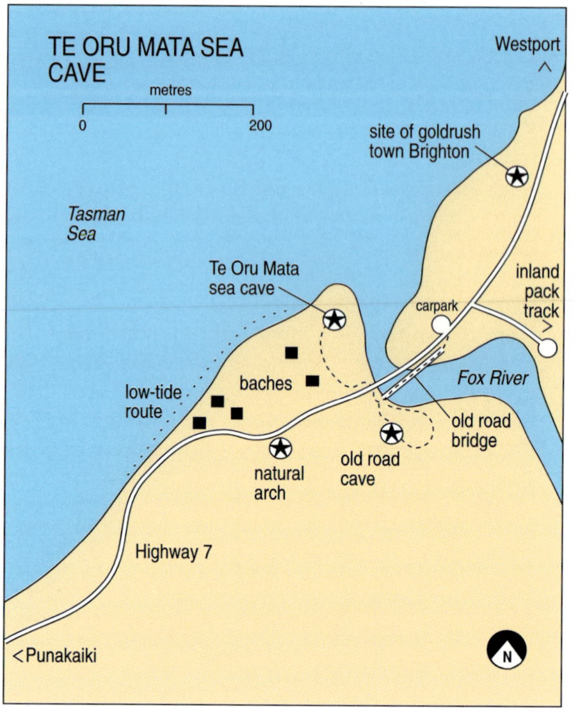

Many years later Julius von Haast stayed there and found it 'draughty', a not unreasonable conclusion.

There are sea caves further south at the Te Miko coastline that were clearly also used by Maori, and further coastal caves at Motukiekie and Point Elizabeth. So although the coast was difficult for the Maori traveller, there was plentiful food and a regular supply of sea caves and rock overhangs for shelter – just about one for each day of travel.

Maori installed ladders and ropes on several key bluffs on the West Coast, notably at Te Miko (described as 'very shaky and rotten'[2]), but this may have been for the benefit of the hardier parties. All the coastal bluffs were negotiable via inland routes and it is a fair guess that the more heavily laden groups, perhaps with older people, young children or mothers with babies, would have taken an inland trail if there were one available. In places the ladders and ropes might have served the dual purpose of providing access to good fishing spots or shags' eggs.

'Bright Town'

The West Coast goldrush in 1865 caused a new type of traveller to tackle the Paparoa coastline. Notoriously impatient, the digger was interested only in rushing to the next gold strike – but he did not count on the difficulties.

> The heavy rains of the past few days have made the journey along the coast from the south exceedingly tedious and difficult, the various streams which have to be crossed being flooded. Several persons have been jammed between the rivers, unable to go forward or retreat, and without any food. Others have narrowly escaped drowning, and many have lost themselves in the bush.[3]

Old Fox River bridge

In 1866-67 the gold town of Brighton sprang up on the spit just north of the Fox River. Some historians have suggested that it was actually known as Bright Town but there is no evidence to support this attractive theory.

It's been said that this was *the* fastest-growing gold town on the West Coast. Fifty establishments sprang up in the first three weeks; two weeks later there were 160 buildings and 53 hotels. At its peak, Brighton boasted about 6000 people. The river was named after the gold prospector Bill Fox, who made his reputation on the Arrow diggings, near Queenstown (see Sawpit Gully story).

Fox River canyon

There's nothing left of the town now, except for the remains of the old cemetery slightly up the Fox River. No doubt there are a few gold-diggers buried there who were drowned or swept away on this majestic but unforgiving coastline.

Footnotes and Further Reading

1. *Early Travellers in New Zealand*, ed. Nancy M. Taylor, Clarendon Press, 1959.
2. Ibid.
3. *The Southern Journey*, Mark Pickering, 1993.

BIG RIVER

FEATURES
Well-preserved mining site, with poppet head tower and winding plant, cyanide tanks, packtracks and old dam site, beech forest, DOC hut.

HOW TO GET THERE
From Reefton briefly take State Highway 7 for 1km toward Greymouth and turn off into Soldiers/Big River Road. This road winds into Devil's Creek valley, slowly climbing 10km to the Alborn's Coalmine carpark.

The Big River road is signposted 100 metres on and it is a 4WD vehicle track, winding through beech forest some 16km to the old Big River settlement. Although generally the road is in good condition it is not being maintained and windfall and snowfall can block the road, and the fords can flood. Ordinary cars will not get very far beyond the Alborn's carpark. Allow about 2-4 hours one way to drive from Reefton.

WALK/TRAMP DETAILS
If you have arrived by 4WD vehicle then you can drive right on in and explore around the open site. The old cyanide tanks, winding plant, boilerhouse and the magnificent poppet head are all within 15-20 minutes' walk of the DOC hut. The hut has 20 bunks and sits on a low hillock overlooking the ruined settlement – a fine outlook. There's also a 20-minute one-way walk to the old dam site.

There are two tramping tracks into Big River: both take nearly a day and people should be well equipped. One starts from Waiuta township and takes 4-5 hours along an old benched packtrack.

The other starts from State Highway 7, 10km from Reefton and over the Inangahua River swingbridge. The track turns into Deep Creek for some 4km to the fine 10-head Golden Lead stamping battery – worth a walk in its own right. The Deep Creek Track climbs 700 metres and eventually picks up an old tramline near the Golden Lead Mine and follows this to Big River. Allow 5-6 hours one-way tramping time.

If you can arrange transport then it is a fine weekend tramp from Waiuta to Big River, then out to Deep Creek.

If you don't have a 4WD and have no plans to tramp, there is a short walk (1-2 hours) from the carpark to Alborn's Coalmine.

'The Worst Road I've Ever Driven On'

Big River Mine was worked from about 1882 to 1942 and up to 100,000 ounces of gold were extracted from the quartz-bearing rocks, from a shaft that penetrated 535 metres underground. Cages were brought up under the poppet head, powered by a steam winding plant. The gold was crushed by the 10-head stamping battery and sifted through covered cyanide tanks that separated the gold from the quartz and refined it.

The Big River mine had its own coalmine, the Golden Lead, which together with the timber resources of the bush provided enough power for industrial and domestic use. It had its own private dam and a 2km water-race.

At an altitude of 670 metres the climate is hardly salubrious, but once there was a whole community living here, with its own school, post office, shop and (inevitably) pub. There were family homes and a row of single men's quarters dubbed Tin Town.

Although Reefton was just over the hill, Big River felt itself to be isolated and this

Poppet head

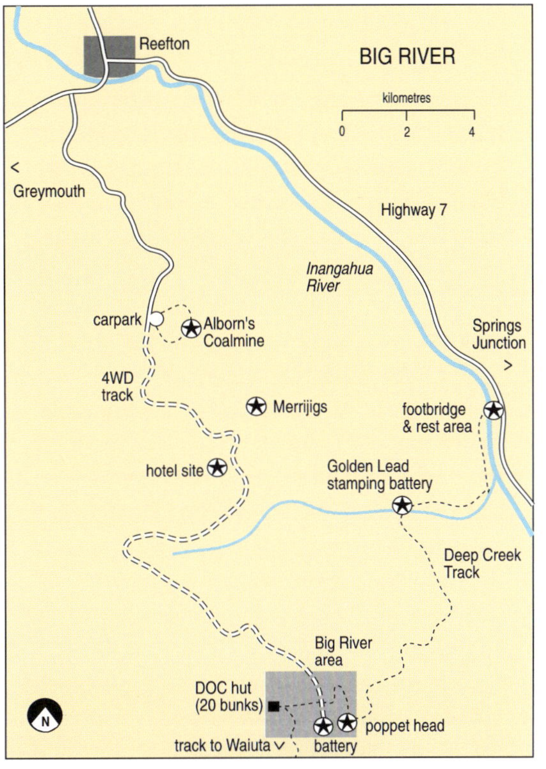

bred an independence that has stuck to this day. The road is still a shocker.

> It was 18 miles to Big River and I would say for the length of it, it was the worst road I've ever driven on in New Zealand. It used to take three hours in the truck and two in the car. That was going fairly well. I only got into top gear twice a week, when I went into Reefton on Tuesdays and Fridays and got on the main road. When I was carting coal from Alborn's mine in Merrijigs it was all gear work, all the way. No top gear at all. Up and downhill. There was one turning place at Merrijigs, one at the Scotia mine, one at the foot of Deep Creek, and that was all until you got to Big River. In the Fargo

ALBORN'S COALMINE

The short circuit walk of 1-2 hours from the carpark to Alborn's Coalmine embraces an area of several small coalmines. Coal was as useful as gold in the Reefton mining community, for running steam engines and for heating homes in the damp Reefton winters. The first coal extracted from this area was in about 1880 and the remains of the tramway and aerial cableway can still be found. The Alborn family took over the coalmine in 1923 after the Progress Mine had closed three years earlier. It was a do-it-yourself family-type operation: witness the Leyland truck used to lower the coal trucks down the incline to the coal bins. Fluming the coal on concrete and wood viaducts was tried but the abrasiveness of the coal wore out the concrete base.

THE SINGERS AND THE SONGS

On any packtrack you can still 'see' them: young, brawny men with straggling beards and Celtic accents. Dressed in moleskin trousers, with bowyangs tied below the knee, leaning on their shovels and yarning to a packman, with his patient horses standing by. You can see the blue smoke of their pipes, the surreptitious clink of a bottle and a sudden laugh, and feel the thin drizzle wetting the bush all around.

A couple of hard potatoes for lunch, another nip of 'cold tea', and an attempt to brush off the daily mud grimed into hands that are dry and raw with the physical effort. Channelling culverts, felling timber, ditching, clearing, and the same again next day as the packtrack patiently wends its way to a thumping sawmill or a raucous gold claim.

You can hear the jokes, the foot-stomping political arguments and the dream of a girl left behind. Anxiety about feeding the family, and arthritic aches in 20-year-old bodies. The restlessness and the hope; the bush that is both promise and prison.

Gold gave these men the chance to start a new life at the very end of the world and saw a daily parade of the incorrigible and the inspirational. Men making good, or on the make, from every walk of life, literally walking toward the goldfields and their golden dreams.

And yet you can also see the continuous claustrophobic environment dampening hopes and diminishing desires, the bodies broken down by hard work at only 30. The fear of begging charity, the poor-house and the workhouse. It was a case of making the best of your choices, with nothing to fall back on. You worked until you dropped, getting solace where you could – and that was mostly of a liquid kind.

There do not seem to have been many bush poets in mid-Victorian New Zealand – perhaps there wasn't time – but there was the working-class poetry of the songs. The evils of transportation and women told in the jaunty 'Black Velvet Band', or the sentimental tush and yearnings of a half-imagined girl in 'Gentle Annie'. As the packtrack turns another interminable corner you can almost hear these old songs and you could try out a bar or two yourself. Don't be too surprised if you hear a ghostly chorus join in.

> truck there was one corner near Deep Creek where I had to back and fill three times, and I think there were 11 others I had to have two goes at. Couldn't get around. The Diamond T truck had a shorter wheelbase, and with it – tightly – I could get around the corner. [1]

Visitors still regularly drive up the umbilical track and poke around, puzzling over pieces of disconnected machinery.

Deserted 50 years ago, Big River still looks recently lived in, with junk strewn everywhere. Perhaps if gold prices soar Big River will be reborn, though its more likely that piece by piece Big River will be souvenired back to town. The dense beech forests and subdued valleys are often wreathed inmist and there's a feeling that not all the old ghosts have been laid to rest.

Footnotes and Further Reading

1. *Big River Quartz Mine*, Les Wright, Friends of Waiuta Inc.,1993.

Alborn's Coalmine Walk (DOC pamphlet).

Big River Track (DOC pamphlet).

CROESUS TRACK & THE BRUNNER MINE

FEATURES
Miners' rainforest packtrack, stamping battery and sawmill sites, Croesus Mine site, Croesus Knob, panoramic views of Paparoa Range, Brunner Mine site.

HOW TO GET THERE
From Greymouth take State Highway 6 toward Westport, turning off after 2km and following the north bank of the Grey River past Taylorville and the Brunner Mine site, turning into Blackball after 18km. From the township take the road to Roa and turn off past the rubbish dump onto a narrow bush road that climbs steadily for 5km (with some small fords) to the Smoke-Ho carpark on the saddle.

WALK DETAILS
Croesus Track is a well-graded miners' packtrack that crosses the Paparoa Range to Barrytown, a tramp of 7-9 hours one way. Most of the historic sites are in the first section of the track up the Blackball Creek.

From Smoke-Ho carpark the one-way times are: 30 minutes First Hotel site, 1 hour Second Hotel site, 2 hours Garden Gully Hut, 2 hours 30 minutes Garden Gully stamping battery, 3 hours Ces Clarke Hut, 4-5 hours Croesus Knob.

Croesus was a king of Lydia in Greece, whose wealth was legendary and whose court attracted such fabulous figures as Aesop (of fables fame) and Solon (of law-making). It's an optimistic name for a goldmine, perhaps even cynical – few wise men search for gold.

But it was such fabled riches that drew the gold-diggers to this wilderness valley. In 1864 George Cundy and his party found gold in the lower Blackball Creek and a rich gold strike was made in the upper Blackball in 1873. Bellbirds, grey warblers and wood pigeons providing a vocal backdrop to the historic remains, which come thick and fast.

Throughout New Zealand during the 1929-35 Depression there was a brief resurgence in goldmining, and a reopening of old mine sites. The Second Hotel site dates from this second spell of goldmining when the hotel was shifted upriver and large-scale sluicing demanded a better water supply, hence the water-races.

A side-track goes for five minutes to sawmill debris of Perotti's Mill (1898) and 25 minutes to the 1898 Croesus battery site, crossing the Wessel's and Roaring Meg water-races on the way. One hour further, past well-made stone drainage channels and over the Roaring Meg water-race again, there is a track junction, where a side-track leads over a low saddle down to the pretty Garden Gully Hut. This was one of several huts built during the Depression.

Another 20 minutes further up the track is the showpiece of the goldmining era, the Garden Gully battery. Restored and largely intact, the 10-head stamping battery was last used in 1905, and berdans, pelton wheels and other machinery lie in grateful retirement among the ferns.

The main Croesus Track starts to climb from the Garden Gully turnoff, passes the ruin of the old Top Hut and turns the corner to the

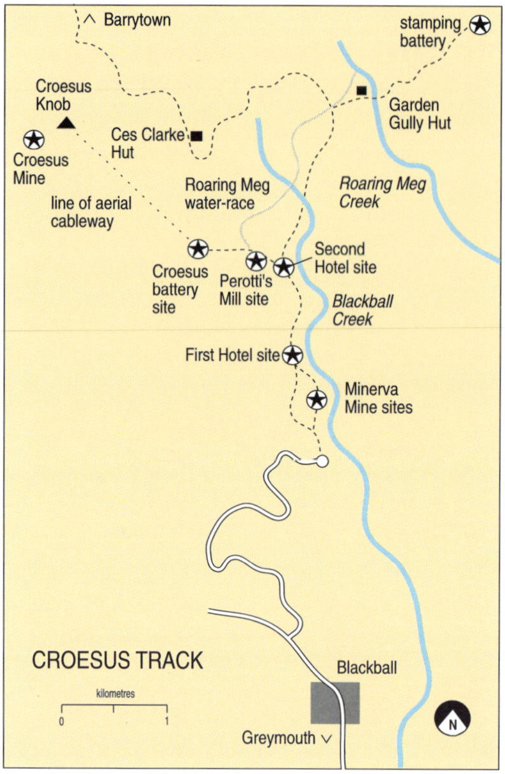

Ces Clarke Memorial Hut – probably the only mountain hut in New Zealand to be opened by a prime minister (David Lange and no, he didn't walk).

The track launches out onto the open tussock tops and a side-route leads up to Croesus Knob and the tangled ruin of an aerial tower.

Croesus Knob

BLACKBALL & THE LABOUR PARTY

Early goldmining was individualistic and creative; coalmining was collective and unimaginative. Gold brought men to the Blackball area but it was coal that provided the jobs.

Coalmining began in 1889 and by 1891 coal was being conveyed across the Grey River to Ngahere by aerial buckets. Some of the towers are still standing. For a long time Blackball could only be reached by ferry or the goldminers' track to Brunner. The railway reached Blackball in 1909.

As the mining population grew a coal culture developed out of this isolation. The work was hard, the town site primitive, the housing crude. A Board of Trade inquiry in 1919 criticised the housing, poor bathing facilities and inadequate town drainage, blaming the continuing industrial unrest on the social conditions. There was some truth in this, but Blackball was also a close-knit community, a working-class pit village where the boss had a fancy gabled house and the miners had shacks in a line. It was a fertile breeding ground for militancy.

The successful Blackball crib-time strike of 1908 launched the Federation of Miners, which was formed in Greymouth and became the Federation of Labour in 1909 – the Red Feds. After the failed 1913 waterfront strike this federation became the Labour Party in 1916. One of the leaders of the crib-time strike was Paddy Webb, who ironically became Minister of Mines for the first Labour government in 1935.

The mine manager's house in Blackball is now the community centre.

BRUNNER MINE

The Brunner Mine site is one of the emotional hearts of the West Coast: the sentinel chimney, the 1876 suspension bridge over the Grey River, and the staring statue of a coalminer.

It was here, halfway between Greymouth and Blackball, that Thomas Brunner in 1846 spotted a seam of coal, and here in 1864 that Matthew Batty dug out 30 tons from the West Coast's first commercial coalfield. Development was quick and by 1868 coke ovens were built. Soon over 200 men were employed in the Brunner industrial complex. Taylorville became a miners' town and on a winter's morning kids might be served warm pieces of coke, which they tossed from hand to hand as they walked to school. Early photographs show smoking industries on both sides of 'coal gorge', workshops piled precipitously. Only the stumps on hillside show where the forest once was.

Then on 26 March 1896 a large explosion killed 65 men in the Brunner Mine, and that's why the granite miner stares across the river.

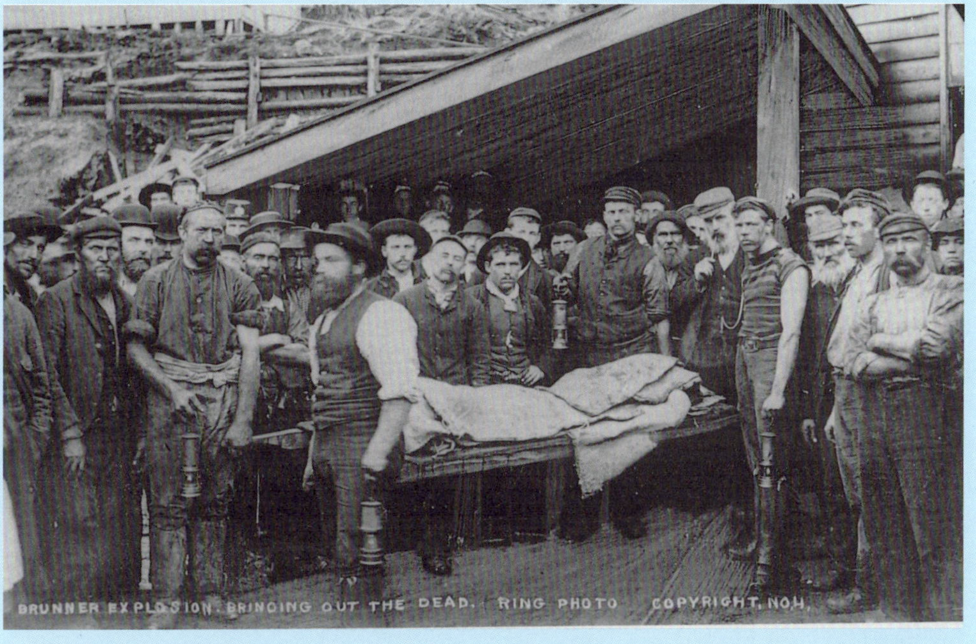

Bringing out the dead after the Brunner Mine explosion, 1896

There's a majestic view of Mt Cook down the long curve of the West Coast. Quartz ore was taken from the Croesus Mine from 1898 to 1903, just five minutes below the knob, and hauled out on an aerial cableway down to the stamping battery in Blackball Creek. If the miners hoped to match the classical riches of Croesus they were quickly disappointed; one hopes that at least they enjoyed the view.

Further Reading

The Past Today, Historic Places Trust, 1987.

Historic Buildings of New Zealand, Historic Places Trust, 1983.

Croesus and Moonlight Walks (DOC pamphlet)

HISTORIC HOKITIKA

FEATURES
Customshouse and wharf, replica of shipwrecked schooner *Tambo*, signal mast, museum and Carnegie Library.

HOW TO GET THERE
Hokitika is on the West Coast 30km south of Greymouth.

WALK DETAILS
The old wharf by the Hokitika River has been preserved and the customshouse has been turned into an information kiosk. The museum is open daily and next door is an original 1908 Carnegie Library that is being restored. Other interesting buildings are the Government Building (1908), the clock tower (1903), and Teichelmann's House.

The Hokitika cemetery contains the grave of explorer Charlie Douglas, a monument to several early explorers who lost their lives, and also several distinctive Chinese gravestones.

A concrete replica of the schooner *Tambo* lies by the rivermouth. The original *Tambo* was built in Australia and worked as a coastal trader on the West Coast last century, surviving 26 crossings of the bar before being shipwrecked in 1866. On full-tide evenings the replica looks uncannily as if it has just sailed in.

It's a short easy walk to the beach, which is as wild as it was the day the first diggers and store-owners scrambled ashore in 1865.

'One Mass of Driftwood'

It would have been a remarkable scene. One wild West Coast beach, with a bashing surf and a thick mist of salt spray blowing over the conglomerations of driftwood locked together in unlikely scrums, the wood polished white by the resonant wind. Immediately behind the beach kahikatea and rimu stood pristine and root-saturated in the coastal swamps that backed the dunes.

The beachline was broken by a huge river pushing dark tea-stained water into the tides, and a regular foamy battle took place where the tide and river argued on the bar. Beyond the trees and river was a continual line of mountains, blue and blurred for the most part, with a few white-cowled and remote, like a line of prayerful monks in a Cistercian chapel.

But on 20 December 1864 the wilderness got a shock. The 123-ton steamship *Nelson* eased across the 'Okatika' river bar with a bunch of boistrous men: some seasick, some half-drunk, one or two half-mad and certainly all besotted with gold fever. Captain Samuel Leech had inspected the river on foot some days before and decided to give it a go. G.O.

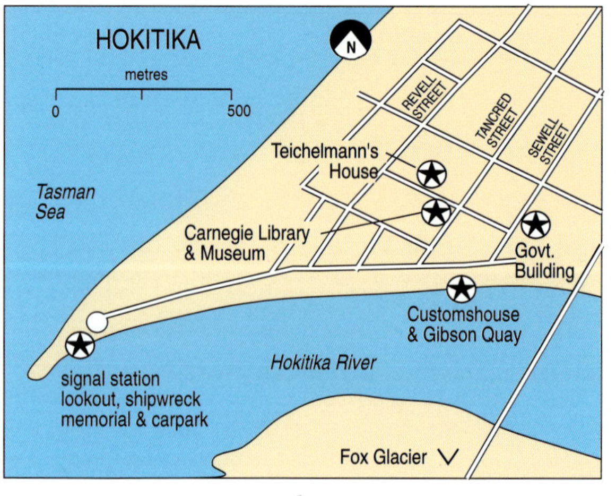

Preshaw, a banker working for the Bank of New South Wales, witnessed the event:

> The river was full of snags, many of which could not be seen at high water, and were therefore dangerous for vessels entering without a pilot. A boatman named James Teer acted on this occasion. The sea was as smooth as glass; so smooth that he crossed the bar alone in his boat and piloted the vessel in in safety. She was full of cargo, and crowded with passengers. Brohan and I were on the South spit, and assisted to make her fast. The passengers were taken to the north side of the river – where the township of Hokitika now stands – by boat. The place at that time was one mass of driftwood, so thick, that it was impossible to get a horse or waggon through without clearing it away.[1]

In a goldrush there was only one speed for all events: panic. Preshaw observed:

> When I returned to Okatika next day I scarcely knew the place, it had so changed in appearance, even in that short time; buildings were going up in all directions. The inspector of the Bank of New Zealand decided to put up a building, which he did as soon as timber was procurable. I agitated for an office, and was informed that one would be provided if the rush turned out to be a good one.[2]

It did. Two months earlier on 1 October 1864 two enterprising shopkeepers, John Hudson and James Price, had erected a 12ft x 20ft (4m x 6m) store of saplings and calico on Hokitika River's north spit, the only place free of bush. It was a bold business venture

Monument to the pioneers of Westland

and looked likely to go bankrupt as various prospecting parties disappeared into the bush and all went quiet for several weeks. Then one morning Jimmy Liddle and a Maori team turned up with substantial amounts of gold from the Totara River and despite their best efforts to keep the fact quiet, by dusk the same day 300 miners with pine torches had formed a garish parade and were trampling down the coast from the Taramakau to the Totara.

Gold strikes at Donnelly's Creek near Ross and then in Waimea Creek kept up the momentum and the excitement spilled into neighbouring creeks and streams, diggers probing every possibility until the whole area between Ross and the Taramakau seemed gold-bearing. A bewildering number of rushes occurred north and south of Hokitika – Kaniere, Grey, Moonlight, Jones, Donoghue's – until one exasperated digger grumbled: 'In this country a man need live with his swag always on his back.'

The crossing of the bar by the *Nelson* in December brought the bankers, the publicans and the shopkeepers and launched Hokitika into serious existence.

Shovels and Shanties

The day the *Nelson* crossed the bar, William Horton Revell, the goldfields warden, was already marking off street frontages and sections. The second ship, the *Wallabi*, crossed the bar, and on 22 December two cutters arrived: the *Petrel* from Jacksons Bay and the *Nugget* from Invercargill. Many miners were arriving down the beachline from Greymouth; the town was booming.

The 'buildings' were calico at first but within days slab-walled and raupo-roofed shanties sprang up. As the value of sections increased, so did tempers.

> 28th December 1864
>
> A dispute arose this morning between Messrs. Cassidy and Price about one of the business sites. Mr Revell was called, and decided in favour of Cassidy. Price persisted in putting down his pegs and digging post-holes. Mr Revell interfering, Price made a blow at him with a shovel ... Price apologised to Mr Revell for his conduct, and was let off with a severe lecture.[3]

By March a town was made.

AN AUSSIE PORT

For three years Hokitika enjoyed unchallenged supremacy as the great West Coast entrepot. It became the sixth town in the Colony, and, in terms of customs revenue, shipping and immigration, one of New Zealand's chief ports.[5]

Like Greymouth and Westport, Hokitika was an 'Australian port': closer in practical travelling terms to Australia than to Christchurch. Diggers would leave the Australian fields and sail direct to the West Coast and the new fields at Ross and Waimea, bypassing both Otago and Canterbury – a fact that caused much anguish to the businessmen of those provinces.

The river bar was the bane of shipping and it took a brave captain to try to get across. There were 27 beachings between May and September 1865, of which 15 were total wrecks. The *West Coast Times* sometimes had an ironic column on 'Vessels Ashore' and it was a common sight to have several boats stuck at odd positions around the rivermouth. The business of getting these vessels afloat was lucrative – up to £1000 a time. A new class of salvagers sprang up – 'beach rakers' who would be out on moonlit nights to drag in spars, planking or whatever had been washed off the wrecked ships.

More often ships anchored in the uncomfortable roadstead and ferried their passengers ashore, but even this could entail long delays for the impatient diggers. 'The schooner *Wallace* lay off the bar for twelve weeks before entering.'[6] The river, too, could change, and in one notable period it was blocked up for four months. When it suddenly cleared 41 vessels came into port between 12 and 15 September 1867. The port closed finally in 1954.

> Some two thousand people had spread themselves along the crooked length of Revell Street and up the curving river frontage; substantial buildings were in the course of erection and a newspaper was projected. Hotels were no longer a yard of canvas and two poles. Skittle alleys, billiard rooms, devil's pool [sic], and a Maori chief who had tomahawked seventeen rebels (admission one shilling) were numbered among its various attractions.[4]

It was glorious mayhem. At its peak Hokitika boasted 102 hotels, which lined up serendipitously on Revell Street. The hotels were required to have lights on outside after dark, which gave the place 'the appearance of a Chinese town during the feast of lanterns'. Other novelties included the Weld Street skating rink, Madam Sohier's waxworks, vaudeville troupes from Australia, minstrels, dancing girls and, in the euphemism of the day, 'the nymphs of the pave'.

Revell Street is still slightly twisted but Hokitika is a good deal quieter now and, one trusts, cleaner. In April 1866 customs duties of £2669 were paid on the importation of spirits and a mere £18 6 shillings on soap.

Footnotes and Further Reading

1. *Banking in New Zealand*, G.O. Preshaw, Edwards Dunlop, 1888.
2. Ibid.
3. *The West Coast Gold Rushes*, Philip Ross May, Pegasus Press, 1962.
4. Ibid.
5. Ibid.
6. Ibid.

THE FERRYMEN

David Millar Graham was an adventurous man. He sailed from Southland in a whaleboat with three others around Farewell Spit to the West Coast goldfields, but their boat got blown 100 miles south and they ended up in Jackson Bay, where they were lucky to get through the surf alive. They were looked after by the local Maori and then had to face a hard tramp back up the coast to the Five Mile diggings. At the Five Mile Graham met and married a nurse, Isobella Garland, who could remember sitting on Charles Dickens's knee in London before her uncle and aunt took her to Bendigo goldfields in Australia.

Graham tried goldmining and running a bakery before accepting the government position of ferryman across the Three Mile Lagoon. He also had to maintain the three miles of horse track to Okarito. The Grahams raised a large family by the Three Mile, including Peter and Alex, who became near-legendary mountain climbers and guides.

The necessity for ferrymen was well demonstrated. Building your own raft was no fun; it was also dangerous, and drowning was such a hazard all over the country at the time that it was dubbed a national disease.

In 1874 the authorities established a subsidy of £50 a year to employ ferrymen. Licence conditions would be commonly like this: 1) the ferry to be worked by boat; 2) subsidy £50 per annum; 3) 25 acres of land thrown in (to augment the ferryman's meagre income); 4) statutory protection from private ferrymen half a mile either way; 5) five-year lease; 6) horse and rider 5 shillings; 7) police and prisoners free.

Ferrymen were a unique breed, jacks of all trades: carpenters, diggers, fossickers, philosophers and most of all yarners. Joseph Collyer is another interesting example. He became a sort of institution as the ferryman and storeman at Okuru River (near Haast) during the 1880s and 90s and was described as a man 'happy in his solitude'. Collyer kept his daybooks on chips of wood, shingles or pieces of bark, and officiated as 'harbour-master, signalman, boatman, wharfinger, guide, philosopher and friend to all who visit Okuru'. Charlie Douglas asked:

> Can any one explain why ferry-men are in general Characters, do ferries make them so? Or are they a special case born to create Ferries and how is it that they are in general sociable & talkative, while the Tollman, who's occupation is about the same, is a gloomy Misanthrope?[6]

Of Bill Hindley on the Waiatoto River Charlie Douglas (himself a ferryman for a while on the Paringa) remarked.

> ... in fiction Bill is unapproachable. He is compound of the Ancient mariner, Sinbad the Sailor and Baron Münchhausen ... His stories always put me in mind of those rivers which rise no one knows where, then they flow on for miles in a steady defined channel, till entering flat country they branch into a hundred mouths and finally disappear in the sand. But long may he and others rule the ferries south, but for their eccentricities we would have nothing to talk about.[7]

DONOVAN'S STORE & THREE MILE PACKTRACK

FEATURES
Donovan's store (oldest wooden building in Westland), Okarito Lagoon and wharf, monument to Abel Tasman, Three Mile Packtrack, Three Mile Lagoon, Okarito trig lookout.

HOW TO GET THERE
From Hokitika it is about a 120km drive south down State Highway 6 to the Okarito turnoff, and 7km down the sealed road to the township.

WALK DETAILS
There are several good walks. The old wharf shed has some good historic photos and it's interesting just to walk around the township and estuary shoreline. The track to Okarito trig starts from further down the road and a steepish climb to the lookout platform gives you a superb view over Okarito Lagoon and the Southern Alps.

The packtrack to the Three Mile Lagoon (Totaraiti) diverges off from the Okarito trig track and is in excellent condition. Alternatively, you can follow the beach at low tide past Kohuamarua Bluff and the Three Mile. Watch out for seals on the beach. There are tide tables pasted up on a noticeboard by the carpark. For the beach-packtrack circuit allow 3-4 hours return. The trig is about 2 hours return.

At the Three Mile Lagoon there's a bridge and by following the coast you can get around Blanchard's Bluff to the Five Mile Lagoon. Often the lagoon exits are 'gravelled up' and the bridges are superfluous.

'Its Glory Has Departed'

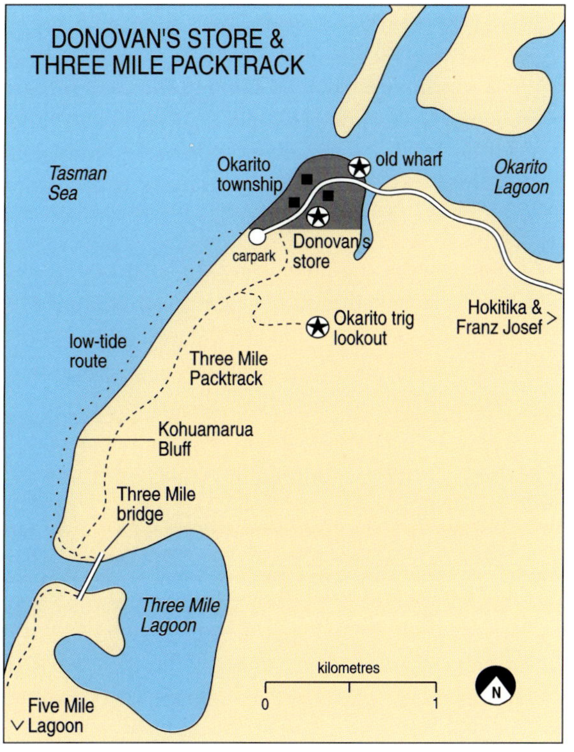

In late 1865 or early 1866 the Club Hotel was hastily erected on a prime street frontage on the Strand. The section cost the owner about £160 but it was a bargain. Okarito's main street jostled with thirsty men dressed in a sort of gold-digger's uniform of a flannel open-neck shirt, 'moleskin' trousers (made from a thick cotton material) and 'wide-awake' hats with a broad brim.

At least a dozen different languages could be heard in the bars as men bought 'nobblers' at outrageous prices and huddled in secret cabals to discuss where the next rush would be. They worked hard and played hard, and at its peak Okarito's 1500 men supported 25 hotels, numerous stores, three theatres, two banks and a harbour-master – 'everybody who does not dig sells grog, and everybody who digs drinks copiously'.[1]

Down the coast it was the same story at the Three Mile and Five Mile lagoons. The Five Mile (Totaranui) was regarded as the richest sea beach in Westland and in July 1866 could boast five hotels, 40 stores, two butcher shops and two bakeries, with a population of 1500. Local identity and observer Charlie Douglas remarked that it was:

> One of the most flourishing places on the coast for several years, and when at the height of its prosperity had a double, sometimes a treble line of stores and shanties extending nearly the whole length of the beach. There were Stores, Pubs, Shanties, Dance houses and other places of even less repute, but never a church or a schoolhouse. Like Gillespies it was never a surveyed township but it passed the calico era and nearly arrived at the weatherboard. But like other famous places its glory has departed. One or two diggers' huts are now all that is left of the once famous Five Mile.[2]

Likewise Okarito never gained any respectability of tenure. All too soon the rich beach sands were exhausted; Okarito's glory years were two, perhaps three in number. The black sands were incredibly rich but quickly exhausted.

JIMMY & EVA DONOVAN

The original Club Hotel was blown down in a storm after a year, then rebuilt from kauri, rimu, kahikatea and baltic pine, the latter possibly scavenged from shipwrecks. The concrete foundations were innovative for 1866 and the store is regarded as the oldest building in Westland.

Jimmy Donovan was born in Hokitika in 1867 and worked at various jobs, including managing the Lake Mapourika store. In 1890 he and his wife Eva took over the Club Hotel and ran it as a store until 1950, an incredible 60 years. Jimmy didn't change much so the store didn't either and it became a veritable time-capsule.

> **Camp ovens and other ironware hung from the roof of the store, racks of sweets fought for space with whale bones, and the shelves were cluttered with old irons, kerosene lamps, butter churns and horse harnesses. People in more recent times entering to buy an ice-cream would end up staying for hours browsing among Okarito's past.[4]**

Under Keith Robertson the store kept going part time as late as 1965 but the writing was on the wall. The Robertsons bequeathed the hut to the Historic Places Trust, which has it listed as a Category 1 site. The Department of Conservation is slowly restoring it and hopes to replace goods on the shelves to look as they would have in the 1890s.

'THIS FINE PIECE OF QUEEN'S HIGHWAY'

This was what Gerhard Mueller disparagingly called the stretch of coast between Okarito and the Three Mile, around Kohuamarua Bluff. It was a route that Jimmy Donovan would have known well from his packing runs down the coast.

> **It used to be a study watching a long line of loaded pack horses with perhaps only one man driving. Going round a bluff in heavy weather, the loads were usually from 250 to 300 lbs of very mixed character. The horses that were up to the work could watch the seas far better than most men. A good packer never swore, or threw stones at his horse, but let them take their own time, the animals would all stop and watch as sea coming in, then make a run for it. If by chance they got caught, they had a way of propping themselves face or back to the waves, and holding their own, then as the sea receded off they went at a trot.[5]**

Oddly enough, it seems that plants could travel as quickly as diggers and would often settle in long after the miners had left. One visitor to Okarito noted: 'I recognised several [plants] indigenous to the lake country in Otago, amongst which were the wild fuchsia, convolvulus, geraniums ...'[3]

Footnotes and Further Reading

1. *The Southern Journey*, Mark Pickering, 1993.
2. Ibid.
3. Ibid.
4. 'Donovan's: a window to rich past', Trish McCormack Ross, *The Press*, 13 May 1996.
5. Pickering, op. cit.
6. Ibid.
7. Ibid.

Peter Graham: Mountain Guide, Peter Graham, A.H. & A.W. Reed Ltd,1965.

Three-mile Beach

PARINGA CATTLE TRACK

FEATURES
Well-graded cattle track, old roadmen's huts, mature forest and kaka.

HOW TO GET THERE
The easiest access is 5km short of Lake Moeraki on the inland side, about 80km south of Fox Glacier, on State Highway 6 on the West Coast.

WALK/TRAMP DETAILS
From the Lake Moeraki end a good packtrack crosses over to the Moeraki (or Blue) River to Blowfly Hut (6 bunks). From here the excellently graded track climbs slowly up to Maori Saddle Hut (10 bunks). Allow 1 hour to Blowfly one way, 5 hours to Maori Saddle. There is no marked route up to the Mataketake Range from the saddle, though a bush-bash should bring you to the tussock in about 1 hour.

To continue along the cattle track to the Waita River you need to allow another 5–6 hours. Parts of the track have been eroded away before Coppermine Creek Hut (6 bunks) and the route follows the shingly river for the last section down to the main highway. The complete crossing is a tramping rather than a walking trip and bad weather could delay you.

'Run or be Damned'

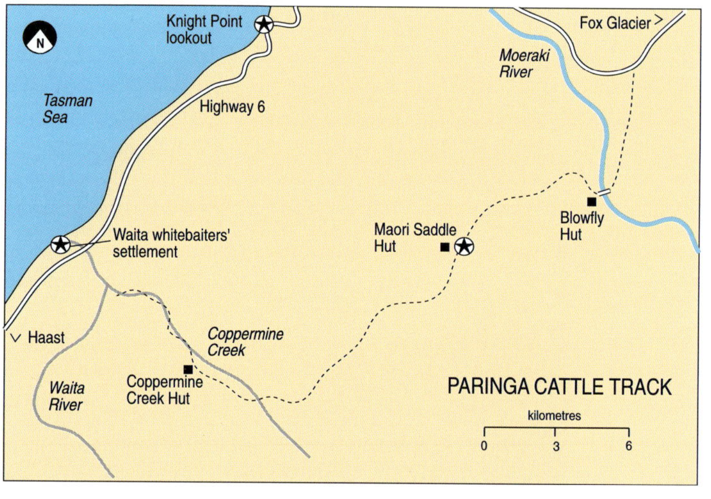

Between Bruce Bay and Haast is a coast steeped in dark headlands, with lonely lagoons and smidgins of golden beach. A rolling sea crashes continually into offshore reefs and generates an unceasing spume that hangs like a mist on the rainforest. But the stunning scenery may have been lost on many an anxious traveller in the 1880s.

> Sometimes but very rarely this point can be rounded by doing a smart piece of running, but it is hardly worth the risk. In the early days some of the diggers gave this point the ominous name of run-or-be-damned – there is a fine cave under the cliff but as might be expected people have no time to admire it.[1]

To avoid the awkward tangle of coastline around Knight Point the Maori found an easier inland trail over a low 700m saddle and the Europeans developed it further as a packtrack for travellers.

In 1871 the Westland County Council issued contracts for clearing tracks south from Bruce Bay to Haast, offering £1380 for 37 miles (60km), and £800 for 19 miles. Charlie Douglas, McGloin and Julies Matthies won the contract for a five-foot-wide clearing track from Abbey Rocks to the Waita River, which included the Paringa Cattle Track.

Contracts were subsequently let for forming the gradient and metalling the top. The result was a 'road' capable of taking horses and packing mules, and it could later be enlarged for a dray road. Progress was slow and expensive. Nine miles and 30 chains of the 'Mahitahi-Haast' track were completed in 1882 for the total sum of £2779, and Gerhard Mueller in his report to Parliament talked of only 'three and a half miles' of track left to finish in 1883 – that's over 10 years to build 50 miles (80km) of road.

Roadmaking was hard labour. A pick, shovel and wheelbarrow might be the only tools, and the workers lived in a tent beside the track. On the West Coast this sort of work went to unemployed goldminers, and councils used road schemes as a means to soak up surplus labour that might otherwise prove troublesome. The pay was 10-12 shillings a day.

50,000 cattle

Originally the Paringa Cattle Track was designed as a communication and supply link to Haast, which was acutely isolated from the rest of the West Coast. There was a bridleway over the Haast Pass, but this route involved almost 80km of rugged travel, with a boat trip down Lake Wanaka to reach Pembroke (the old name of Wanaka). The Paringa Cattle Track offered a shorter route for the cattle farmers, and cattle were already being taken over the saddle to the yards at Whataroa by 1875.

'A CORRUGATED-IRON BOX'

Basic roadmen's 'tin shed' huts were established at either end of the track and were intended as little more than rest stops for the cattle-drovers or the benighted traveller.

In the 1920s Maud Moreland and her companion crossed the Moeraki River in the dark to the old Blue Hut, on the site of the present-day Blowfly Hut.

> But that night it was dark; it was wet; we were both tired and hungry and longing for a decent resting place, and when we pushed open the door of that hut what did we find? It was nothing but a corrugated-iron box, eight or nine feet square, with a rude bunk, covered with fern ... A more truly uninviting place would be hard to find; and all the time a booming, like a swarm of bees round our heads, warned us that though we might find a resting-place, we should not find rest.[2]

Blowfly Hut

They had a 'desperately uncomfortable night' in the Blue Hut and the mosquitoes were not much put off by the lighting of 'Himrod's Powder'. They fled at first light 'while there is any of us left'.

THREE ROADMEN

A road is not just a link with living communities, it has a whole history to itself, starting with the men who worked on it. Charlie 'Mr Explorer' Douglas, 'Arawata Bill' O'Leary and Joe Driscoll were three notable South Westland identities, who all worked as roadmen on the Paringa Cattle Track.

Douglas worked on the track in the mid-1870s, clearing the bush and tidying up the surveyed line. He was paid 700 acres of land and had an unsuccessful stint at cattle farming near the Paringa River, but his real love was exploration. On a casual basis at first, Douglas began work for G.J. Roberts of the Survey Department and slowly acquired a reputation and semi-official position as an 'explorer'. With this financial assistance at his back he was able to do what he most preferred: wander through the wilderness valleys of Westland, far away from people, thinking his own thoughts.

Charlie Douglas was one of the great men of Westland. Explorer, hermit, acute observer, humorist, and in his writings sardonic, cynical and thoughtful, there is scarcely any valley in South Westland that he did not explore – Fox, Franz Joseph, Paringa, Clarke, Waiatoto, Arawata, Turnbull, Okuru, Cascade – usually to the headwaters, and usually on his own.

> There is a fascination in living in such places, away from all communication with the outer world which attracts many people – especially the failures.[3]

Some time early in this century another 'failure' had a stint as a roadman on the Paringa Track, 'Arawata Bill' – 'you should have been told Bill, only in you was the gold'. William O'Leary was a roadman, packer, ferryman on the Arawata River and itinerant prospector, made famous by Denis Glover in his sequence of poems. He fossicked in the country around the Dart, Arawata, Cascade and Hollyford but he seems to have found little actual gold. He had extraordinary resilience.

> In 1937 the Olivine explorer Jack Holloway was amazed to come across 'Arawata' clad in thigh gumboots cutting steps in the ice on O'Leary Pass with a long handled shovel. No mean effort for an old timer of 71![4]

In 1939 Robert Monteguoy Nelson, alias Joe Driscoll, deserted from the army and spent five years in the Paringa-Haast region, evading the military police and living off the land by hunting the tops around the Mataketake and Thomas ranges. He sold venison and skins to local runholders and when he was finally arrested at the end of World War II, he found himself to be something of a local hero. He was sentenced to a year's hard labour but recalled rather enjoying his stay in Paparua Prison, where he mostly looked after the horses.

On his release he took on the 30km stretch of Paringa road from Coppermine Creek to Chasm Creek and lived for 12 years in a comfortable three-roomed cottage at Coppermine Creek with five horses and a 'fiery' wife. He died at the age of 54.

His story formed the basis for a novel called *Moving Target* by Jack McClenaghan, and a novelised biography called *The Loner* by Ivan Agnew.

Cattle were taken in mobs of about 200 from the South Westland river valleys such as the Arawata and Cascade, mustered along the beach to the Waita River, and brought to graze near Coppermine Creek Hut. In the pre-dawn the cattle were broken into smaller mobs to stop them bunching on narrow parts of the track, and pushed over the saddle to be coralled at the Moeraki River, near Blowfly Hut. The next day involved getting them across the river and onto the roadhead at Lake Paringa.

It took two weeks to get cattle from the Cascade Valley to the Whataroa yards. The last mob was driven through in 1961, after which cattle were trucked south over the newly completed Haast Pass road. In 1965 the main highway down the coast was finally breached through.

Most of the history associated with the track has gone and the best historical relic is the track itself, which has stood the test of time remarkably well. For almost 100 years some 50,000 cattle are estimated to have been taken over this unlikely trail, bellowing in the pre-dawn starts and moving sluggishly up into the white mists that wreathe the tops in solitude.

Footnotes and Further Reading

1. *The Southern Journey*, Mark Pickering, 1993.
2. *Through South Westland*, Maud Moreland, Witherly & Co., 1911.
3. Pickering, op. cit.
4. Ibid.

Haast-Paringa Cattle Track (DOC pamphlet).

WAITAKI POWER STATION

FEATURES
Concrete dam and power station, hydro village.

HOW TO GET THERE
From Oamaru it is 8km to the Pukeuri Junction and 65 m up State Highway 83 to the Waitaki Dam.

WALK DETAILS
There is a viewing platform and information centre at the dam, and a quick walk around the site and village won't take more than 15 minutes. The hydro village is private property so you have to look in from the outside.

The power station is an uncompromising concrete blockhouse, yet some unknown poet in the Public Works Department added a touch of Regency to the facade, incorporating large, airy and elegant windows. The dam does not have a separate spillway so when the lake is high it cascades over the entire arc of the dam – a genuine piece of concrete poetry.

The Depression Dam

In the Waitaki Valley the light is hard and vivid. Summer browns the valley to a toast-crisp texture, then winter extends a long gnarly grip over the landscape. Snow sneaks down to the riverside and frost lies on the frozen river flats for weeks, mocking the efforts of a weak sun in a steel-blue sky. There seem to be only two seasons, for spring is a quick dash of roadside flowers, and autumn is a moment of red brittle golds.

The river is true to its glacial origins and always runs like a thick milkshake, while the wind cuts down the valley like a chisel. The men building the Waitaki Dam lit braziers and between shifts huddled around the warmth.

Yet they were the lucky ones. The Waitaki Dam was built through some of the worst of the Depression years and every day men were trudging up the valley looking for work on the dam site. If the project was in expansion they got a job, for the government of the day used Waitaki as a gigantic on-again, off-again work scheme. Picks and shovels were used in order to soak up workers, and the Waitaki was the last great dam to be built without any substantial mechanical means.

FACTS & FIGURES

The Waitaki River has a mean flow of 342 cubic metres a second (cumecs) and investigation into a site for a dam began in 1925. The first 'accommodation' for single workers was by way of canvas tents in early 1928 but by later that year most were housed in an 'army camp' of new wooden shacks. The first concrete-block house, used by senior staff but intended eventually for power station maintenance staff, was built in 1929.

The first coffer dam was finished about 1930, designed to divert and hold back the river while the real dam was built behind. Huge amounts of shingle had to be removed; 500,000 cubic metres in all was dug out, mostly by pick and shovel, though a light rail system was used to move material in and out of the works site. The Depression cut into progress dramatically and, because it also reduced power demand, the original plan of having the power station up and running by 1931 was quietly shelved.

Average pay during 1930 for a labourer on the dam site was about £3 10s a week. A loaf of bread cost 6d (sixpence); a pint of milk 3d ('thruppence'). In 1931 the Depression caused wages to be cut by 10 per cent and the workforce at Waitaki fell from 1200 to about 1000. In 1932 there was another 10 per cent cut and the workforce was halved. By 1936 things were picking up again but most people were still being paid less than they earned in 1920.

The powerhouse was almost complete by 1932 and the turbines were slotted in. The main dam was finished by 1934 and by September of that year the last of the sluice gates were closed and the dam filled up. The opening ceremony on 24 October 1934 was a grand if ironic occasion. No turbine was actually operational, so when the Governor-General touched the switch and the lights came on, the power came from Lake Coleridge.

Genuine Waitaki power flowed in early 1935 and since then the powerhouse has been extended to add two more generators. The dam is a curved gravity dam, 36 metres high.

The Waitaki scheme is the largest in the country, incorporating eight dams and several cross-country canals. Each droplet of water that falls onto the eastern side of the Southern Alps into Lake Tekapo is thrashed, propelled, pummelled and spouted through eight power stations on its nearly 200km journey to the sea.

These power stations are now operated largely by remote control so there is little need for permanent maintenance staff. The original hydro village at Waitaki sits tidy and forlorn. The whole thing was up for sale in 1996 – lock, stock and fruit trees.

THE SOCIAL CONTRACT

Michael Joseph Savage led the first Labour government, which came to power in a landslide victory in 1935. Labour gained 53 seats to the opposition's 17. The Maori seats were split evenly, with two supporting Labour and two supporting the United-Reform coalition.

Labour promised more for the working man – a pension, social services, better housing – and by and large they delivered it. Indeed, such was the charisma of Savage that people hung his portrait in their homes, and as late as the 1993 election a candidate for Sydenham in Christchurch recalled walking into sitting rooms where the portrait of Michael Joseph Savage still hung in pride of place.

Savage visited the Waitaki Dam in 1934 and stayed with the energetic local doctor and his wife, Gervan and Ethel McMillan. At that time the Presbyterian minister at Kurow was Arnold Nordmeyer, and along with others working on the dam site (schoolmaster Andy Davidson, Labour Party representative Tom Butler and union leader Jerry Skinner) they talked about the grim social conditions of working people and what could be done to alleviate them. McMillan formed a cooperative medical insurance scheme, he and Nordmeyer joined the Labour Party, and through the sweltering summers and bitter winters of the early 1930s the doctor and the priest developed the notion of a cradle-to-the-grave social security system.

The idea was not new but the determination was – and the timing was perfect. The Depression, the tired government, the food-kitchen queues and the kids in sugarbag playsuits all touched off an explosion of anger and frustration at the existing system.

Both McMillan and Nordmeyer won seats in the new Parliament (Dunedin West and Oamaru). Members of Parliament were poorly paid then and McMillan 'slept in a [Wellington] garage in order to make ends meet'.[1] Along with other firebrands, such as John A. Lee, they pushed for change. McMillan had written in 1935 a pamphlet entitled *A National Health Service, New Zealand of Tomorrow* and both he and Nordmeyer were on the social security committee.

After the usual debating and in-fighting period the Social Security Bill was introduced in 1938. It promised universal free health care and a pension for everyone at 65 without, at Nordmeyer's and Savage's insistence, a means test. The opposition fought it all the way.

It has been described as the crowning achievement of the first Labour government and probably the single most important piece of legislation in New Zealand's history. Aspects of the legislation predated and influenced similar moves in Britain and other Commonwealth countries, and in western society today there is not a single country that does not have a social security system, some less comprehensive than others. The principle, although only 50 years old, is quite ingrained.

So the Waitaki Dam not only conquered the river but in a strange fashion it also supplied a political bulwark against the despair of the infirmity of old age. From now on people would get power, and a pension.

Dam and intake

The dam was both a symbol of an engineering triumph – stopping a great river and providing a huge power boost for the economy – and a symbol of the tyranny of the Depression – ants toiling on a concrete leviathan. In an age where physical exertion was a matter of pride and mana, the dam came to be used as a boast about the prowess of the Kiwi working man. But it was also a potent political weapon. It was no accident that Michael Joseph Savage visited the site of the Waitaki Dam twice in his campaigning before the great Labour landslide in 1935.

Footnotes and Further Reading

1. *From the Cradle to the Grave*, A biography of Michael Joseph Savage, Barry Gustafson, A.H. & A.W. Reed Ltd Methuen Ltd, 1986.

Cast in Concrete, Geoffrey Thornton, A.H. & A.W. Reed Ltd, 1996.

Waitaki Dammed, G.C. Natusch, Otago Heritage Books, 1984.

OAMARU: THE WHITESTONE CITY

FEATURES
Historic precinct of whitestone buildings (including banks, warehouses and industrial buildings), wharf and old promenade, penguin colonies, and Grave's Walkway.

WALK DETAILS
Most of the commercial buildings and banks in Oamaru's historic precinct are part of the city centre on Thames Street. Just over the railway line (and around the corner from the information centre) are the warehouse and office blocks of Tyne Street and Harbour Street.

The interesting buildings lie conveniently close together, and a stroll about the precinct would take 1-2 hours.

Allow 4-5 hours if you are visiting Grave's Walkway and the wharf area.

Oamaru has the most unified historic precinct of any town in New Zealand: better than the Anglican stonework of Christchurch or the scattered Art Deco buildings of Napier. Lower Thames Street is lined with buildings and banks created in a sort of grandiose Grecian style, with imposing pillars and sumptuous decorative detail. The whitestone shines cleanly in the Oamaru air and the buildings reflect the prosperous and pompous times in which they were built. This was the main street, and designed to impress, but around the corner in Tyne and Harbour streets are the backyard working districts, the dynamos that kept the economic juices flowing in Oamaru.

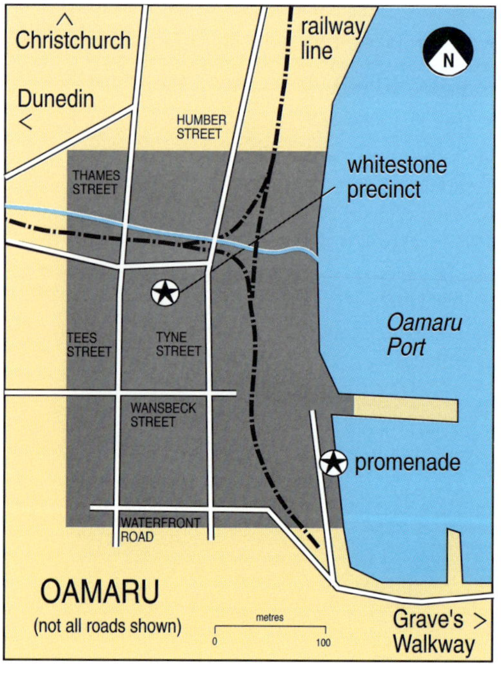

Both streets are mostly intact Victorian terraces of Oamaru stone, with Italianate decorated offices and huge monolithic warehouses. It has been likened to an empty film set, or an Italian street scene, but what saves the precinct from unreality is that it is still lived and worked in.

Warehouses are still full of wool bales, cubiform as the masonry around them, with wool hatches and hooks protruding from the walls. Cars are jammed in awkward possies and the large articulated trucks manoeuvre cautiously in the confined alleyways. Garages and engineering shops are full of busy blue boiler-suited men, there are storehouses, a truckies' outfit, a book-binder's workshop: it is a used landscape.

The industrial integrity is enhanced by the railway line slicing down the back and swinging across Thames Street to pass a giant grain warehouse, where the blocks of stone are piled up like a barricade of wool bales.

A walk up the Oamaru Stream has been created underneath the 1860 Thames Street bridge, linking both sides of the inner city.

Oamaru's glory days were 1870-80, when many fine buildings were erected. Sheep and wool were the backbone of the economy and the practically inexhaustible supply of excellent building stone encouraged the Oamaru élite to build big. Architects such as Robert Lawson emphasised the Grecian style, while the architectual partnership of Thomas Forrester and John Lemon favoured Venetian styles and went about creating a most unlikely South Island Rialto.

Oamaru stonework

By the turn of the century the competitive building boom among the landed and mercantile classes was over. The money had run out and Oamaru gradually declined, with the port dwindling away after World War II, and closing in the 1970s. Out on the wharf today all you find are the lonely fishermen and leg-balancing gulls. Penguin homes have been made for the little blues that come ashore each evening, a different sort of parade from the couples who once strolled along this now sadly down-at-heel promenade.

Ironically, the closure of the port and the loss of Oamaru's prosperity saved the historic precinct from 'modernisation', and calls for conservation of the precinct gradually grew in momentum from the 1970s. The Whitestone Civic Trust was founded in 1988 and the ongoing maintenance programme is admirable. Chimney and vehicle fumes turn Oamaru stone a dirty grey after a while, but after cleaning makes it painfully white, as if bleached by the long, hot Oamaru summer.

Further Reading

Whitestone Oamaru, Peter Shaw, Craig Potton Publishing, 1995.

MATANAKA AND JOHNNY JONES

FEATURES
Oldest farm buildings in Otago (1842-43) including double-storey stables, granary, privy and schoolhouse, fine seascape views and Waikouaiti beach, St John's Church at Waikouaiti.

HOW TO GET THERE
From Waikouaiti on State Highway 1 (21km north of Dunedin) turn down the signposted road to the beachfront for 3km, then turn north along the road and up a steep gravel lane 1km to a signposted carpark.

WALK DETAILS
It is 15 minutes' walk to the farm buildings, painted a blood red that goes well against a lively sea and rare Otago blue. What is currently on view are the fine stables, with dormer windows (and wooden louvres over the side windows), the schoolhouse (shifted to this site) and the curious three-seater privy. The homestead (about 1846) is still private.

Waikouaiti has several interesting and quirky buildings. The church, schoolhouse and parsonage were all deliberately English-village in conception and since the town's founder, Johnny Jones, provided the cash, he could fancy himself as the local squire. The 1858 Mountfort-designed St John's Church is made of pitsawn timber, and the much later Waikouaiti grandstand is built on a truly heroic scale.

'A Law Unto Himself'

The first farm buildings in Otago stand on a bold bossy headland, a commanding and exposed site – not a bad metaphor for the man who put them there. Johnny Jones was something of a legend in early Otago and he liked it that way. Short, squat and used to getting his own way, he was likened to a gorilla by his enemies and lauded as the saviour of Dunedin by his friends.

His origins are obscure but he was probably the son of a convict. He was born in Sydney in 1809 and at 16 was working as a sealer in New Zealand waters. By some unexplained means he had raised the capital to own shares in three whaling ships by the age of 20, and by 1839 had established a chain of shore whaling stations from Foveaux Strait to Waikouaiti Bay. With the slump in whaling Jones moved into property dealing and, armed with a sheaf of dodgy land deals with the Maori from the Otago coastline to Lake Wanaka (which by and large the government did not recognise), organised a migration to Waikouaiti in 1840 aboard the ship *Magnet*.

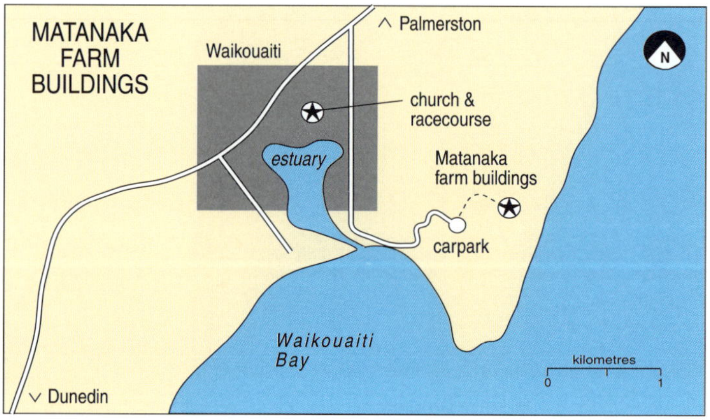

Johnny Jones

The new colony stuttered into life but Jones had to stock up on new migrants after the first lot became disillusioned. Some time in this period to 1843 the first pre-fabricated buildings were established on the headland overlooking the lovely Waikouaiti Bay, which was a reasonable anchorage and originally a shore whaling station.

Matanaka farm buildings

What launched Johnny Jones firmly on his mercantile career was the arrival of the Dunedin settlers in 1848. Jones supplied them with wheat, meat and fresh vegetables and soon involved himself in all sorts of trading enterprises. His farming and shipping interests prospered to such a degree that by 1854 he had shifted his family to Dunedin, where he became heavily involved in the business community of the growing city. It was said that Jones had £20,000 of his own private banknotes in circulation in the city, which were accepted without question.

> He could make a corner in grain, determine plenty or scarcity, and disarrange the small money market. A law unto himself and to other people, he was always ready in time of need to support his will by force of fist. Yet he was generous and ever ready to help any scheme to advance the settlement.[1]

At Johnny Jones's funeral most of the gentry of Dunedin joined the procession and it was said that 'the history of Dunedin followed him'. Another version has it that they were there 'just making sure the bugger was buried'.

Footnotes and Further Reading

1. *Mobil Travel Guide: South Island*, Diana & Jeremy Pope, A.H. & A.W. Reed Ltd, 1990.

Matanaka, Hardwicke Knight & Peter Coutts, John McIndoe Ltd, 1975.

MAPOUTAHI PA

FEATURES
Pa and peninsula, sea caves, beach and coastal cliffs, natural sea arch and tern colony, low-tide route to Doctors' Point.

HOW TO GET THERE
From Dunedin you can reach Mapoutahi Pa by driving via Port Chalmers 10km, Blueskin Road 4km, Hayward Point Road 1km and Purakanui Road 1km. Then turn into Osborne Road, which plunges steeply to the estuary and skirts it for 4km to a rough and ready carpark. Don't be tempted to go further: the 'road' is sandy and boggy.

WALK DETAILS
From the carpark it is an easy stroll to Purakanui Bay and along the beach sands to the short track onto the pa site. Good views both ways along the coast, 1 hour return.

With a low tide it is possible to follow the coastline north as it rounds the headland to Doctors' Point. Conglomerate rocks form attractive patterns on this lonely stretch of coast and there's a noisy tern colony just above the double sea arch. On the other side of the arch it's an easy stroll to Doctors' Point, though it's impossible to get through the arch at high tide. Allow 2 hours one way to Doctors' Point.

This is an attractive pa site, last occupied in the 18th century, and the remains of terraces and trenches are disappearing under the windblown grass and cabbage trees. On a soft summer's evening it is hard to imagine the harsh lives of the inhabitants – constant searching for food, looking out for enemies. This was a good defensive position, with ready access to estuaries and tidal creeks, but it was obviously not strong enough.

Tradition suggests that the pa was sacked in winter during an inter-tribal feud. The story goes that the defenders set up dummies beside the pallisade walls so they could retreat to the warmth of fires, but the besiegers realised the ploy and attacked, overwhelming the defence. Most of the pa inhabitants were killed and, in the traditional way, some would have been eaten and the survivors taken as slaves.

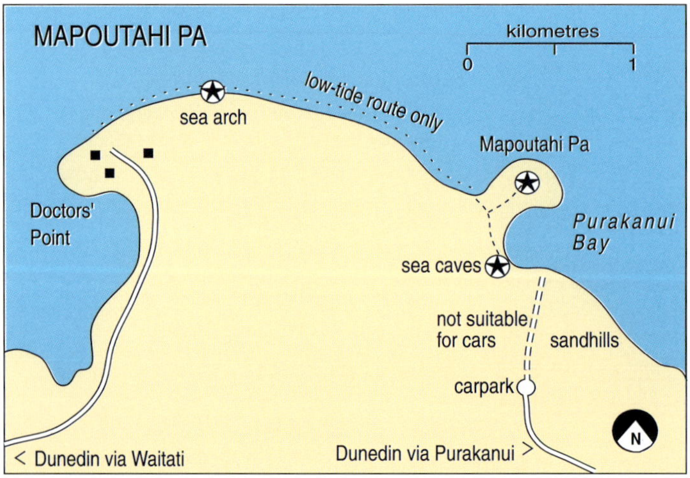

Obsidian flakes in the excavations indicate some trade with the North Island, the only source of the volcanic material. Evidence from midden sites indicates that the Maori ate mostly barracouta and red cod, with a

Sea arch, Doctors' Point

liberal supply of shellfish and nesting local birds such as shags and penguins. Maori dog (kuri), seals and rats (kiore) were also part of the diet. Sugar would have been extracted from the pith of cabbage trees, a rare treat in a monotonous diet. Judging from the discarded wrappers on the beach, we have much more plentiful supplies today.

Further Reading

Mapoutahi Pa (DOC pamphlet).

DUNEDIN CITY

FEATURES
Many notable Gothic-style buildings, university quad, Botanic Gardens, Olveston House, Ross Creek Reservoir, a working 19th-century dam with ornamental valve tower.

HOW TO GET THERE
For the Ross Street Reservoir from George Street, turn onto Duke Street and Malvern Street to the Rockside Road junction and signpost. There are also entrances further up Rockside Road and Tanner Road.

WALK DETAILS
A 2-hour walk should cover most of the buildings in the city centre (see map) and in another 2 hours you could include the university and Botanic Gardens.

The 1901 Victorian terrace houses in Stuart Street are now fastidiously and richly painted; the 1880 Municipal Chambers and the 1919 St Paul's Cathedral are both built of Oamaru stone. 'Gingerbread George's' ornate railway station was built in 1906 to a design by Sir George Troup. The ornate and relatively young 1928 Allied Press building houses the *Otago Daily Times*, which started in 1861, making it New Zealand's oldest daily newspaper.

It is also well worth looking out for recent buildings that are quite different in style, notably the Art Deco of the St John's Ambulance and the former New Zealand Railways bus depot. It's this peculiar clash of the codes that gives Dunedin an eclectic and eccentric air.

Dunedin is a porridge of personalities. Town and gown, brain and brawn, cappuccino and whisky. A stern history of Presbyterian values has to endure an annual influx of hedonistic students. Recitations of Robbie Burns's 'Ode to a Haggis' and James K. Baxter's 'Ode to Mixed Flatting' are equally likely to be heard, as is tribal chanting from the terraces of Carisbrook. Dunedin is well known for its fanatical rugby support, yet it is also an abiding centre for the arts.

This southern city has a sorry climate and

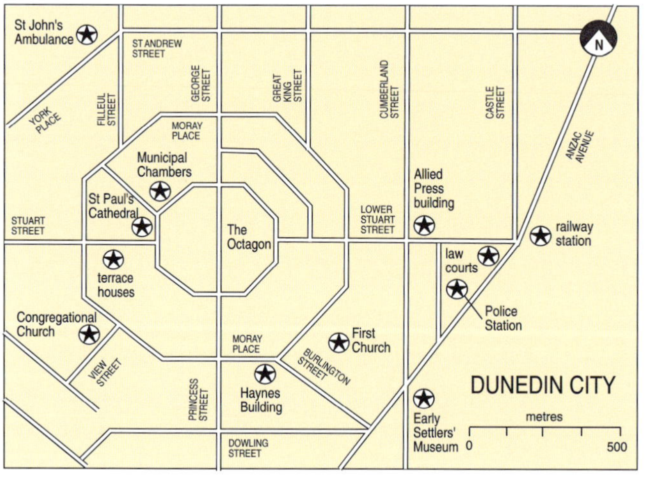

The Octagon in 1874 taken from the spire of First Church

dark winters encourage conversation and cafe philosophy. The buildings cling crustacean-like to steep hills but as a consequence the city centre is cramped and most of the fine assemblage of Dunedin's stone buildings can be seen in a short stroll.

European settlement began on March 1848 when the first settlers arrived aboard the *John Wickliffe*. The town grew slowly until the remarkable news of Gabriel Reed's finding of gold at present-day Lawrence in 1861. This put Dunedin on the map and it entered a prosperous period from the 1860s to the end of the century. For a time Dunedin was the leading city in New Zealand and most of the best buildings were built in this affluent period.

Dunedin has been declining defiantly ever since, struggling to hold its population as people drift north. Yet, perversely, this slow stagnation has preserved a lot of buildings that would have disappeared in a more upbeat economy.

It does not take long to walk from the city centre to the university – about 10 minutes. A population of 120,000 people receives a 10 per cent increase in March that enlivens the streets in a somewhat raucous fashion.

The centrepiece of Otago University is the Clock Tower Block, built in stages from 1879 to 1922. The tower finally received its clock in 1931. Behind it is the Geology Block, also in the high Gothic style and built between 1879 and 1913. Four professors' houses were also built (St David Street) in 1879 and 'startled observers by their extraordinary complications and inclinations of window and roof ... and in a tint of the darkest and most inflammatory red'.[1]

ROSS CREEK RESERVOIR

Ross Creek is a mossy bush ravine only 2km from the city centre, yet not particularly easy to find. Locals use it all the time of course but out-of-towners might need a map. Allow 1-2 hours for visiting the reservoir, where a pretty circuit can be made through a mossy gorge and woodland.

In 1867 a dam of local stone and puddled clay was built across the creek to provide a water reservoir to supply the new and bustling gold city. Today it also serves as a sojourn away from the suburbs, with woodland promenades only a whistle away from the surrounding houses. The dam is one of only two working 19th-century dams in the country, the other being the West Eweburn Dam near Naseby.

From Rockside Road the track turns into a narrow stream gorge, with steep damp bluffs and moist native bush. Gradually climbing for 20 minutes, the track crosses a bridge before coming onto the lawns surrounding the water-treatment plant. It's one minute onto the top of the dam itself and the jetty to the piece of puffery that is the valve tower. This was designed by Ralph Donkin and makes a nice foreground to a restful vista.

An easy circuit of the reservoir can be made by taking the west-side track to the top pond then down the other side past a rock-lined overflow channel. A track leads past the caretaker's house to the big iron gates at Rockside Road, and this road can be followed down a steep switchback to the starting point.

The Water of Leith is a somewhat grandiose name for a wet concrete ditch that cuts through the university and houses an occasional white heron. From the university it is only five minutes' walk into Dunedin Botanic Gardens, the oldest in New Zealand, with a mix of formal and woodland settings, rhododendrons and azaleas – spectacular when in full bloom – rock gardens and a tearooms. If you've walked from the city you will need some refreshment.

Footnotes and Further Reading

1. *From Sea to Silver Peaks*, Graham Bishop/ Antony Hamel, John McIndoe Ltd, 1993.

Buildings of Dunedin, Knight & Wales, John McIndoe Ltd, 1988.

Bricks and Mortar, Lois Galler, Allied Press, 1982.

Portrait of a City, Shona McFarlane, Whitcombe & Tombs Ltd, 1970.

OTAGO PENINSULA

FEATURES
Convict-built roads, Rongo memorial, Fletcher House, Pukekihi church (1868), dry-stone walls and steadings, Sandymount lime kilns, boatsheds, stunning coastal scenery and beaches.

HOW TO GET THERE
From Dunedin follow the signs to the peninsula coast road as it edges up the harbour past Broad Bay (Fletcher House) some 15km to Portobello. A narrow road goes over the saddle to Hoopers Inlet, skirts the estuary and climbs onto another low saddle at Sandymount Road (lime kilns) onto the main summit road. Follow this back to Dunedin through Pukekihi (cheese co-op and church) and past the turnoff to Boulder Bay (dry-stone walls), then down Centre Road (steadings) to Tomahawk Lagoon and the city.

DRIVING TIME
Allow at least 3-4 hours' driving and looking time for this peninsula circuit; more if you are doing the guided tour around the Fletcher House and Larnach's Castle.

The Coast and the Convicts

This peninsula undoubtedly has personality: an awkward finger of narrow roads and knotted land, where albatrosses steer over the headlands and Hooker's sealions snooze on painfully beautiful and empty beaches. A deep stillwater harbour on one side and the rolling Pacific on the other. On the west there is a harshness, with deserted steadings and dry-stone walls that stick out like ribs from a thin man's chest. On the eastern side there is a plump contentment in the snug seaside colonies, where every bloke has his bach and his boatshed.

From Dunedin there's a fine stretch of coastal highway right out to the heads at Taiaroa, but it was wrought at great cost. In the 1860s is was common to use convict labour on public works (an idea that continues to resurface from time to time). The Andersons Bay causeway, along with other roads in Dunedin, was built by Taranaki Maori who challenged land confiscations between 1862 and 1882 at places such as Parihaka and were imprisoned in caves here, often without trial.

The Rongo is a rock that was brought to Dunedin from Parihaka to commemorate bonds forged between the Taranaki and Ngai Tahu tribes. It was laid in March 1987 by Governor-General Sir Paul Reeves and it can be seen on the corner of Portobello Road and Shore Street.

Further along the coast the stretch of road at Macandrew Bay was built by convicts in the 1860s. They were housed on the ironically named *Success*, a hulk that was dragged along as the prisoners progressed. The tidy stone walls between the road and the sea also date from this time.

Dry-stone Walls and Steadings

From Portobello you can drive up the narrow lane over a saddle to Hoopers Inlet, and the road skirts the estuary and then climbs up to another low saddle. As you come up the Sandymount Road something like a little fort can be seen: a squat turrett standing on a grassy paddock, with an unbeatable view. This lime kiln was built in 1865 by a Scottish stonemason and good deposits of limestone were quarried and burnt in the two kilns, one on the left of the road and one on the right.

Indeed, Pukekihi was looking prosperous at this time, and New Zealand's first co-operative cheese factory was founded here in 1865. The church dates from 1868 and note the tiny library.

Around Pukekihi and Highcliff and the narrow side-road to Boulder Bay are many massive dry-stone walls. These are sturdy memorials to thrifty settlers, who were obliged to use local materials for fences until the arrival of post (broadleaf) and rail (kowhai) fences and barbed wire in the 1870s. Many of the settlers were from the Scottish Highlands and so put their existing skills to good use.

Sandymount lime kiln

Dry-walling is a lost art. It takes patience, selectivity and skill to snug the boulders in place. Some walls reach two metres above ground and 60cm below for a good foundation. They make spectacular and lovely fences and it is a pity that so many are in a dilapidated state.

From the Boulder Bay side-road return to the main summit road and continue toward

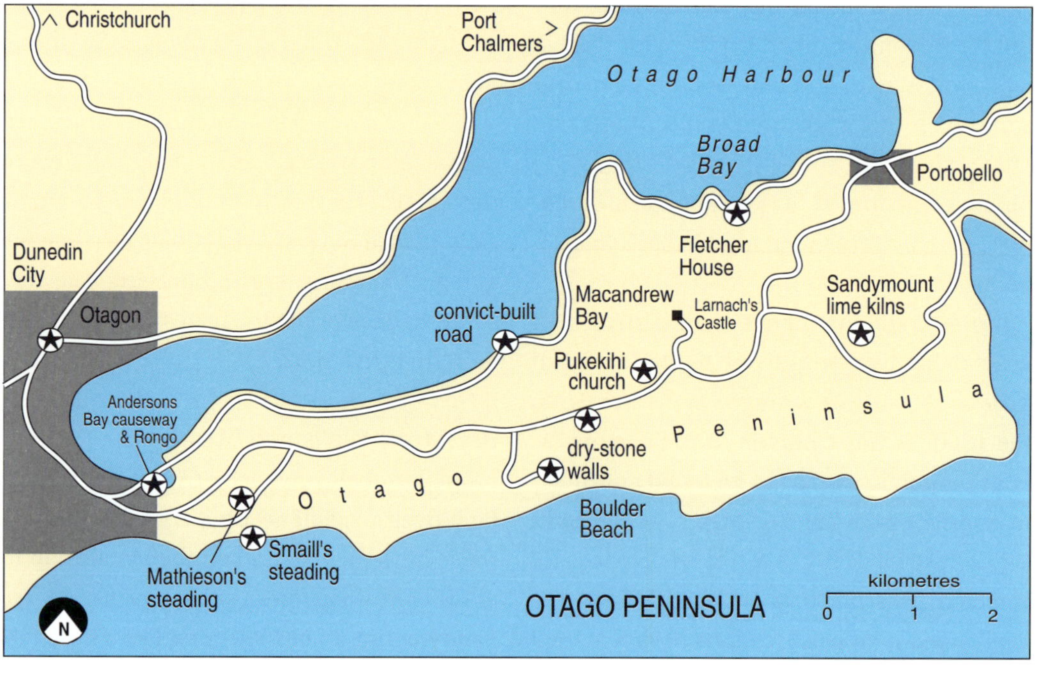

THE HOUSE THAT JIM BUILT

James Fletcher 'arrived in Dunedin from Scotland in 1908 with little more than a nailbag and a £12 bank deposit'.[1] With his partner Albert Morris he lodged a tender to build a house for Hubert Green of Broad Bay for £375. The bay had just been reached by the coastal road, though there was still a launch service. Farming was becoming unprofitable and cheap sections were coming up for sale, and many 'cribs' (holiday homes) were built at the bay between 1900 and 1910. A 1910 photo shows a pretty and prosperous seaside township.

Hubert Green was the general factotum of the bay – storekeeper, postmaster, keeper of the cemetery book, watchdog for the crib-owners. It was he who was telephoned whenever any of the patients escaped from Larnach's Castle, which was a psychiatric hospital at the time. If he had any spare moments he reverted to his original trade of bootmaker. He married Agnes Galloway in 1909 and the newlyweds needed a house.

The Fletcher House is a classic double-bay, return-verandah Victorian villa, with a central passage leading to two bedrooms, a sitting room and a living room. Built of heart rimu with weatherboards outside, it was noted for its ornamental verandah and the pressed zinc dado panels in the hall, which rise over a metre from the floor.

Fletcher and Morris worked long hours on the house, charging themselves wages of 1 shilling and sixpence an hour and no increase for overtime. Their grand profit was 3 shillings and sixpence, but the smartly finished house drew other offers of work and they slowly established themselves and set up a joinery factory in 1911, calling themselves Fletcher Construction by 1919. In 1981, after many mergers and acquisitions the company became Fletcher Challenge, New Zealand's largest company.

Dunedin, turning down Centre Road. About halfway down is Alexander Mathieson's steading, built of bluestone and once described as one of the finest steadings in the country. A steading is an old-fashioned word for a collection of farm buildings, usually including the farmhouse, stables, shearers' quarters, cowsheds and the like. Mathieson's was built in the 1870s.

At the foot of Centre Road if you turn left into Smaill's Bay there is another substantial steading. Smaill's is partly in ruin but the farmhouse and outbuildings still make an impressive grouping of bluestone buildings.

Footnotes and Further Reading

1. *The Fletcher House*, Peter Shaw, 1992.

MT IDA WATER-RACE

FEATURES

New Zealand's longest functioning water-race (123km), siphon and Hogburn gold workings, Naseby cemetery and Chinese graves, goldtown buildings in Naseby.

HOW TO GET THERE

Naseby is 8km off State Highway 85, about 12km from Ranfurly. Metric stress has not reached Naseby yet, for the signpost at the town entrance says the town is '2000 feet above worry level'.

WALK DETAILS

There are several good walks at Naseby. The whole town reeks of nostalgia and the museum in particular is worth seeing. Up the Hogburn Gully there is a pleasant picnic area and a detailed information board of the various tracks.

The One Tree Hill Historical Walk starts 50 metres above the sign, climbs and crosses the Mt Ida water-race and winds through the 'badlands' sluicings back to the amateur gold-panning area in the Hogburn. Allow 1 hour return.

Or you can continue on to the mining claim area, where a small amphitheatre of sluicings contains quite a few iron remnants of the gold days, including pipes and a sluice gun. This track continues briefly and meets a side-track to the water-race, and you can return along the vehicle track to the Hogburn – about 2 hours return.

For the grand tour lasting 3-4 hours, take the One Tree Hill walk to the mining claim, then follow the Mt Ida water-race south past the road and swimming hole to a turnoff to the cemetery. Keep a lookout for the small signpost on the tree.

Nothing more clearly illustrates the antipathy the European diggers felt toward the Chinese than where they put their graves: tucked under trees at the back; the headstones even face away from the main burial plot. From the cemetery follow the road back and through Naseby to the Hogburn picnic area again.

There is a confusion of logging roads, bridleways, trail-bike tracks and paths throughout the pine forest immediately behind Naseby – great for orienteering but walkers can get easily muddled. The water-race wriggles above the town and is a convenient reference point if you get lost.

'Poor Man's Diggings'

Central Otago in the 1860s was as bare as a baby's bottom, but a good deal drier. When gold prospectors ranged into the Kyeburn and Naseby area in 1863 they found plenty of dry hills and alluvial gold in the dry gravels, but little water to sluice it out and no wood for flumings even if they had water. Firewood for cooking and keeping warm was a luxury item. That did not stop the gold-diggers; it just made their lives more miserable.

William and Richard Parker found gold at Naseby in May 1863 and by July 2000 people had set up camp in the Hogburn, a small creek behind the present-day town. It was a 'poor man's diggings', which did not mean that no one made a living but rather that the workings needed little equipment (only a pan and shovel) and therefore poor men could dig out the gold. At least they could if they had water.

Water is life in Otago and much of its history has revolved around the acquisition and maintenance of water, at whatever price. The gold-diggers needed water for sluicing. The gravel was dug up by pick and shoveled into a sluice box, where running water pushed the paydirt over riffle boards that trapped the gold. Bigger gold-mining operations used hoses to wash against the gold-bearing cliffs, washing away the gravels and leaving the distinctive moonscape that is so obvious in the Hogburn today. But these hoses needed a constant supply of water and diggers would go to enormous lengths to build water-races.

Numerous small water-races were built around Naseby through the winter of 1863 and the owners had a monopoly and made more money than the diggers. By 1871 there were calls for 'government water', not only to deepen the sluicings and develop new fields but to flush out the accumulation of tailings that were choking the Hogburn and piling up in six-metre mounds everywhere. Naseby was literally choking on its spoils.

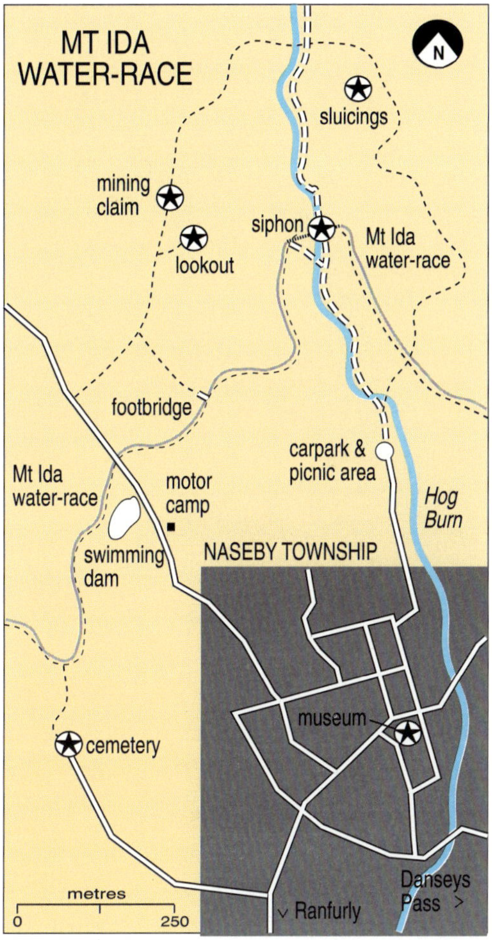

The miners actually got much more than they bargained for and it's a curious story. The original scheme was to take water from the Little Kyeburn River, some 8km east of Naseby. The alternative was the headwaters of the Manuherikia, a river draining into the Alexandra and St Bathans catchments, some 25km as the crow flies from Naseby.

The task of bringing water from Manuherikia was considered by H.W. Robinson, the Naseby warden, to be 'formidable'. Then someone must have whispered in his ear.

In 1870 Sir Julius Vogel raised an enormous loan in England for public works projects in New Zealand, some £10 million. This money was earmarked for the development of railways and by a strange bureaucratic logic it was decided by central government that since the goldfields were *not* to have railways, perhaps they *could* have water-races.

So by 1873 work was started on both the 123km-long Mt Ida water-race and the 16km-long Sludge Channel, finishing by July 1877. Both were dug by hand of course. The Sludge Channel was about 2m deep and 2m wide, paved with stones on the bottom and for 1m up the sides. It had a drop of 1 in 40 to 1 in 100 and it tended to block with

Goldminer with sluicing hose

tailings at these changes in grade. It was the longest sludge channel in the country when it was built, but there is nothing of it to see today.

Not so the water-race, which can still be followed throughout its tortured length as it wriggles around the barren hillsides like a crazed serpent. It was basically an open ditch 1m deep, 1.25m at the base and over 2m at the top, mostly unlined, with 140 metres of tunnels cut through the spurs in places. Its fall is remarkably accurate – 1 metre for every 540 metres, or 1 inch to every 45 feet.

Hogburn sluicings

When the work gangs reached a gully they had to make a decision. They either built a bridge or aquaduct to carry the water over – a fluming, as they were known – or they went underground with a siphon. Despite the shortage of timber they flumed most gullies, though gradually as the timber deteriorated these were replaced with siphons. The longest flume, over the Wedderburn, was 40 metres.

The completion of the Mt Ida water-race encouraged a burst of prosperity in Naseby, but despite the fact that the goldfield was almost entirely dependent on its water the race became less and less profitable. The cost of maintenance was high. The four racemen each had 25-30km to look after and it was difficult to do repairs quickly. Heavy snows blocked the race, and hard frosts would make it inoperable for long periods. Then spring floods washed away the race walls or destroyed the intakes. An inspection in 1892 revealed that the race was in poor condition, full of vegetation and slip debris.

But this was beside the point, for the gold returns were diminishing, people were drifting away, and Naseby was in decline. The government took full control of the water-race in 1893, cleaned it up, built the West Eweburn Dam in 1900, and in 1915 replaced the fluming across the Hogburn with the present-day siphon. This energy did not bring any more profit.

Even in 1877 only about 130 miners were being supplied with water and the rot had set in: only 65 miners in 1900, 50 in 1910, and a mere 10-15 in 1920. So the water-race was adapted for irrigation and, although it substantially follows the same line, there is very little of the original hand-dug race left. The walls have been made saucer-shaped by mechanical diggers, a vehicle track has been built up on one side, and most tunnels have been converted into cuttings – only one remains.

Chinese miner's grave tucked under trees at the back of the cemetery

For all that, the Mt Ida water-race remains one of the most remarkable efforts of the gold-digging community, and as an example of pick-and-shovel precision engineering it is impressive. It is now over 120 years old and the water still flows, as clear, as cold and as expensive as champagne.

Further Reading

Goldminers and their Landscapes at Naseby, Dr Jill Hamel, New Zealand Forest Service, 1985.

Naseby Forest (New Zealand Forestry Service pamphlet). This pamphlet is rather old but the forest headquarters might still have some copies.

THE DUNSTAN TRAIL

FEATURES
Historic goldminers' trail, alpine tussock plateau, Great Moss lake and rock outcrops, old Styx Hotel and jail (Paerau).

HOW TO GET THERE
The entire Dunstan Trail runs from Clarks Junction (off the Middlemarch highway) to the Poolburn Reservoir and Moa Creek, but this chapter covers only half the trail – from Clarks Junction to Paerau, 50km in all (10km sealed, 40km unsealed).

This road is suitable for ordinary cars in good dry weather only. Winter snows close the road; in spring and autumn the wet makes the roads slippery and frosts create a false hardness in the morning that changes to sludge by lunch. Take an adequate repair kit and food and drink in case you get stuck. Make sure someone knows where you are going, and take good topographical maps. Obviously a 4WD vehicle would be useful.

WALK DETAILS
From the Dunstan Saddle a vehicle track climbs up to McPhee's Rock at 4300 feet (1300m), with a splendid view of everything, 2-3 hours walk return. The Great Moss Swamp is now the Great Moss Lake, and a signposted side-road leads down to a boat ramp and a large flat area good for picnicking. The dam is an easy 20-minute return stroll. Just where the Dunstan Trail joins the valley road at Paerau a vehicle track drops down to the river flat and across quite a big ford to the old secluded locality of Styx. The massive schist stables are still in good condition, as is the old hotel and and jail, an iron fetter still in place. The Styx Hotel is now a private bach.

87lb of Gold

Central Otago is hard country, severe and beautiful at the same time: it repels some people and deeply satisfies others. The weather can be appalling but often it is dry and fine – after all, it is virtually a desert. The Dunstan Trail exists because of the gold believed to be waiting at the end of the proverbial rainbow, but for many diggers there was more gold in the moody rich sunsets than they ever got out of the ground.

It is curious that the name Dunstan has almost vanished from the maps but it was a word on everyone's lips when the *Otago Daily Times* published a news report on 19 August 1862 that two American goldminers, Horatio Hartley and Christopher Reilly, had deposited 87lb of gold in a Dunedin bank. To put that in perspective, with gold worth about $350 an ounce nowadays, it's as if two strangely secretive, bushy-bearded and smelly men with Yankee accents had arrived in your town bringing with them $400,000 worth of gold.

It was unbelievable; it was suspiciously staggering. For a further £2000 the two men claimed the gold reward offered by the Otago government and Hartley went with a government prospecting team to show the spot. Of course the rush was already on and the banks of the Molyneaux (Clutha) River near present-day Cromwell were full of expectant miners.

The story goes that the river was up and

Hartley's first shovel-loads produced only wash dirt, whereupon the disgruntled miners threatened to whip him. The diggers had expected to find the gold in the terraces, as at Gabriel's Gully (near present-day Lawrence), and were not used to working the rivers in the manner that Hartley and Reilly had learned on the Californian fields. But the next day the river had dropped and Hartley waded into the stream, dug a shovel-load of gravel and an ounce of gold was washed out. That was enough.

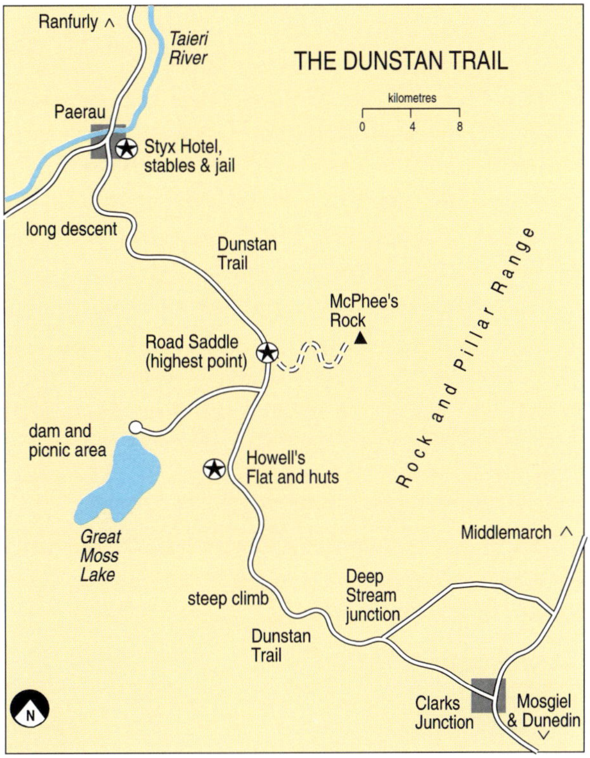

The Most Impatient Men on Earth

The problem was how to get there. A route up the Clutha River from Gabriel's Gully seemed the most direct way, but it required several deep crossings of the river and there was no practical way to get a dray road up the banks. The only alternative was unlikely and risky.

The Dunstan Trail went first from Dunedin to Outram, crossing the Taeiri River by ferry, which was then run under contract by Donald Borrie, whose family lived in a sod house by the river. Then there was a long climb to Clarks Junction, and after negotiating Deep Stream the trail climbed up onto the Lammermoor tussock plateau at almost 3000 feet (1000m). It skirted the Great Moss Swamp, rose to the Rock and Pillar Range saddle at 3500 feet (1200m) and dropped sharply down to Styx (present-day Paerau).

Landscape on the Dunstan Road

The trail toiled on over Rough Ridge at 3000 feet (1000m), dropped to Moa Creek, then over the relatively mild Raggedy Range at a mere 1800 feet (600m), then followed the Manuherikia River to Lower Dunstan (Alexandra).

The trail quickly developed offshoots: the

FIXING A THIRST

It has been said that there were three types of gold: (1) the yellow stuff in the ground; (2) the sparkling stuff that was used to sluice out the yellow stuff; and (3) the brown stuff used to sluice out a miner's dusty throat. Which was the most important? Well, if you travelled the Dunstan Trail in 1862 there was no doubt which was the most available.

A whole string of hotels, wayside shanties and sly-grog shops opened up along the Dunstan: as many as 10 licensed premises and an unknown number of illegal ones. Lee Stream stone hotel still stands (and was used until the 1950s), as does the ruined Oasis Hotel near Rocklands Station, just before the big climb up onto the Lammermoor Range. Clarks Junction Hotel was opened in 1867 by Glens, then taken over by Clark. Howell's Flat had a sly-grog shop (possibly this is the same place that someone called McDonald had an iron shanty) and one Mother McPhee ran a halfway house on the Dunstan Saddle at McPhee's Rock. She must have been made of iron.

The Styx Hotel was opened by a Mrs Potter in 1861 and the gold escort would halt there, storing the gold in the secure lock-up of the Styx jail. Just beyond Styx is the ruin of the Blackball Hotel at the junction of the Dunstan and Serpentine roads, then over the dry Raggedy Range was the Moa Creek pub, the last stopover before the magical field of the Dunstan.

Styx lock-up

Serpentine Track over the Lammermoors direct to Roxburgh, another from Styx to the Kyeburn diggings, the Rise and Shine Road (Thompson's Gorge) to Bendigo. Soon a whole *ad hoc* network of gold trails rushed about the Central Otago peneplains, making little sense on today's maps but matching precisely the explosive growth of the Otago diggings in the 1860s. The gold-digger was the most impatient man on earth.

In all the Dunstan Trail was about 175km long, an exposed, arduous journey. Wagoners often travelled in teams to help get themselves out of the bogs, and could expect to take a week or more to get to the diggings. Firewood was a real problem and they tried anything, including 'buffalo chips' (dried dung), 'yellow pine' (straw), and 'kaladdies' (the flower and stem of flax).

The first Cobb & Co coach left Dunedin in November 1862. The journey took three days each way, but by January 1863 that was down to a day, changing horses five times. By 1864 the Dunstan Trail had passed its peak but it still continued to provide access for many years to obscure diggings that were deep in Central.

AT THE FOOT OF THE OLD DUNSTAN TRAIL

There's a green grassy slope by the boundary fence,
With the scrub bushes sheltering round,
A hollow that shows where a building has been,
And there broken black bottles are found.
A water-race too, that's been dry for long years
Coming out of a creek at the back.
It's all that remains of a shanty that stood
At the foot of the old Dunstan track.
Oh, the days when the track was a road, boys,
The rollicking days of old,
When the bullockies came with their load, boys,
The days of the first of the gold.[1]

A lonely furrow of a road, climbing onto the brow of history, then disappearing.

Footnotes and Further Reading

1. *Station Ballads*, David McKee Wright, 1897.

Clyde on the Dunstan, Betty Veitch, 1976.

Accommodation house, Otago

TINKERS TOWN & DRYBREAD CEMETERY

FEATURES
Matakanui township with sun-dried brick buildings (including store and houses), old hotel, isolated goldfields cemetery.

HOW TO GET THERE
To reach Tinkers Town, these days called Matakanui, from Omakau on State Highway 85, turn into Racecourse Road for some 10km towards Thompson's Gorge (or the old Rise and Shine Road). Turn left into Glassford Road for 1.5km and right into Naylor Road for 1km.

Drybread Cemetery is signposted 3km from Matakanui north-east along Glassford Road. A farm track leads to the cemetery so it is probably better to walk the last stretch as it gets boggy in places (5 minutes one way). It's an isolated cemetery, standing obscurely in a paddock 1km from the main road, a fact that has probably saved it from the attention of vandals. The graveyard is in good condition with many headstones still readable.

Otago in autumn takes your breath away. Poplar trees like standing flames, willows loosening a gentle rain of golden leaves; even the briar, the most charmless plant in the province, turns out in a pretty yellow dress dotted with red beading. For the gold-diggers autumn was a signal to hurry up before the freezing winds from the Antarctic came blasting over the unprotected plains and water-races froze.

If you intended to more than survive an Otago winter you needed some sort of hut but your choice of building materials was limited. Wood was prohibitively expensive so schist rock was often used, but at Tinkers Town nearly the entire original settlement was built of adobe or sun-dried brick.

> A wide range of soil types may be used for making the bricks provided there is clay and sand present. The size of early bricks varied; they could be up to 600 mm (two feet) in length and from 200 mm (eight inches) to 300 mm (twelve inches) thick. Although they are commonly referred to as sun-dried, it is more usual to dry them out slowly in the shade to avoid undue shrinkage cracking. The natural colour is an attractive yellowish putty hue, thus the character of the adobe building, as with other early earth structures, is unmistakeable; it appears to have grown out of the soil and is truly in harmony with its natural surroundings.[1]

Adobe brick and letterbox, store at Matakanui

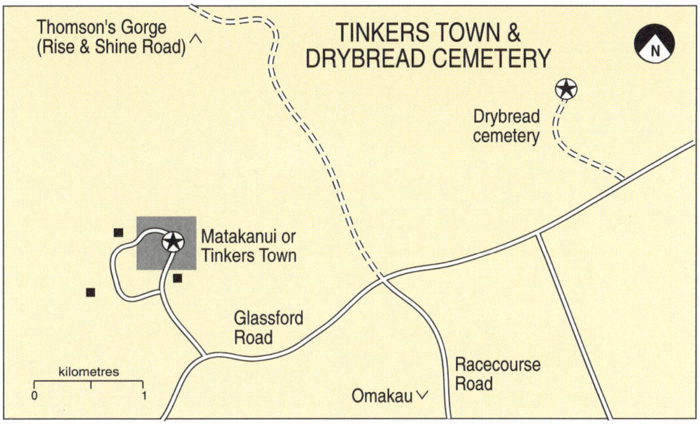

Cob is a variation of adobe, using much the same materials and methods but building up in layers rather than separate bricks. Rocks were sometimes incorporated into cob structures for strength.

The adobe buildings that remain in Tinkers Town include the restored local hall, the Matakanui store and a couple of houses. The Matakanui store was built in 1889 and was originally the dancing hall. In the 1890s it became a store and also served as a post office and the office of the Mt Morgan Sluicing Company Ltd. The store was still operating up until the 1980s, but the Newton Hotel has lost its licence and today's thirsty travellers have to go elsewhere.

Drybread Cemetery

Just the name brings on a thirst. This was an old diggings at the base of the Dunstan, isolated and lonely, one of a string of gold-working communities between Alexandra and St Bathans. Their lives were short, and often so were the diggers'. Mine collapses and slumps of tailings were common causes of fatalities, as were (ironically in this desert) drownings. But what is startling about Drybread cemetery is the record of child deaths. There are almost a dozen headstones over the graves of children and babies, the earliest one visible dating back to 1870. One can only guess at the accidents or illness that led to the heartbreak corseges that travelled up to this lonely paddock.

The massive macrocarpas have partly obscured the splendid views the graves once had, but the Dunstan Range is still dissected by the purposeful lines of the water-races feeding the derelict diggings at Matakanui and Drybread, a permanent reminder etched in tussock.

Drybread cemetery

Footnotes and Further Reading

1. 'Earth and Stone Buildings of Central Otago', Geoffrey Thornton, *Historic Buildings of New Zealand: South Island*, Reed Methuen Ltd, 1983.

Gold Trails of Otago, June A. Wood, A.H. & A.W. Reed Ltd, 1970.

BANNOCKBURN SLUICINGS

FEATURES

Dramatic 'badlands' gold sluicings, tunnels and shafts, paved water-races and sludge channels, sun-dried brick huts, stone and earth dam, Young Australian waterwheel and stamping battery.

HOW TO GET THERE

For Bannockburn sluicings from Cromwell take the Bannockburn Road 5km across the Kawarau River and turn into Fenton Road – 2km to the carpark and information sign. Please note that all the gold workings are on private land, which is closed between August and October for lambing.

WALK DETAILS

This is a 2-3 hour circuit, taking in Stewart Town. The track initially goes up through canyons and crumbling cliffs of the sluice claims – the pillars that remain are often at the corners of claims. After a lookout over the diggings the track climbs up and crosses the water-race, passing the dam and reaching Stewart Town, a ruined place of sun-dried brick buildings and old orchard trees that have become so ingrown and twisted they look like matagouri. The track returns via some of the remaining paved tailraces.

The Young Australian waterwheel is not so easy to reach. The shortest way is to drive 1km from Bannockburn and turn into Schoolhouse Road for 1km to the carpark at the end. Carricktown is 4km up the four-wheel-drive road and the waterwheel a further 3km, virtually on top of the range.

Another option is to drive up the Nevis road to the saddle, which crosses the Carrick water-race near the top. A vehicle track goes down the ridge from Watts Rock some 5km and the waterwheel is obvious – in clear weather. However, it's easy to get 'geographically embarrassed' up here.

Allow 2-3 hours return from the Nevis road; 3-4 hours right through to Carricktown and Schoolhouse Road. This should be treated as a tramping trip, so take a good topographical map and a compass.

Cowboys and ... Diggers

In the American west a legend was created: a legend of cowboys and Indians, of corralls and shootouts, of gunslingers and scalping. The language of the American west has entered our English so thoroughly that nobody fails to understand such expressions as 'he was buried on Boot Hill' or 'he was the fastest gun in the west'.

There were plenty of cowboys in the 1860s in Otago but they called them diggers, or new chums if they were raw. New Zealand's 'cowboy' era lasted 20 hectic, raucous gold-mining years from the 1850s to the 1870s, but such words as 'nobblers', 'riffle-boards', 'pay-dirt' and 'a duffer's rush' mean next to nothing to a modern New Zealander. There were great hardships, glittering prizes, madcap rushes, vile murders and tragic deaths, yet the stories died when the gold ran out. No great storyteller wrote the legends down, the half-truths that could be spun into a mythology. Schoolboys don't play at diggers and shysters.

The Bannockburn sluicings could be in the American west – it's a tortured landscape, the river terraces eaten out into canyons and cliffs by the hunger of the miners. Hot, dry, brown:

you half-expect John Wayne to come riding around a butte, squinting into the sun as the director says 'cut'.

Bannockburn was unusual because after the initial flurry of activity (1862-65), when all the easy gold was won, a little community established itself and settled in to win the deeper gold that lay under the old river terraces. At first they tunnelled, trying to intercept the gold-bearing layers and hauling out the paydirt in trucks on rails. It was hard physical work and it was also slow, and the miners looked for faster methods to get the gold-bearing gravels out. The answer was sluicing, and for that you needed lots of water.

In 1873 the Bannockburn water-race was completed, and the Carrick race in 1876. The latter still supplies water to Bannockburn, wriggling over the high-country tussocks, through tunnels and

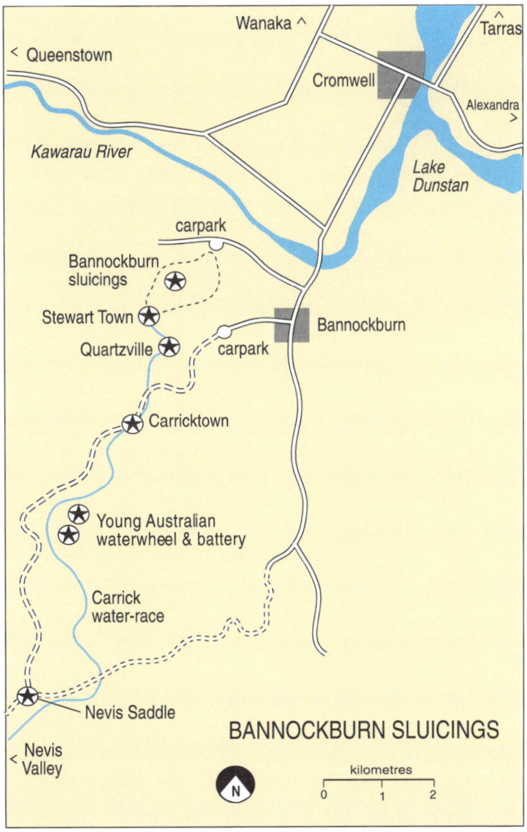

YOUNG AUSTRALIAN MINE WATERWHEEL

At 1500 metres on the slopes of the Carrick Range is the huge 7.9m waterwheel of the Young Australian Mine. There's also a five-head stamping battery and some ruined stone huts. The quartz reefs of the range needed heavy machinery to process the rock and water to run the machinery so it wasn't until the Carrick water-race was cut in 1874 (at 25km the longest high-altitude water-race in Otago) that the Young Australian was made possible, and profitable. For two years they got one ounce for every ton of rock crushed, but by 1877 the mine was closed, though the battery was run sporadically until 1898. Visitors today have the luxury of pondering the enthusiasm and folly of those heady days in a landscape that makes no excuses and no explanations.

Badlands Bannockburn

The ruins of Stewart Town

fluming from Coal Creek in the Nevis Valley. It was all very well sluicing the gravel out, but where were the tailings and sludge to go? The Kawarau River was the obvious answer and huge sludge canals were constructed to link the sluice workings with this natural sewer.

There was at least as much money in supplying water to the diggings as there was in getting the gold out. Sludge channels were also profitable, especially if the owner paved the channel and had a 'second go' at the spent tailings. Water was supplied on an eight-hour basis but ran for 24 hours, so the water company could sell three days' water in one day and some poor sod had to rise at midnight to collect his share although, as with electricity today, the night rate was cheaper.

By the 1870s sluicing was in full swing but because of the large operations involved Bannockburn was a company field and men worked for wages. By 1900 the diggings were in decline and farming and orcharding were on the increase, ironically made possible by the gold-diggers' water-races.

What is left now is a stark and strangely beautiful landscape, vigorous and exhausted at the same time. Every inch of ground has been gone over probably several times, first by the shovel-and-pan diggers, then by the tunnellers, then by the sluicers. The last popular invasion was the gold dredges, of which some 23 were operating on the Kawarau and Clutha rivers around Cromwell in 1900. In the 1920s the *Lady Ranfurly* dredge made the exceptional return of 1273 ounces of gold from four and a half days' dredging. It was the area's swansong.

Further Reading

The Past Today, Historic Places Trust, 1987.

SKIPPERS BRIDGE

FEATURES
Historic suspension bridges, Shotover River canyon, narrow and difficult road, Mt Aurum schoolhouse and farm, remains of Bullendale generator and dam.

HOW TO GET THERE
The Skippers suspension bridge is a tough place to reach, as it lies halfway up the Skippers road, 25km from Queenstown. The Skippers road requires a certain suspension of disbelief as you find yourself teetering on tight bends, wondering whether your insurance policy will cover you along some 15km of tortuous driving – and that's one way.

Allow a good 2-3 hours for the return drive to Skippers, an area that now forms part of Mt Aurum Station.

WALK DETAILS
Mt Aurum schoolhouse has been beautifully restored and sits prettily on the terrace above the river. Some parts of the nearby homestead were built in the 1860s, and this building is also being restored. This is an attractive area to walk around in, particularly in autumn. Allow 1-2 hours.

Another good walk follows the vehicle track into Skippers Creek and up to the site of the old Bullendale generator and dam, 2 hours return. A vehicle track continues in easy zig-zags up the creek for 3km, then picks up an old packtrack to the overgrown site of the Bullendale Mine. There was a settlement here, and a school, and mine relics abound in the broom and beech forest. Allow a full day from Mt Aurum carpark to reach Bullendale and return.

Skippers Canyon is the golden road following alongside the Shotover River, once dubbed the richest river in the world. For once the metaphor was not overblown, for the Shotover was rich, and when you added to it the Arrow River, and Skippers Creek leading to Mt Aurum ('the golden mountain'), you had one of the highest densities of gold-bearing gravels anywhere in the world.

Gold-diggers are not by temperament great recorders of history. For one thing they hardly had time, in a constant nervous hustle, jostling from one rush to another. For another thing they were notoriously secretive. One man's gold was his; two men's gold and you might as well tell the whole world. What they did leave behind is a landscape riven with water-races and sluices; piles of tailings still stand everywhere and undoubtedly every ruined stone hut tells a tale.

Their best monuments are the Skippers road itself, and the two fine suspension bridges at the Kawarau and at Skippers.

The original Skippers road was just a bridle track constructed to the diggings at Maori Point in 1863. Parts of it can still be seen, particularly on the opposite side of Long Gully. Obviously this is a job for the passengers: drivers have to concentrate. But the present road to Skippers was surveyed by J.S. Morrison in 1882-83, and four contractors were hired to complete various stages. By 1888 it was finished, the toughest job being at Pincher's Bluff.

Pincher was the roading contractor and it took his gang two years to shape the 275m-long section. Road workers were lowered on ropes and chipped away at the rock with chisels and hammers, then others would go down and lay small dynamite charges. If the charges were too big they risked destroying the road foundation as well as the material they wanted to remove.

After winding about steep bluffs and sharp corners for 15km it is remarkable to see the Skippers bridge. It replaced the original 1868 bridge and at 90 metres above the river is the highest suspension bridge in the country. It has a span of 96 metres and the towers are 11.5 metres high. These were built in concrete, an unusual material for that time in Central Otago. The bridge was opened in 1901 and the splendid occasion was marked by a banquet and ball.

But why on earth is it here? It seems an excessive structure for such a remote locality. It was an engineering triumph but an economic mistake – Skippers was already in decline.

Skippers was a thriving gold community settlement from 1863 to the early 1900s and every ravine and side-stream off Skippers Creek and Stony Creek was prospected and developed. Colourful names are amply scattered on the maps – Dynamo Flat, Dandys Saddle, Boomerang Terrace. The school was

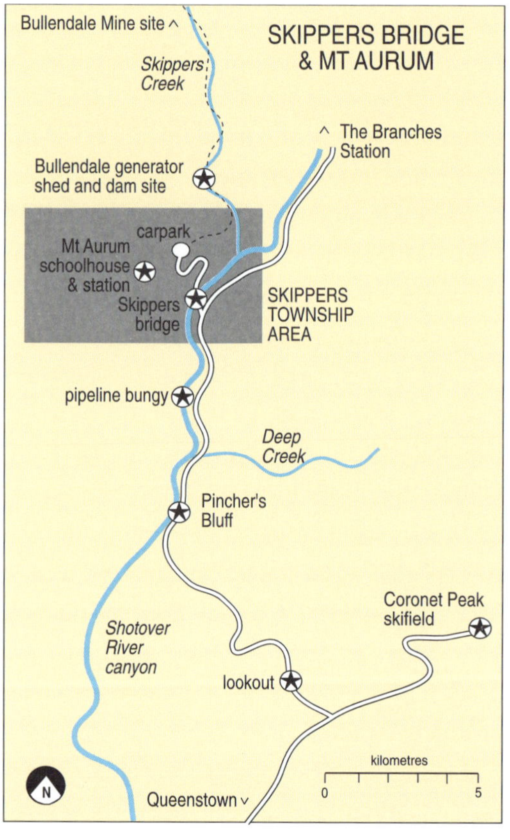

KAWARAU BRIDGE

The Kawarau suspension bridge is about 20km from Queenstown on State Highway 6 and a large carpark overlooks the famous bungy site. The bridge was built in 1880 and, if you can forget about the bungy frenzy, it is well worth looking over the structure itself. The bridge is public so you are free to walk across it, and on the far side the cables are buried deep into the rock and edged with decorative stone porticoes.

Detail, Kawarau suspension bridge

Skippers suspension bridge

opened in 1879 and ran to 1927, and the teachers were expected to run the post office as well.

But the real industry was at the head of Skippers Creek, the famous Bullendale Mine underneath Mt Aurum. It was worked from 1866 to 1907 and New Zealand's first hydroelectric plant was established here in 1885, used for driving the powerful crushing machinery. Yet despite its impressive array of buildings and the great amount of gold that was won, the Bullendale hardly ever made a profit and it finally closed only six years after the Skippers bridge was opened with such fanfare.

So there it hangs, balanced above the canyon in a masterwork of elegant engineering. When early snowfall dabs the hillsides and bridge it makes the cables look frail, and perhaps they are, for soon the bridge will celebrate its 100th birthday.

Further Reading

Cast in Concrete, Geoffrey Thornton, A.H. & A.W. Reed Ltd, 1996.

The Road to Skippers, Danny Knudson, A.H. & A.W. Reed Ltd, 1995.

SAWPIT GULLY

FEATURES
Bridle path and packtracks, water-races, ruined miners' hut, tussock landscape and Arrow River Gorge, monument to William Fox.

HOW TO GET THERE
Arrowtown is 20km from Queenstown and can be reached either via the Arthurs Point road or via Lake Hayes. The track to Sawpit Gully starts by the Chinese settlement carpark and information sign. Toilets in Arrowtown.

WALK DETAILS
This elegant circuit track goes through the heart and soul of the Arrow goldfield, where every footstep for the miners of the 1860s was a golden one. From the carpark beside the Chinese gold village, cross the Arrow River and follow the uninspiring pipeline into the maple and pine forest of Bush Creek. This track follows the old bridle track to Big Hill, and it is a surprisingly steep haul out of the creek onto German Hill or Eichardt's Flat.

From the junction with the Big Hill track the Sawpit Gully track drops down to a melancholy miners' hut, then sidles down the creek and drops down to the sheer-sided Arrow River Gorge. The track cuts around schist bluffs, passes the monument to William Fox and returns to the Arrowtown carpark. Allow 2-3 hours return.

'Hunting the Fox'

In 1862 a strange new game was being played in the obscure hills and deep furrows around present-day Queenstown. It was called 'hunting the Fox', and there were only human foxes in New Zealand then, as now. This particular specimen was six feet tall, burly, individualistic, ill-tempered and cunning. Bill Fox had spent 14 years in California as a 'forty-niner' and he had a good eye for country. He and his mate John Callaghan had drifted up from the Dunstan diggings in September 1862, following the Kawarau River, and he liked the look of the Arrow River Gorge. But they could not cross the river and went on to Lake Wakatipu, where they met the station cadet Alfred Duncan, who described them as:

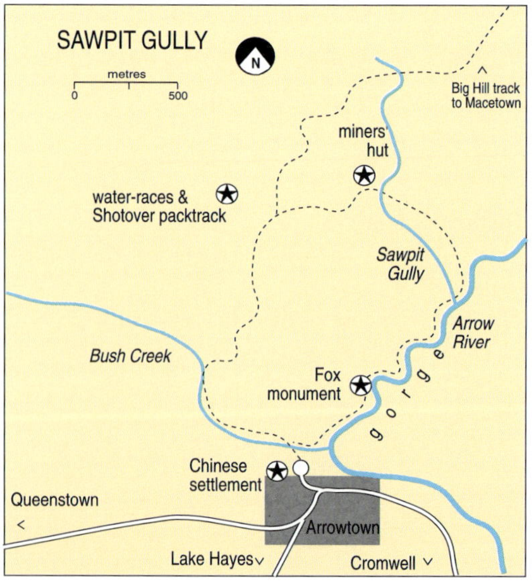

> ... men with swags on their backs, and picks and shovels in their hands, who looked as if they had not seen food for days, which was indeed the case, and yet the first thing they asked for was not food but tobacco.[1]

William Rees was the only station-holder in the district, and he took the diggers across the lake and sold them provisions. A Maori hand working on Rees's station, 'Jack' Tewa, tipped Fox off about 'colours' he'd had seen in the Arrow River and when Fox arrived at the Arrow Gorge on 6 October he found another man, Peter Stewart. Fox was torn between caution and eagerness and a dour goldminers' conversation probably ensued:

'Got any gold?' asks Fox nonchalantly.

Stewart shrugs dolefully: 'I can raise the colour but there's nothing payable.'

He was lying, of course. Stewart had found payable gold, and Fox was to do so a couple of hours later – well out of Stewart's sight.

The Arrow is an attractive gorge, steep-sided and with deep pools, but gravels in the bed make for easy travelling. Bill Fox and his mate moved upriver, trying prospects and getting more excited at each romantic bend in the river.

Like all gold prospectors Fox faced two bugbears. The first was provisions, for which he had to go back to the Dunstan diggings or to Rees's station. The second and more difficult problemwas unwanted attention from other miners. By this time three parties were engaged in the Arrow River: Fox's, Stewart's and that of a man named West. They were also joined by another party, who stalked the men to Fox's camp in the gorge.

Fox laid down the rules; he was the 'commissioner'. No telling tales, each man had 60 feet of frontage (double the normal width on a proper goldfield), and anyone claim-jumping would have to fight him. There were no takers for the latter job and it was in any case a dream situation. A secret gorge, no other diggers, and gold oozing out of the incredibly rich gravels.

Fox's party earned 40lb of gold in two weeks' work, Stewart and McGregor 82lb in four weeks. Gold was worth £3 an ounce in 1862, now it's worth $350 an ounce, so in today's money Fox's party had earned $224,000 in a fortnight. It was said that gold nuggets were found scattered among the

ARROWTOWN CHINESE SETTLEMENT

This quiet collection of stone houses and shelters is the best-preserved Chinese settlement in Otago. The Chinese were imported into New Zealand as cheap labour as early as 1866, single men only, and only slowly spread onto the goldfields. Because of the prevailing prejudice they were only allowed to work over abandoned European gold claims.

The 'celestials', as they were known, arrived in Arrowtown in larger numbers by 1869 and Chinese labour was used on all sorts of public works locally at a wage rate of 5 shillings a day, about half the European wage. The Bush Creek settlement was deliberately sited just out of Arrowtown, and distinctive Chinese stores served the small community with such specialities as pickled shrimp sauce, preserved ginger, teas, rice and gambling pieces.

At one stage there were 5000 Chinese in Otago and 1200 Chinese on the Wakatipu goldfields, but as gold fever subsided many returned home. They had left China to escape poverty and to amass some money so as to return to the family with wealth and honour. £100 was equivalent to 20 years' wages in China at that time. Only a few stayed on in the settlement, generally the older and the infirm, and by the 1920s most had died.

Ruined stone hut, Sawpit Gully

gravel like peas and beans – they simply could not believe their luck.

Of course it couldn't last, and the provincial geologist, Dr James Hector, was 'hunting the Fox' as he put it. When he located the secret goldfield there were 40 men there at least. Within a week of Hector's arrival a flush of 20 miners came over the hill into the gorge and asked breathlessly, 'Are you Fox?'

The rush of new chums into the Arrow caused chaos and when Sergeant Major Bracken arrived men were roaming about flourishing revolvers. But he was more than a match for the miners and he established 'law and order whether they liked it or not'. Remarkably, the miners were so impressed by Bracken's performance that at a farewell banquet Bill Fox gave the sergeant major a ring of Arrow gold 'dug by my own hands'.

By Christmas 1500 men were working the Arrow. But it was Fox who claimed most of the credit for the discovery of the goldfield, and he got the memorial.

The tussock hillsides around Sawpit Gully retain the imprint of the goldminers' work. Water-races interlace and interlock everywhere and some create very peculiar optical illusions – you'd swear some of them are running the wrong way. From German Hill you can see the old Shotover packtrack as it crosses the brow of the hill, and a melancholy miners' hut stands in the gully. It's a landscape that has become an ode to the shovel and the wind.

Footnotes and Further Reading

1. *The Wakatipians*, Alfred H. Duncan, 1888.

The Arrowtown Chinese Settlement (booklet), Otago Goldfields Park.

CASCADE HUT

FEATURES
Old recreation, musterers' and cullers' hut, Bridal Veil Falls, fine valley and mountain views, Aspiring Hut.

HOW TO GET THERE
From Wanaka drive up the Matukituki Road about 50km to the Raspberry Creek carpark. There are some 13 fords and ditches on the last 8km of road, some of which can become impassable after rain.

WALK DETAILS
It is easy, inspiring walking up the Matukituki Valley to Cascade and Aspiring huts, with broad river flats and mountains that look as if they were cut out of the Southern Alps with a knife. Allow about 3 hours return to Cascade; 4 hours return to Aspiring. Aspiring Hut has good historical information panels on the early history of the valley.

Mountain huts. There are hundreds of them, standing apart in landscapes that illustrate their solitude and perseverance. Four walls, a tin chimney leaning slightly askew, an old stone fireplace cracked with a thousand brews. The puff of smoke drifting down the valley evokes companionship and warmth. They are part necessity, part luxury: a bulwark against the weather, and perhaps also against the loneliness of the mountain environment.

Bar a few explorers and pioneers, the first men and women who worked in the mountain regions did not much relish their high-country solitude. Boundary keepers, shepherds or musterers, gold-diggers, trackmen on the water-races – all had a job to do, and they built squat huts and faced out hard winters with just the company of a dog or the whisky bottle.

Even the first pioneer families had few illusions of romance. The Camerons moved into the Matukituki Valley in the 1870s and lived in a slab-walled and thatched whare. The terrible winter of 1885 drove them out: there

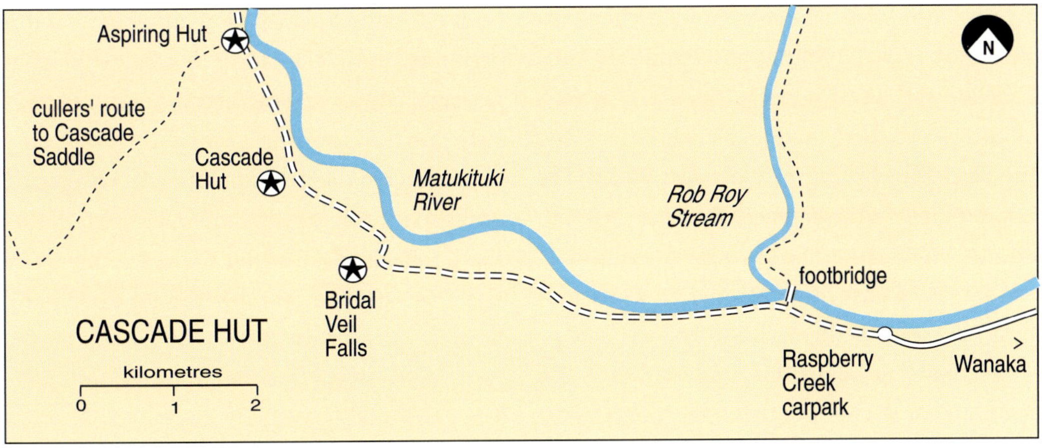

was a metre of snow on the ground for four months.

Sadly, many traditional high-country huts have had their day. These lonely outposts of civilisation were once at the heart of the manifold operations of the sheep stations, but 4WD vehicles and trail-bikes have made access to the high country much easier for the runholder and recreationist alike and rendered many of the old huts superfluous. Apart from such times as the autumn muster, many high-country huts are seldom used. The farmer hasn't the time to fix things up and the recreationist is usually not interested.

Many of these early huts still remain, tucked away in backblocks niches, and some are still fondly tended and enjoyed. Most, however, have crumpled under the weight of too many heavy winters and half an hour of vandalism. Once the roof starts to deteriorate it can mark the start of the end of another piece of history. A hundred years is a good life for a high-country hut, and Cascade is a comparatively young 'un.

In 1932 the recently formed Otago section of the New Zealand Alpine Club brought two Works huts from Dunedin, joined them together with a common porch and formed Cascade Hut. It is a quixotic affair, with a chimney at either end and a cattle bar to stop the beasts fossicking in the wood lobby. The hut looks down the valley to the Shark's Tooth and the mists that fill the valley overnight.

Increasing ease of access and the construction of Aspiring Hut in 1949 made Cascade somewhat redundant for climbers but it has been put to use as a musterers' hut, a deer-stalkers' and cullers' base and a stopover for trampers and daywalkers, though on an average weekend these days you will see more mountain bikers than climbers.

Cascade Hut

Cascade was one of the earliest purpose-built climbing huts in the South Island and is certainly one of the oldest to survive. The hut has seen almost 70 seasons of Aspiring hopefuls, some plodding down the valley sun-blistered and triumphant with weariness, others with rain beating against their retreating parka hoods. Starlight and storms, glory and frustration: alpine climbing is rarely dull. You have either wasted a week watching the rain, or (to quote someone famous) you have 'knocked the bugger off'.

HOMER TUNNEL & HOLLYFORD VALLEY

FEATURES
1km-long tunnel through granite, superb scenery in the Darran Mountains, Hollyford museum and camp.

HOW TO GET THERE
From Te Anau it is 60km along State Highway 94 to the Homer Tunnel, and 15km on to Milford Sound. The Hollyford camp and museum are 8km down the signposted Hollyford Road. The museum has many relics and photos from the Homer Tunnel works and the early pioneering days in the Hollyford Valley. It is worth stopping at Homer Saddle and admiring the awesome scenery and the old route up onto Grave-Talbot Pass.

The Perils of Finding a Pass

As soon as the wonders of Milford Sound were publicised – the deep fiord and the striking Mitre Peak, Sutherlands Falls (touted as the highest in the world when it was first discovered) and the Milford Track (called then as now, the finest walk in the world) – everyone wanted to go there.

Walkers could do so, of course, via the Milford Track, but they rather fancied a return route other than retracing their steps. For the general run-of-the-mill sightseer Milford Sound remained a mystery, available only as a splendid photo in a magazine. There was no road to break Milford's majestic solitude. Could there possibly be a low pass to the sound, yet undiscovered?

In 1889 W.H. Homer and George Barber discovered the Homer Saddle at the head of the Hollyford Valley, but the precipitous sides made it 'quite useless as a route to Milford', according to the government surveyor Wilmot.[1] What about the Gertrude Saddle? William Quill, who had just completed three hair-raising ascents of the Sutherland Falls in 1890, the first two solo, went to have a look – and was never seen again. His brothers traced some footprints in the moss walls on the Cleddau side of the precipice on which he had presumably slipped and plunged to his death.

Milford Sound remained resolutely isolated. From 1907 to 1910 a group of amateur climbers and explorers, led by W.G. Grave, attempted various routes out of the Cleddau River (on the Milford side) and the Hollyford, getting baulked every time. But in January 1910 Grave and Talbot climbed up onto Homer Saddle from the Hollyford, scrambled up the perilous ridge to McPherson's Peak, then sidled steep snow slopes down into the Esperance Valley, which drained into the Cleddau. Just on darkness they ended up on precipices, with only a short rope and meagre snow tussock to hang on to.

> We had now cut off all chance of climbing back. Downward we must go. Each further stage was accomplished by tying the ends of a piece of snowgrass with a piece of string,

> and passing the rope through. There was not much danger of the snowgrass giving way. The chief risk was that the string might slip off the grass. When our supply of string gave out we used pieces of our bootlaces.[2]

This bootstrap method worked – just – and apart from the Milford Track, this was the first overland crossing to the Milford Sound.

The government now took an interest in the so-called Grave-Talbot route. Huts were built on either side of the 'pass' and wires were politely fixed on the tricky bits, where the ridge was the width of a man's body and bluffs peeled off for 500 metres on either side. In 1925 the pass route was completed and incredibly it was considered suitable for the 'active tourist'. In fact it was a semi-suicidal route that made it abundantly clear that Henry Homer was right after all – there would have to be a tunnel.

Henry Homer's Tunnel

> No timber wanted, no climbing over ice and snow; no repairs and open all year round. The size of the tunnel 7 feet 6 inches high by 6 feet wide, at say £1 15 shillings a foot to a total of £2100. This should open a good horse track all through. A party can be found to accept the work at the figures tomorrow and glad of the chance.[3]

This letter to the *Lake Wakatip Mail* in 1889 from Henry Homer did not immediately result in any action, but it sowed a seed that bore fruit in the Depression when the government looked to find roading projects capable of soaking up unemployed labour.

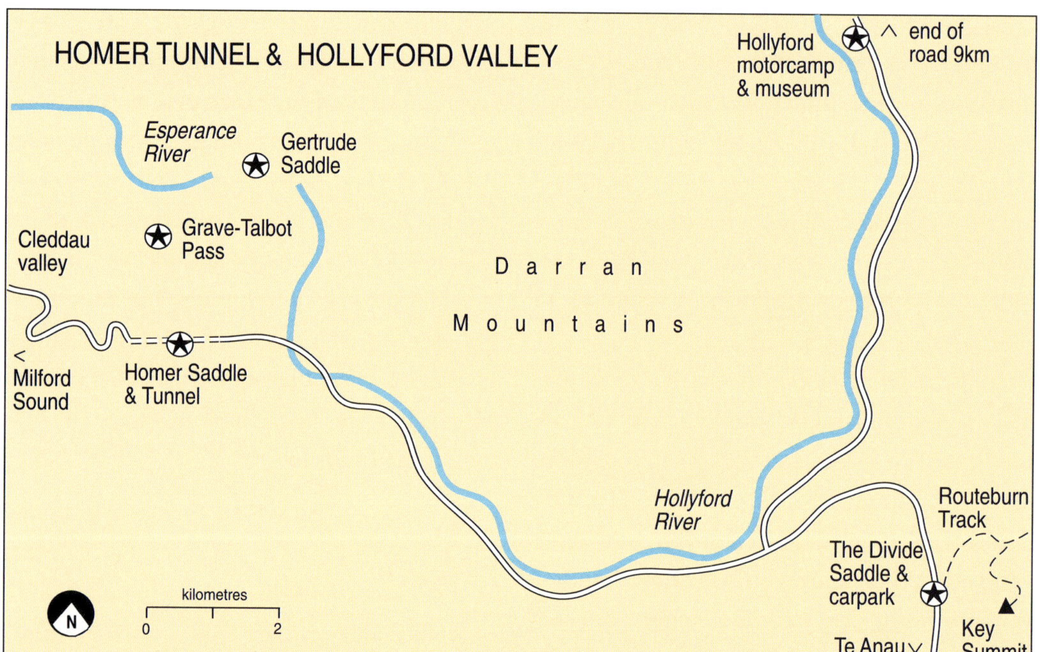

Signpost at Hollyford camp

Unlikely picnic spot: the entrance to Homer Tunnel

The Milford Road was started from Te Anau in 1929 and eventually reached Homer Saddle in 1934, and the tunnel proper was started in 1935.

Five men with tents, picks, shovels and wheelbarrows were taken to the site and told to go for it. It was a year before they had got through the outer scree and reached the granite itself.

The tunnellers faced all sorts of difficulties, not least the dismal weather, and the harsh winters with continual avalanches. The tunnel head was under an amphitheatre of rock walls, potentially lethal, even if you had a man with a whistle standing by. Time and time again snow blocked the tunnel entrance; rock blasting caused an avalanche in 1936 that killed one man and two more were killed in another avalanche the following year.

Because the tunnel faced downhill the pumps had a full-time job keeping the work face clear of water. An estimated 6000-10,000 gallons came in every hour, mainly through rock fractures from the permanent snowfields above. One winter the entire tunnel filled up with water. The camp in which the men lived was charitably described as 'never a garden suburb at the best of times': it was a row of single cabins and sheds that never saw the sun between May and September.

Communications with the Milford gangs was also a problem. J.H. Christie was an engineer on the Waitaki Dam and like many others left for the Homer Tunnel as work on the Waitaki wound down. He was an accomplished climber and in 1935 he was surveying the Homer Saddle and needed a quick way to get down the Milford side. He led a team down the diabolically steep 500m western face and fixed ropes on it, an extraordinary achievement.

This 'Homer Rope' subsequently became a route for the post and the pay. The paymaster had to climb up from the Hollyford some 500 metres to the saddle and meet the guide, who would take the bag of money down into the Milford side. Later a telephone line was put over the pass.

The tunnel was pierced through in 1940 and a car was driven through in 1942, but the war stopped the tunnel's enlargement and it was not until 1954 that it was officially opened. Since then the single lane has been enlarged to the point where two buses can pass each other – just. At 1219 metres long it looks as raw and hewn as the day it was first cut, and it is estimated that the final cost was $1 million.Rock and snow avalanches still regularly close the Milford road, and such is the power of Fiordland that many people find the drive into Milford Sound itself a wilderness experience.

Footnotes and Further Reading

1. *Men of the Milford Road*, Harold Anderson, A.H. & A.W. Reed Ltd, 1975.
2. *Beyond the Southern Lakes: The Explorations of W.G. Grave*, ed. Anita Crozier, A.H. & A.W. Reed Ltd, 1950.
3. *Fiordland Explored*, John Hall-Jones, A.H. & A.W. Reed Ltd, 1976.

Bush locomotive, Pourakino

POURAKINO BUSH TRAMWAY

FEATURES
Restored bush locomotive and tramway, concrete 'bridge to nowhere' and abutments, forest and bush birds.

HOW TO GET THERE
From Invercargill take State Highway 99 for 30km towards Riverton. Just before Riverton turn onto the Riverton-Otautau road for some 9km to Mitchell Road, then 4km to the turnoff to Harrington Road. It is a 7km drive through bush and cutover forest to the pleasant picnic area and locomotive beside the Pourakino River. Picnic tables and toilets.

WALK DETAILS
An attractive short bush circuit of 1-2-hours takes you through surprisingly tall beech forest with emergent rimu. Historic plaques illustrate the tramway and bridges. The Pourakino River is a picturesque honey-coloured river, with mudstone banks and several good swimming holes. The chirrup of bush birds, the sun dappling through the canopy and the running trickle of water all seem a long way from the sweat and sawdust of timber milling. The Pourakino is now a peaceful place amidst the relics of a great and noisy New Zealand industry.

In the Longwood Forest is Southland's own 'bridge to nowhere', a substantial concrete arch over Granity Stream that carried the tramway for the sawmill run by the Otautau Timber Company between 1900 and 1940. Concrete abutments sit oddly in the tannin-stained waters of the Pourakino, but pride of place goes to the restored bush locomotive.

The loco looks all ready to steam, with gauges set and the black sides gleaming in the rain showers. It is a Johnson locomotive called a Black Maria, and was built in Invercargill in 1902 and worked for 50 years. It hauled timber from the bush-felling site to the railhead at Longwood along a 25km private railway, and has been restored by volunteers Jock MacRae (whose father drove it for 20 years) and Ned Ramage.

Also in the picnic area is an old boiler, the only known survivor of five such boilers imported from England. It powered a 20-horsepower engine and the sawmill ran on steam for all its life. Originally teams of horses pulled the wagons along the tramways but these were later replaced by bush tractors. The timber logged included miro, totara, kahikatea and rimu, and in the 1940s the sawmill cut silver beech for the Australian motorbody-building trade.

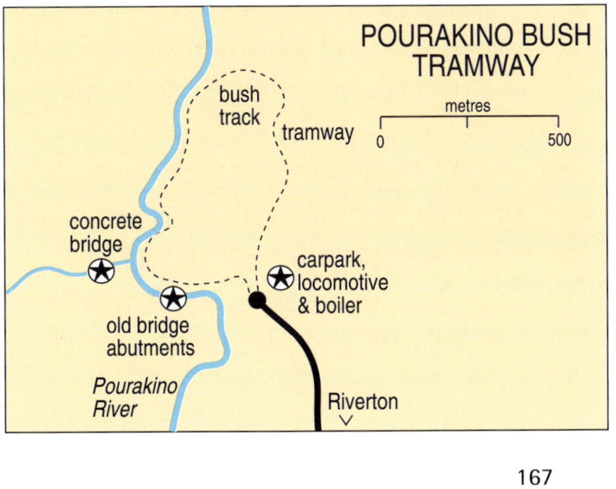

QUEEN'S PARK, INVERCARGILL

FEATURES
Victorian and Edwardian-style park, tree-lined avenues, aviaries and deer enclosures, ponds and waterwheel, statues and rose gardens, a beastly pool for children.

HOW TO GET THERE
Queen's Park is about 1.5km from Invercargill city centre, via Dee Street and Gala Street. The water tower is off Gala Street on Doon Street.

WALK DETAILS
Allow 2-3 hours to stroll about Queen's Park and also to see the Invercargill water tower. There is also a museum and art gallery next door.

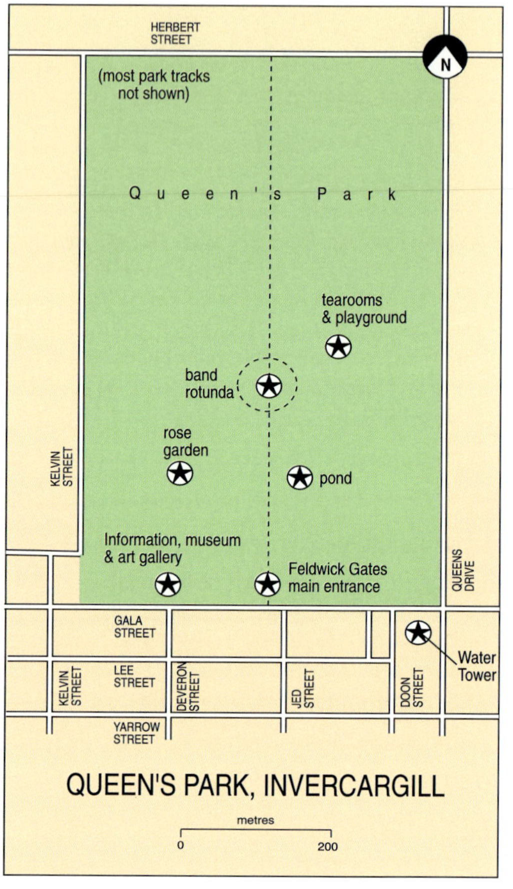

The Victorian and Edwardian municipal garden was not just an assemblage of flowers, nor an idle space for a few elderly nature-lovers. It was a place to promenade and preen, where the brightly crinolined ladies would stroll down avenues of stately English trees listening to the sounds of a brass band in the rotunda. To be seen was as important as to see and the arrangement of straight paths, and seats at conspicuous corners, was designed to show off the visitors as much as the flowers.

It was a chance to meet and mingle; the best-dressed working classes found themselves beside the affluent 'middles', who in turn got a chance to bump into aristocratic blood. Matronly gossip changed hands under the silver birches, there was tea and madeira cake in the tearooms and for some perhaps a discreet liaison near the rhododendrons.

The gardens then were filled with the 'special effects' that Victorian and Edwardian society loved: aviaries with colourful parrots, richly sown herbaceous borders, statues of a playful Pan or Puck, a circular rose garden arranged like a sliced cake and elegant and roomy avenues of trees. There may even perhaps have been a few innovative fashions: Japanese gardens with ponds and bridges were all the rage in the late 19th century.

All around New Zealand these Victorian

INVERCARGILL WATER TOWER

The Invercargill water tower is an excellent example of how you can take a basic utility and decorate it with aplomb. It can be seen from the entrance to Queen's Park and is only a short walk away. The Invercargill visitor centre at the museum will tell you the opening hours and the view from the top of the tower is a regular Sunday treat for visitors.

Built in 1898, the tower is 42.6 metres tall, an impressive landmark on the flat city plain. The architect was William Sharp, whose decorative design was an improvement on the originally proposed cast iron structure.

> ... instead of a huge iron skeleton, we will now have an ornamental and useful structure from the summit of which we can show visitors a view which would gladden their hearts.[1]

The tank held 300,000 litres of water but the tower fell into disrepair during the 1930s and the cupola was removed in 1934. It was restored in 1989.

The polychromatic brickwork, arch detailing over the narrow windows and italianate and romanesque touches on the facade should have resulted in a big ugly mess but somehow it works: an achievement of both engineering and architecture.

and Edwardian-style gardens remain a feature: Hagley Park in Christchurch, Pukekura Park in New Plymouth, Dunedin's city park, Ashburton domain. But none, perhaps, better exemplifies the style than Queen's Park in Invercargill.

Though to a Victorian style, much of the ornamental planting in Queen's was done from 1911 to 1917. Many details of statuary and ponds were added later and the process continues today. The rose garden was put in in 1917, the Feldwick Gates in 1924.

It can hardly be an accident that the Roman statue of Minerva (which stands beside the museum near the entrance to the gardens) is uncannily like Britannia. These kinds of gardens were showpieces of the empire: English to the core, orderly and well managed, and one can feel that attitude today. Invercargill's modern municipal gardeners still battle against loose leaves and wanton flowers, and the New Zealand botanical section in Queen's Park is absurdly tidy and seems rather out of place. Wilderness is nasty stuff.

Footnotes and Further Reading

1. 'Utility and Beauty', Hamish Carter, *Historic Places*, July 1993.

PORT CRAIG & PERCY BURN VIADUCT

FEATURES
Four bush viaducts, old schoolhouse (now a tramping hut), ruins of jetty and rail trucks, wilderness coast with rainforest and blowholes.

HOW TO GET THERE
As they say, half the fun is getting there. From Tuatapere drive south 12km to the Blue Cliffs Road and then on to the prominent DOC signpost and the start of the beach walk.

TRAMP DETAILS
A walk of about 6km along the beach will take you to the start of the tramping track to Port Craig. A low tide is best as it is fast travel on the exposed sand. Even at high tide you can usually get along the beach, but more slowly. A big surf would make it dangerous.

Most trampers make this a three-day trip: one day to Port Craig, a day visiting the viaducts and one day out. In this case a low tide in the middle of the day is useful.

The bush track is now very well graded and follows the coastline for 4km to Breakneck Creek and a low-tide route along the beach for some 3km. This is well worth taking, as the permanent high-tide route is a quagmire and the log book at Port Craig chronicles much discontent and gnashing of teeth. After a steep climb up from the beach another well-graded track goes 1km into Port Craig and the hut.

Tramping times: 2-3 hours along the beach, 4-5 hours one way to Port Craig, 2 hours one way from Port Craig to Percy Burn viaduct.

Men tend to leave quite a mess behind them and Port Craig looks like a junkyard of dreams. Old wire hawsers tangled in the bush, bogey wheels drunk in the creeks, half-ruined brick walls and railway sleepers melded to the rock foreshore by rust. Wagons are perched incongruously by a wharf that is slowly being gnawed to pieces by the sea.

Port Craig, at just about the end of the earth, is both desolate and romantic – a wet, hard, stubborn place. Yet there are moments of quiet beauty, where wisps of cloud mingle with the spumey shoreline, and the morning sun can reveal a glassy sea and briefly redden the rimu trees.

What were men doing here? Sawmilling. Port Craig was one of the biggest and most sophisticated sawmills in New Zealand, the brainchild of Christchurch entrepeneur Daniel Reese, who imagined a big American-style timber operation. Since most of the easily reached New Zealand forest had already gone, or was under licence to someone else, Reese had to come right down to Port Craig to get access to a sufficient volume of forest to make his scheme pay.

Before work began everything had to be shipped in: the machinery, the buildings, the men, and later their wives and families. There were enough kids to justify a schoolhouse, now a Department of Conservation hut. A wharf had to be built, and a bush tramway of course, with the four viaducts bridging side-creeks. It was a huge engineering effort with over 100 men working in the 1920s. At its peak the sawmill was producing 1800 cubic metres of sawn timber a month.

But bad luck dogged the scheme right from

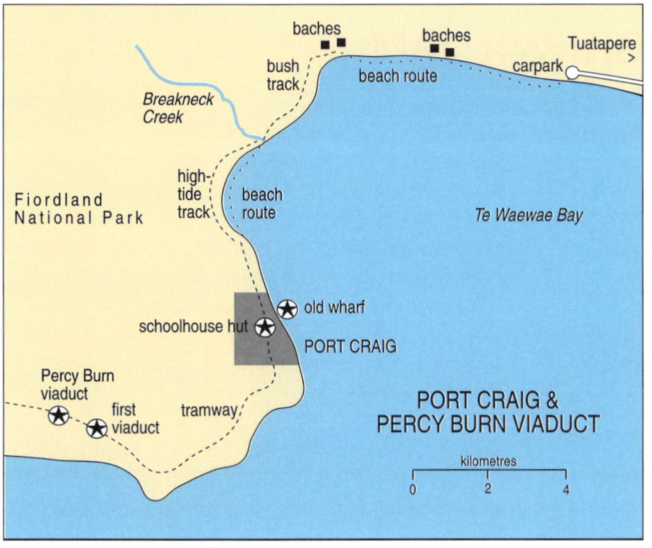

Percy Burn viaduct

the start when the first manager, John Craig, drowned in the surf. His brother died a year later when a box of blasting powder exploded. Then the timber turned out to be of poor quality and there was a 40 per cent wastage rate to get down to sawn logs. Shipping was expensive, and getting skilled workmen to live in such a remote place was not always easy. Despite economies of scale Port Craig was always a marginal operation and the Depression finally killed it. In 1929 everyone left, bringing an abrupt end to Southland's greatest sawmill.

Most of the machinery was removed in 1938-39, leaving only the schoolhouse, the viaducts and the garbage remaining. In the 1970s the Forest Service renovated the schoolhouse and re-planked the viaducts. Further restoration work was done in 1995 and the viaducts have become something of a feature of the area.

The Percy Burn viaduct, the first of the four, is about two hours' walk from the schoolhouse. It is the largest at 36 metres high and 125 metres long, and is in remarkable good shape considering the atrocious weather at this end of Fiordland. Built purely for pragmatic reasons, these logging bridges have retained a workmanlike elegance. Ironically, they are all made of Australian hardwoods.

They are certainly the largest wooden viaducts remaining in New Zealand – some Southlanders claim the world. They have a stubbornness of character that reflects the harsh working conditions of the sawmillers, between a bitter sea and a formidable forest.

Further Reading

Otago Daily Times, 29 September 1921.

'The Port Craig Viaducts', Paul Mahoney, *Historic Places*, July 1993.

PORT WILLIAM

FEATURES
Site of Shetland Islanders' settlement at Port William, remains of sawmill at Maori Beach, wilderness coastline, DOC hut.

HOW TO GET THERE
Stewart Island is serviced by regular plane and ferry services. The planes leave from Invercargill airport, the ferry from Bluff.

WALK DETAILS
The track to Maori Beach starts from Lee Bay, 4km from Halfmoon Bay. There is plenty of Stewart Island mud but the track is well graded, as it was once the main land route to the sawmill settlement at Maori Beach.

It's about 30 minutes and 1km to Little River, and the track skirts the sand at a lower tide. Upstream from the bridge there is a pleasant picnic site, with a toilet, and some splendid rata and rimu trees. After Little River the track climbs steeply, glimpsing the bouldery coastline as it cuts across the headland at Peters Point and drops abruptly to Maori Beach (2 km). At a lower tide you can cross directly to the beach, and there is a very muddy high-tide alternative track if you get stuck.

Maori Beach is a 1km-wide sweep of sand – golden when the elusive Stewart Island sun emerges. There is a designated camping area at the east end, with a cooking shelter and toilet. The track from Maori Beach 2km onto Port William does a big up and down climb of 150 metres before dropping to Magnetic Beach, which you can follow around to Port William.

'The Anchor Stone'

Port William's history has been formed in dribs and drabs, rather like its weather. Sudden squalls of activity interleaved with long periods of languishing solitude, and then sunlight unexpectedly illuminates a moment. The port could easily be considered a romantic place today but history tells a gaudy story – of exploitation, misery and death.

In Maori legend Stewart Island is known as Te Punga o te Waka a Maui, the anchor stone of Maui's canoe, used while he fished up a great flat fish known as the North Island. The current Maori name is Rakiura, which has been translated as 'glowing skies', a beautiful transcription of the light that can illuminate the land in unexpected fashion. Maori used many coastal sites around Halfmoon Bay and Port William for hunting and fishing and at Port William was the settlement of Pa Whakataka. Few Maori seemed to live permanently on the island, but made annual trips for muttonbirds and eels.

The early meetings of the European sealers and the Southland Maori were fractious to say the least. In 1823 the superbly named but ruthless Abimeleck Riggs had a sealing depot in the bay. He was an American captain of the brig *General Gates*, and had a reputation for cruelty to his own gangs and the Maori. For utu (revenge) the Maori attacked the depot when it was guarded only by the boy, Ebenezer Denton, who was murdered.

Another visitor to Port William was Captain Edwardson of the *Snapper*. He had sailed to New Zealand looking for flax but had picked up a half-starved sealing gang (one of Riggs's) in Fiordland and taken them on to Port William to pick up a cache of seal skins. They were met by a war party of Maori, one of whom was a tattooed white man who addressed the surprised and apprehensive crew in excellent English. He turned out to be James Caddell, who at 16 in 1810 had been one of a party of sealers who had been massacred by Maori on one of the muttonbird islands. His life was spared by the chief's daughter, who threw a cloak over him and claimed him for her own. Subsequently married and duly tattooed, he seemed to have taken to his new life with gusto.

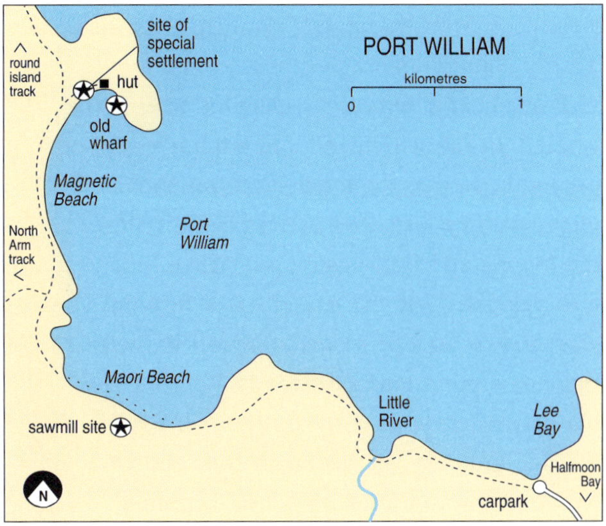

Edwardson invited him on board and later Caddell and his wife Toki-Toki sailed with the boat to Sydney, where they attracted much attention. Edwardson's chart of 1823 is the first map of Port William.

Port William even had a gold strike. Louis Longuet was an itinerant gold prospector who found gold on Magnetic Beach in 1866, enough to cause a rush. Sergeant Morton of the police was stationed there, in a small hut and office, but his services were not required and the rush died stillborn.

Pearson's Paradise

In the 1870s and 1880s various provincial governments had a fling with the idea of 'special settlements' to populate remote areas. It was somehow abhorrent that the wilderness should be left untamed, 'going to waste'. Karamea, Jacksons Bay and Martins Bay, all on the West Coast, all proved more or less disastrous, but perhaps the fastest failure of all was at Port William.

The idea came from James Macandrew, the Superintendent of Otago, but the dream merchant behind the scheme was Walter H. Pearson, the Commissioner for Crown Lands.

Port William

Here was Stewart Island 'wanting' for a 'sturdy population' to civilise it.[1]

Pearson had very clear ideas of who he wanted for the settlement, and did not think giving the settlers too much land was a good idea, lest they 'prove as useless colonists as the Maoris and Half-castes, who have hitherto vegetated on the island'.[2] Sea farming was the way, and he seems to have regarded the seas around Port William as a cornucopia of whales, seals, fish, oysters, all ready for the larder. In his vision of how settlers would live he conjured up a desk-scribbler's nostalgia for the simple life.

> While trawling, if he sees a whale he can, if prepared give chase, and if he gets his monster fish, tow it home and try it out at his leisure; if he loses it, go on trawling; always sure of a return of some sort. He lives in a genial climate, with the means of subsistence, nay wealth at command, and surrounded with such comfort as few of his calling experience in the home country, or the bitter winter of Nova Scotia. To the fishermen the Government proposes to bring out, or Nova Scotians, Stewart Island will prove a very paradise.[3]

MAORI BEACH

Halfway between Port William and Halfmoon Bay is Maori Beach, the site of a prosperous sawmill from 1913 to 1931. It was to be the last sawmill on Stewart Island and was well established, with horse-drawn trucks pulling the cut timber on wooden tramlines to the sawmill and onto the wharf. Houses were built for the sawmillers and their families and a school established, which functioned until 1935, four years after the sawmill had shut up shop.

A boiler, steam engine and log haulers still remain on site, though much of the 800 hectares of cut bush has regrown into vigorous second-growth forest. A scattering of bluebells can be seen in the sand dunes.

Old whaling hulks, Stewart Island, 1930s.

PADDY GILROY – HAVING A WHALE OF A TIME

Whalers often used Port William as a base, for 'trying-out' the captured whales, and having a 'gam' (whalers' talk for gossip) with other ships. Nothing gave more scope for conversation than the activities of the rough and ready whaler Paddy Gilroy. His ship *Chance* might have looked 'carelessly rigged and vilely unkempt', but he knew his business, and knew the coastline of Stewart Island intimately.[4] He was already a local legend when Frank Bullen recorded his observations.

> He was a queer little figure of a man – short, tubby, with scanty red hair, and a brogue thick as pea-soup. Eccentric in most things, he was especially so in his dress, which he seemed to select on the principle of finding the most unfitting things to wear.
>
> ... the poor *Chance* looked like some poor old relic of a bygone day, whose owners, unable to sell her, and too poor to keep her in repair, were just letting her go while keeping up the insurance, praying fervently each day that she might come to grief, and bring them a little profit at last... She looked what she really was – the sole survivor of the once great whaling industry of New Zealand.[5]

But appearances can be deceptive, and the other whalers in Port William quickly realised that their brisk, efficient enterprises were no substitute for local knowledge, a loyal crew and 'a little philanthropist' of a captain.

> The old Chance, like some shadow of the past, haunted Foveaux Strait, and made a better income for her fortunate owners than any of the showy, swift coasting steamers that rushed contemptuously past ...
>
> There were sixteen white men on board the Chance, including the skipper, drawn as usual from various European and American sources, the rest of her large crew of over forty all told being made up of Maories and half-breeds. One common interest united them, making them the jolliest crowd I ever saw – their devotion to their commander.[6]

The other whaling captains disliked Gilroy because he took on deserters from other ships, and 'but for his Maori and half-breed bodyguard, I have little doubt he would have long been killed', wrote Frank Bullen. However this did not seem to faze Gilroy, and let's leave Port William in the sort of style that Gilroy managed.

> Characteristically theChance was away first, before daylight had quite asserted itself ... Paddy lolled on the taff-rail near the wheel, which was held by an immense half-breed, who leant back and carried on a desultory, familiar conversation with his skipper; the rest of the crew were scattered about the decks, apparently doing what they liked in any manner they chose. The anchor was being catted, sails going up, and yards being trimmed; but, to observers like us, no guiding spirit was noticeable. It seemed to work all right, and the old ark herself looked as if she was as intelligent as any of them ...[7]

Pearson's report was full of such extravagances: little wonder he was nicknamed 'Paradise' Pearson. But he had energy. A vast two-storeyed barracks was built, and a separate building for single women, and in April 1873 the first migrants from the Shetlands arrived. But by August 1874 the place was deserted, except for the resident magistrate and his family. So what had gone wrong?

The islanders had been led to expect cleared land, not bush down to the waterline. Their fishing techniques were unsuited to New Zealand waters, and when they did adapt they found there was little money to be made from exporting the catch to Melbourne. With no land for farming animals, and fishing a failure, it is hardly surprising they quickly left for the mainland. The planned second boat of immigrants never eventuated.

The great barracks crumbled away and the current DOC hut sits on the site, the only reminder of the special settlement the whispering blue gums behind it.

Footnotes and Further Reading

1. *Appendices to the Journals of the House of Representatives* (1872 D5a), report by Walter H. Pearson, Commissioner of Crown Lands.
2. Ibid.
3. Ibid.
4. *The Cruise of the Cachalot*, F. Bullen, 1907.
5. Ibid.
6. Ibid.
7. Ibid.

Stewart Island Explored, John Hall-Jones, Craig Printing Co. Ltd, 1994.